Poetic Prosthetics

For Abba and for Imma
For Orit and for Me

Series Editors: Victoria M. Basham and Sarah Bulmer

The Critical Military Studies series welcomes original thinking on the ways in which military power works within different societies and geopolitical arenas

Militaries are central to the production and dissemination of force globally but the enduring legacies of military intervention are increasingly apparent at the societal and personal bodily levels as well, demonstrating that violence and war-making function on multiple scales. At the same time, the notion that violence is as an appropriate response to wider social and political problems transcends militaries: from private security, to seemingly 'non-military' settings such as fitness training and schooling, the legitimisation and normalisation of authoritarianism and military power occurs in various sites. This series seeks original, high-quality manuscripts and edited volumes that engage with such questions of how militaries, militarism and militarisation assemble and disassemble worlds touched and shaped by violence in these multiple ways. It will showcase innovative and interdisciplinary work that engages critically with the operation and effects of military power and provokes original questions for researchers and students alike.

Available Titles:

Resisting Militarism: Direct Action and the Politics of Subversion
Chris Rossdale

Making War on Bodies: Militarisation, Aesthetics and Embodiment in International Politics
Catherine Baker

Disordered Violence: How Gender, Race and Heteronormativity Structure Terrorism
Caron Gentry

Sex and the Nazi Soldier: Violent, Commercial and Consensual Contacts during the War in the Soviet Union, 1941-1945
Regina Mühlhäuser (translated by Jessica Spengler)

The Military-Peace Complex: Gender and Materiality in Afghanistan
Hannah Partis-Jennings

Politics of Impunity: Torture, the Armed Forces and the Failure of Transitional Justice in Brazil
Henrique Tavares Furtado

Conscientious Objection in Turkey: A Socio-legal Analysis of the Right to Refuse Military Service
Demet Çaltekin

Poetic Prosthetics: Trauma and Language in Contemporary Veteran Writing
Ron Ben-Tovim

Forthcoming:

Beyond the Wire: The Cultural Politics of Veteran Narratives
Nick Caddick

The Gendered and Colonial Lives of Gurkhas in Private Security: From Military to Market
Amanda Chisholm

War and Militarisation: The British, Canadian and Dutch Invasion of Southern Afghanistan
Paul Dixon

Inhabiting No-Man's-Land: Army Wives, Gender and Militarisation
Alexandra Hyde

Mobilising China's One-Child Generation: Education, Nationalism and Youth Militarisation in the PRC
Orna Naftali

Martialling Peace: How the Peacekeeper Myth Legitimises Warfare
Nicole Wegner

Poetic Prosthetics

Trauma and Language in Contemporary Veteran Writing

RON BEN-TOVIM

EDINBURGH
University Press

Edinburgh University Press is one of the leading university presses in the UK. We publish academic books and journals in our selected subject areas across the humanities and social sciences, combining cutting-edge scholarship with high editorial and production values to produce academic works of lasting importance. For more information visit our website: edinburghuniversitypress.com

© Ron Ben-Tovim, 2022

Edinburgh University Press Ltd
The Tun – Holyrood Road
12(2f) Jackson's Entry
Edinburgh EH8 8PJ

Typeset in 10.5/13 ITC Giovanni Std by
IDSUK (DataConnection) Ltd, and
printed and bound in Great Britain

A CIP record for this book is available from the British Library

ISBN 978-1-4744-9849-4 (hardback)
ISBN 978-1-4744-9851-7 (webready PDF)
ISBN 978-1-4744-9852-4 (epub)

The right of Ron Ben-Tovim to be identified as the author of this work has been asserted in accordance with the Copyright, Designs and Patents Act 1988, and the Copyright and Related Rights Regulations 2003 (SI No. 2498).

CONTENTS

LIST OF FIGURES

ACKNOWLEDGEMENTS

The publication of this book is a milestone on an intellectual journey, the roots of which are far from purely theoretical. While it brings
together analyses that hopefully add to the ongoing discussion of the toll
war takes on those who participate in and witness it, its connections to
my own life make it very personal as well. And so, in acknowledging all
those who have helped me along this path, I must begin with my parents,
Shmuel and Judith Ben-Tovim, for showing me the blank, sometimes
silent, pain that comes after war but also the immeasurable gift of love
and respect amid that pain. Sometimes that love means talking; sometimes it means silence. I would like to mark my love and appreciation for
my wife, Orit, with whom I share this load of pain and love around our
own war, and who has, with her kindness, humanity and love, taught me
much more than can be contained in this book. In many ways, the book
was born from a cauldron of pain and love, and I also dedicate it to my
children, Na'ama, Itamar and Yehonatan. May they always find love and
support in their encounters with pain.

That firm base in real-life experiences, however, would never have
found its way into the final form this book has taken without those
teachers who, with their humanity and intelligence, led and encouraged
me along the way. They include my dear adviser, friend and inspiration,
Prof. Karen Alkalay-Gut, along with the discerning and loving support of
Prof. Shirley Sharon-Zisser and Prof. Milette Shamir. It is one thing to be
able to uplift and support your students; it is quite another to allow them
to form their own voices, and I am not sure what that identity would
have been without their guidance. I would also like to acknowledge the
support of the scholars and mentors who never failed to inspire me and
push me on, even when it wasn't very clear what would come of all this

work. I mention especially Prof. John Limon for his endless compassion and intelligence, Prof. Hans Ulrich Gumbrecht for his uncompromising honesty and love, Prof. David Wellbery for his humanity and patience, Prof. Amir Eshel for his kindness and support, Prof. Eitan Bar-Yosef for his support and priceless advice, Prof. Efraim Sicher for his keen intellect and guidance and Prof. Katarzyna Jerzak for her unwavering confidence and seemingly endless wellspring of hope and inspiration.

I would also like to express my utmost appreciation to the teachers I have met and the friends I have made along this winding path and who have helped me realise this work, whether through reading, listening or teaching; they include Dr Tamar Gerstenhaber, Dr Hanna Freund-Chertok, Dr Nir Evron, Prof. Noam Reisner and Prof. Ayelet Ben-Yishai. It is impossible to name all those who have done their best to help me along the way but I send my thanks to you all.

A special thank you to the editors of the Advances in Critical Military Studies series, Sarah Bulmer and Victoria M. Basham, for their significant support and helpful comments, but mostly for helping this book find its true intellectual, cultural and social home. I will forever be in your debt.

Last but certainly not least, I would like to thank the extended family of authors and poets whose work has been reprinted here, and whose generosity and writings have enabled my own work, as well as creating a greater community of *Poetic Prosthetics*: Graham Barnhart (University of Chicago Press), Chantelle Bateman, Nigel 'Bernie' Bruen, Trace Currall, Maurice Decaul, Elyse Fenton (Cleveland State University Poetry Center), Kate Gaskin (YesYes Books), Nicole S. Goodwin, Colin D. Halloran, Lynn Hill (with special thanks to Vijay Iyer and Mike Ladd), Jaime Lorente, James Love, Gerardo Mena (Southeast Missouri State University Press), Edward Poynter, Brain Turner (Alice James Books and Bloodaxe Books) and Maximilian Uriarte (Little Brown).

Grateful acknowledgement is made to these writers and sources who have granted permission to reproduce material previously published elsewhere. Every effort has been made to trace the copyright holders, but if any have been inadvertently overlooked, the publisher will be pleased to make the necessary arrangements at the first opportunity.

Introduction: Limping Back to Life after War

> Don't be so sensitive to your private death
> Try to dismiss it, even while awake
> Life is filled with water as death with earth
> To drown in life's waters is more terrible than just an end.
>
> The magic of war to the desperate
> Is in its carrying them to dismiss their private death
> But he who wishes to rid of the dream of his death
> Without infringing on the life of his fellow man –
>
> — Meir Wieseltier, 'End'[1]

Soldiers return from war with the distinct feeling that their experiences have sliced them away from their lives, that they have been haphazardly pasted back after war, expected by others and by themselves to fit back in. Instead of sensing the relief of homecoming, they encounter the jagged edges of their incompatibility with who they were. Writing about this sense of 'radical discontinuity' felt by those who survived World War I, Eric J. Leed describes soldiers as 'troubled by the sense of having lived two lives and of being unable to resolve the contradictions between them'.[2] This ill-fitting, disjointed experience is exacerbated by the fact that, in many cases, returning soldiers, at least those who do not bear physical scars, 'look the same' and are thus expected to reintegrate quickly, a fact that produces a profound frustration – one that brings with it, moreover, an urgent need to find a way of addressing and giving voice to that incompatibility. It is precisely that effort to seek new words for a new strange life that I will refer to as the work of the prosthesis, the laborious process of building a new way of speaking out of the rubble of post-war language.

Soldiers seek out a mode of communication from the remains of a language they had once known and used and yet that seems, in the wake of war, like a broken and inadequate tool. Amid the struggle to reinitiate the work of meaning, this new form of communication takes, at times, the shape of what is commonly thought of as literary or poetic language. Literature, as I see it, is not, then, simply an ornate mode of depicting an otherwise 'objective' reality but the result of hard work by veterans and their families wishing to stay alive after trauma and violence, the attempt to keep one's head above the raging waters of personal pain and broken-down communication. The writing of an artificial limb, as with all prostheses, retains in it the painful memory of a now inaccessible past and the anguish of an inanimate construct, a man-made object, rubbing against the still tender flesh of the wound. In terms both practical and theoretical, then, this book focuses on the work required by veterans, as well as by their families, to transform the insufferable pain of silence and disability into a liveable, if uneasy, coexistence with life in the wake of violence. In less theoretical terms, this book also represents a significant part of my own work to do the same, an issue I shall address later on.

This notion of writing as fulfilling a complex prosthetic operation is not my own and is not exclusively the task of returning veterans. Writing in *Prosthesis*, writer and theorist David Wills outlines a way of understanding certain works of literature and art as sharing the structure of the prosthetic limb, arguing that prosthetic writing is motivated by the spectre of an unspeakable pain in the past. In psychoanalytical terms, those works of literature Wills discusses locate the wound of past suffering and allow it to speak. But, importantly for this book's insistence on the 'limping' and painful nature of the prop that is writing, Wills also highlights the imperfect nature of such a contraption, an imperfection that stands at the heart of a simple truth regarding prosthetic work: the pain may subside but it never goes away. Like any artificial prop, the prosthetic text is constructed by linking mechanical and organic, amputated stump and steel rod, dead and alive. And as is the case with any prosthesis, the movement of the textual or written prop depends on an ambiguous relationship between them, one Wills refers to as its 'ghostly transfer', a blurring of the lines between the made and natural, real and unreal. This, I will argue, is the ground of the verbal tool that is poetry. The poetic machine works: it hums, allowing veterans to speak and to live. And yet the ghost of past pain is never banished, haunting veterans in what could be called the linguistic manifestations of sudden bouts of piercing phantom pain. As Herman Melville writes in his depiction of Captain Ahab's false leg, even the most successful of prostheses remains a work of tense friction:

'Had you watched Ahab's face that night, you would have thought that in him also two different things were warring. While his one live leg made lively echoes along the deck, every stroke of his dead limb sounded like a coffin-tap. In life and death this old man walked.'[3] As Wills writes, the two aspects apparent in the prosthetic as seen in Ahab's example, the living and the dead, the organic and the inorganic, inform the structure, movement and use of the prosthetic text. It is a tension that forms an ambiguity that frustrates any attempt to nail down which is which, as the two intermingle – the living parts seem eerily artificial, while the dead are oddly alive – creating a space of ambiguity and poetry that enables a kind of communication. This tension stands at the heart of the work of the prosthesis and will be referred to in this book as the 'poetic prosthetics'.

The operation of the tool that is the poetic prosthesis, a toolness I shall discuss at length in the following chapter and one that falls within the more general tool-making human tradition, is in the attempt to 'come back to life' through writing; it means that, for 'dead inside' veterans, a new set of relations is set up with both life and death, in which one seems to bleed into the other. The extraordinary aspect of their wartime experiences is pushed against the mundane, everyday facts of language and the shocking everydayness of the return home, creating a composite where we may glimpse, as Zoe Wool writes, 'the vanishing point where the figure of a torn world and the ground of an ordinary one come so much together that they are not clearly distinguishable'.[4] While Wool here refers to her observations of the push and pull between ordinary American life and the extraordinariness of the front that veterans endure while hospitalised in Walter Reed hospital, this zone of tension very much speaks to the nature of the poetic prostheses presented in this book. What veterans seek, as Wool points out, is to eke out a semblance of normality from a situation that is anything but normal, as well as, inevitably, to explore the extraordinariness of their new normal. As she writes, it

> matters to injured soldiers who share a feeling of ordinariness in their common lot, a lot that others anxiously render extraordinary. It matters to these same soldiers as they move toward an aspirationally normative civilian future and are animated by an ambivalent desire for a life that others recognize as ordinary.[5]

This desire finds its expression, I would argue, in the impulse to rebuild a language that is composed of both poles of experience: to use the ordinary mode of communication, words, and bend it toward the extremity of war, and back again.

One striking expression of this dual nature can be found in the poem 'So I Was a Coffin', written by American army veteran Gerardo Mena, originally posted online and subsequently published as part of Mena's debut poetry collection, *The Shape of Our Faces No Longer Matters*, in 2014. In the piece dedicated 'To Corporal Kyle Powers, Died in My Arms, November 4, 2006', Mena foregrounds the uneasy link between organic and mechanical in war, the mundane and the shocking, and in the act of writing poetry, as he self-identifies as a series of war-related objects:

> They said *you are a spear.* So I was a spear.

> I walked around Iraq upright and tall, but the wind blew and I began to lean.
> I leaned into a man, who leaned into a child, who leaned into a city. I walked
> back to them and neatly presented a city of bodies packaged in rows.
> They said *no. You are a bad spear.*

> They said *you are a flag.* So I was a flag.

> I climbed to the highest building, in the city that had no bodies, and I smiled
> and waved as hard as I could. I waved too hard and I caught fire and I burned
> down the city, but it had no bodies. They said *no. You are a bad flag.*[6]

In Mena's poem there are two ways to experience the inanimate or the dead tool. The first is that form of life defined by 'doing your job' at war: 'being a spear' or 'being a flag' or, as the poem proceeds, 'being a bandage'. It is a way of life so defined by the tool, in fact, that it seems it is not a living being that is performing these functions, but that, by participating in and witnessing extreme violence, the witness or participant somehow *becomes* a tool.[7] The height of the drama that unfolds between object and person, however, comes in that scene in the poem that is presented as the raison d'être of the poem itself: the death of his friend Kyle, to whom the poem is dedicated, and which disrupts this tool-led life. While each of the speaker's self-identifications as various objects is depicted in a brief stanza, the attempt to save Kyle, one in which the speaker is 'a bandage', is repeated thrice, a fact that speaks volumes as to the emotional desperation of the speaker, his failure as a tool, as well as to his agency as a writer:

> They said *you are a bandage.* So I was a bandage.

> I jumped on Kyle's chest and wrapped my lace arms together around his torso
> and pressed my head to his ribcage and listened to his heartbeat. Then I was
> full, so I let go and wrung myself out.

And I jumped on Kyle's chest and wrapped my lace arms together around his torso and pressed my head to his ribcage and listened to his heartbeat. Then I was full, so I let go and wrung myself out.

And I jumped on Kyle's chest and wrapped my lace arms together around his torso and pressed my head to his ribcage but there was no heartbeat. They said *no. You are a bad bandage.*[8]

Mena's poem, in its ambiguous mixing of the living and the dead, organic (the speaker) and inorganic (the bandage), and the in-between figure of the dying comrade, complicates the dead and the living, creating a third space – that of the poetic prosthesis. This is the space of a waking dream in which the repeated attempt to save a friend's life in an already culmi-nated past is a mark of a very real and painful guilt and grief, as well as of an artistic and personal freedom. Compulsive repetition, flashbacks and hyper-vigilance are all common symptoms experienced on a daily basis by veterans with varying degrees of post-traumatic stress disorder, all of which are repetitions of a traumatic past against which they are power-less. They do not choose when the 'phantom pain' or the phantom of pain makes its return, and this only adds to their inherent sense of lacking control or humanity. However, within the context of the poetic rendering of that event, repetition is a sign of style, of artistic control. This is not exerted, as Nil Santiáñez argues in his study of World War II literature,[9] by way of inserting that void into a narrative of their experience – one would find it difficult to sketch a narrative that would diffuse the internal tick-ing time bomb that is 'failing' to save the life of one's friend. Instead, the poem is a moment of control through relations, through style and form, through the creation of an object made of seemingly opposing forces, one that can have the effect of gaining personal agency via poetry. Thus, a return to a scene of wartime violence, the repetition of its horrid detail, the self-identification as a series of inanimate objects, all these are a part of what I am calling here prosthetic or, as I shall later discuss, 'dream'. This is a work of verbal art that coalesces in the final lines of Mena's poem around the unlikely figure of the coffin. The veteran, who had failed at being a weapon, at being a national symbol or the heroic saviour of oth-ers, finds meaning and power in fashioning the object that remembers and, by doing so, enables a new way of relating to the past:

They said *you are a coffin.* So I was.

I found a man. They said he died bravely, or he will. I encompassed him in my finished wood, and I shut my lid around us. As they lowered us into the ground

he made no sound because he had no eyes and could not cry. As I buried us
in dirt we held our breaths together and they said, *yes. You are a good coffin*.[10]

I will not elaborate further on Mena's poem at this juncture, as arresting as it is, for the simple reason that I shall revisit it several times in this book. But what is clear is that the new form of recounting a painful, traumatic past, created by Mena as well as other veterans attempting to reclaim life who are discussed in this book, paradoxically results in a new, strange kind of life or view into the future: not one endowed with post-war 'healing' or one delivering the much-desired 'moving on', but a persistent insistence on life lived through and with pain. This is a future in which the duality of replacement and displacement remains and that creates a new rhythm of life, a new style, brought forth by the prosthetic.

Through a reading of contemporary post-war poetry and one graphic novel, created for the most part in the last decade or so by American and British war veterans, I propose a poetics, an analysis of post-war poetic works that will both shed light on the veteran's chaotic world of language after war and offer a possible way out. On one hand, these texts are pinned down by the past and thus also invested in the linguistic work required to return to the past. On the other hand, however, once constructed, the 'ghost' or 'dream' that is the result of the attempt to bury the past changes the meaning and use of that past, transforming moments of a concrete past pain into ambiguity-filled instances of poetic and artistic performance. The 'index' of pain, to use a concept from pragmatist American philosopher of language Charles S. Peirce, that part of speech which seems most attached to reality – the date and place of Kyle's death, for instance – is transformed into the axis of a work of art, filled with ambiguity, performance and empowerment. Ultimately, writing created in the wake of war and other equally devastating personal experiences represents the attempt to reinitiate movement in the face of an emotional, intellectual, communicational and communal dead end, of paralysis. The newly constructed 'machine', whether in the form of a poem, a graphic novel or perhaps a film, initiates the movement that defines one's own humanity, the arrest of which, as a result of traumatic wartime experiences, is experienced as a kind of death or loss of humanity. So, to reignite the flame, to 'restart' the machine, could mean not only a bold step forward to return to life, as painful as that life may remain, but also a tool of artistic and personal agency.

The model presented by this book as characterising post-war writing, it should be said, shares the articulated, mechanical–organic structure seen in both Wills and, to an extent, Peirce. The mechanical aspect of both Peirce and Wills, the discussion of which will take up much of the first chapter, is geared toward highlighting a certain sense of technicality and mechanics in the veterans' task of writing a false limb. And, at the same time, that technicality will eventually implode, resulting in the 'dream'. My wish is not to pinpoint those exclusively mechanical and organic aspects of these prosthetic texts; such discrete identification is a slippery task. Instead, I am interested in highlighting the mechanical preoccupation these works represent, as well as one central effect of the movement they create: an indexical pointing toward an absent and inaccessible past, and a dealing with the past using a tool that also serves to remind one of the mechanical, fragmented nature of the present. The organic–mechanic duality of post-war life is echoed in the double process of the poetic prosthesis. It is one in which meaningful words and concepts whose meaning is purely social – Pierce's 'symbol' – are drained of that meaning, while factual anchors – Peirce's 'index' – shift from simple placeholders to an aesthetic focal point. And it is precisely that 'play of the text' – to recall the work of literary critic Wolfgang Iser, to whom I shall return in the concluding pages of this book – that attempts to initiate the oscillation that constitutes a significant aspect of regaining one's humanity after war: to reignite the movement of life, one which had been arrested in the wake of the encounter with violence.

Living Death

The mark that wartime experiences and the first-hand encounter with sudden and devastating violence leaves on those who experience it is the mark of death. In what has by now become a cliché of post-traumatic and post-war writing, words repeatedly fail to describe war, creating a painful gap between soldiers and their communities but also a gaping wound in their own understanding of being 'alive' or 'human'. In *Achilles in Vietnam*, Jonathan Shay, an American psychiatrist noted for his work with army veterans, writes: '"I died in Vietnam" is a common utterance of our patients. Most viewed themselves as already dead at some point in their combat service, often after a close friend was killed.'[11] Describing his sessions with Art, a Vietnam veteran, psychotherapist Edward Tick quotes his patient as saying 'Nobody could survive what I did and still be alive. Sometimes I'm convinced I'm not.'[12] Writing of a similar tendency to describe the change one undergoes in war to death, Eric J. Leed writes of World War I soldiers: 'Many used death as a metaphor describing their distance from the "men and things of the past".'[13] Veterans, then, time and again report a sense of having not survived war, of being emotionally dead or severed from home life, with only other soldiers with whom to share their feelings. Tim, a Canadian veteran of the war in Afghanistan working as part of a veterans' theatre group, expresses the depth of the divide between the living and the dead. In an impromptu address, Tim gives form to this sense of a living death, later adapted by group leaders as part of their performance. In this passage Tim highlights the gap between the 'reality' of war and the uncertainties of post-war life:

> People all around me. But it's not real. None of it's real. Going fucking shopping. Hundred dollar shoes, thousand dollar purses. They don't have a clue. Who cares if your fucking Starbucks coffee's not 180 fucking degrees. FUCK. It's not real. Afghanistan's real. It's something. When I'm there, I'm something. I'm alive. When I'm here I'm just dead inside.[14]

The scene of death, of violence, the index of 'real' experience, becomes then the moment of life, of assured living, of being certain one was alive. On the other hand, the home, the mall, the family dinner become, paradoxically, the site of an imperceptible or deceptive death, or, at the very least, of a profound confusion between life and death.

This death, a sense of extreme disconnect from one's environment, is a slippery experience, one defined by a sense of being nailed down or paralysed. As opposed to other forms of disability, whether physical or cognitive, many of those who return from war, perhaps not unlike Tim, do not appear to be disabled, do not seem 'dead'; nor do they always betray the behaviour that would lead others to mark them as such. And yet they are stamped by death, by the cessation of that movement that is essential to a self-perception of life and humanity, one that is halted by violence and one set back into limping motion by poetry. Thus it seems appropriate to gesture at one key concept that I shall be returning to again and again in my discussion of post-war writing, loss and prosthesis, and that is the importance of movement and the role poetry may have in creating post-war movement. In the words of French philosopher and writer Maurice Merleau-Ponty, as a result of that event that blows out the human flame, the kind of event or experience that arrests life, bringing it to a screeching halt:

> A human body is present when, between the see-er and the visible, between touching and touched, between one eye and the other, between hand and hand a kind of crossover occurs, when the mark of the sensing/sensible is lit, when the fire starts to burn that will not cease until some accident befalls the body, undoing what no accident would have sufficed to do.[15]

For Merleau-Ponty, what we define as 'human' is not a static fact but the outcome, perhaps even byproduct, of an interaction or movement that goes a long way towards explaining what it is that 'goes wrong' as a result of wartime experiences: that movement stops. Frozen in space and time following their injury, veterans stand motionless, detached from that which makes them human to the point of identifying as inhuman. This severing is that which stands at the centre of what this book will claim is post-war 'injury'.

The force of literature, or, better said, the importance literature can have in the general discussion of living with the after-effects of war, is, then, in forging a path out of death. This book could be considered the literary supplement to what is already a wide movement across fields and disciplines to better understand the experience of soldiers after their return from the frontlines. It is a theme evident in the work of Wool's *After War*, already cited above, which uses ethnographic tools in order to survey the slippery twilight zone of US military hospitals such as Walter Reed, in which soldiers and their families attempt the precarious task of returning to an ordinary life informed by the extreme experiences of battle. As Wool writes, this 'zone of life – the space of Walter Reed and the limbo of life blown apart and not yet pieced together, not yet sedimented into life stories of before and after – is full of visceral intensity and uncertainty'.[16] That term 'limbo' is, of course, another associated with a sense of paralysis or lack of movement, a 'stuckness', a 'neither here nor there' that not only is fuelled, as Wool writes, by the uncertainties of the post-war form of life but triggers intense personal unrest. Writing about the intricate linguistic and habitual differences that separate soldiers from their families, Sarah Hautzinger and Jean Scandlyn discuss the 'sticky' codeswitching that takes place in post-deployment military families, concluding that the 'compressed tempo of multiple deployments during the post-9/11 wars made it increasingly difficult for soldiers and families to adapt to continuous oscillations between war and home, absence and presence'.[17]

And yet literature and writing have one other important role, one to which I shall also return later on – reading. Veterans' writing enables us to read texts that bear the mark of wartime death and gain a view into the horrendous personal ramifications of proximity to wartime violence. One work in which non-movement in the face of death has been articulated and which examines how we read or write poetry about war is Simone Weil's reading of the classical war epic Homer's *Iliad*, in her 1941 essay 'The *Iliad*, or the Poem of Force'. Weil's term 'Force' represents the dehumanisation that takes place during war and is revealed through

Homer's poetry, characterised by objectification – of ending movement. In her essay, Weil argues that objectification of the human body is the main thrust of the 'Force' of war:

> that x that turns anybody who is subjected to it into a thing. Exercised to the limit, it turns man into a thing in the most literal sense: it makes a corpse out of him. Somebody was here, and the next minute there is nobody here at all.[18]

Weil, moreover, describes Force as freezing and objectifying not only the dead but also those who killed them, as well as witnesses and unwilling participants. In one startling example she discusses the meeting between Achilles, who had killed Trojan hero Hector in the latter stages of the *Iliad*, and Priam, Hector's father and the King of Troy, who has arrived at Achilles' camp in a bid to retrieve his son's body. In Weil's analysis both characters, while not dead, have in fact been 'stopped' by Force, whether because of the death of a close friend, as in Achilles' case, or, as with Priam, the death of a son. Referring to Priam's turning into an object under Achilles' gaze, Weil writes:

> In their presence, people move about as if they were not there; they, on their side, running the risk of being reduced to nothing in a single instant, imitate nothingness in their own persons. Pushed, they fall. Fallen, they lie where they are, unless chance gives somebody the idea of raising them up again.[19]

Those undone by the death of friends and family and those pinned down by the threat of violence become objects while still alive, an experience further complicated by the idealisation of the often masculine soldierly body. A site of potence, a symbol of national pride, veterans are reduced to emotional paralysis and a living death, placing even more pressure on the impetus to 'be OK' and 'move on'. As Wool writes:

> The fighting soldier body and its nationally configured masculinity has been disciplined and ennobled, decried and obscured, displayed and defaced. And the injured soldier body, which insinuates a threatening display of just one of the many deadly elements that undergird the existence of the modern state, has been subject to an array of additional treatments.[20]

This turning into an object, a 'being dead', the transformation from the kind of body that interacts with others to the kind that is seemingly passively moved by others or by the symptoms of post-traumatic stress disorder (flashbacks, hyper-vigilance, violent acting out and memory loss, among others[21]) is a recurring theme in post-war and post-traumatic literature. A case in point is Randall Jarrell's seminal post-Second World War poem 'The Death of the Ball Turret Gunner', in which a speaker narrates the shift from the movement of the human body and that of human thought to the passivity of an object, or the remains of an object, being washed from the inside of a bomber:

> From my mother's sleep I fell into the State,
> And I hunched in its belly till my wet fur froze.
> Six miles from earth, loosed from its dream of life,
> I woke to black flak and the nightmare fighters.
> When I died they washed me out of the turret with a hose.[22]

The flow of human consciousness, the almost associative movement between place and mind, a present in the turret and a past in the mother or life on the ground, is violently halted by the gunner's death, spilling forth an object that once was a person. A living being, moved by life and the mover of others, has become a thing to be 'washed out'. Jarrell's poem, while explicitly dealing with the moment in which a dynamic, ambiguous life force, a 'dream', is turned into a passive object to be 'washed' out, also exposes the problem with language that may befall those frozen not by the violence of the event, as the soldier's body was, but by the witnessing of it – say, by that soldier in charge of 'washing' his friend out.

Thus the arresting of life's motion leads to objecthood and death. It is the shock of encountering what Merleau-Ponty describes as an unassuming truth, one spelled out by the remains of the soldier being washed from the turret, and one that, it seems, continues to haunt those veterans who sense deeply that they never really emerged from or survived war but remained dead while alive: 'Visible and mobile, my body is a thing among things; it is one of them. It is caught up in the fabric of the world, and its cohesion is that of a thing.'[23] In his *Writing after War*, John Limon discusses the shock that realisation can have, the dark epiphany of experiencing one's body as an object, or any human body as also an object, one experienced in the heat of battle and, as I shall discuss in Chapter 3, also in other forms of sudden violence, such as sexual assault. Limon here uses the example of an anecdote involving Civil War veteran and future US President James A. Garfield. In this narrative, Garfield speaks of an incident in which he attempted to wake fellow soldiers who appeared to be sleeping, and who, to his surprise, turned out to be dead bodies. This incident, according to the account, caused him to lose a sense of what he calls 'the sacredness of life', and he goes on to say 'the sense of the sacredness of other things, of peace, had gone out of some soldiers and never come back again'.[24] Here Garfield relates 'life' to a kind of safety, 'peace', pointing at the fact that men who were thought to be alive but turned out to be dead undid both those states.

Jarrell's 'The Death of the Ball Turret Gunner', however, also aids us in fleshing out the link between such an accident and a breakdown in communication, an explanation that goes beyond the sentiment, made prominent in certain theories of trauma, according to which traumatic events resist representation or communication to others. We must, then, imagine not the soldier who had died, for he did not survive the power of Force – though he is instrumental in the experience of survivors – but another, the soldier who had washed out the human remains with a 'hose', or even one who had just witnessed that horrible scene, perhaps also the soldier who had attempted to awaken the dead Civil War soldiers. If they were ever to use a hose again, they would have encountered the fact that neither tool nor word – 'hose' – had changed in post-war life. One uses hoses in 'civilian life' and one uses the word 'hose' from time to time, the same way one may encounter those who are asleep in everyday life as well: there seems to be nothing extraordinary about either. However, once a person has experienced the unique use of 'hose' or 'sleep' in the wartime context, those words and situations have nevertheless changed in a disturbingly indiscernible fashion, creating an obstacle to representation, yet one that is different from a complete impasse. In short, how does one use 'regular' words to describe 'irregular' situations? The returning, so-called 'demilitarised' veterans must use the hose, then, but cannot bring themselves to use the hose, will encounter a sleeping loved one and are suddenly frozen. Thus, just like the soldier had turned into an object, his movement arrested and dispersed by the 'flak' of the 'nightmare fighters', and just like those soldiers who had had the shocking realisation of other human bodies as objects, so the words available to witnesses of that event similarly lose their plasticity, overrun by the moral and psychological onus of past horrific experiences, of an arrested movement, one that has become anchored or fixed to the moment of its death.

Words like 'hose' and 'sleep', and the objects and situations to which they refer, are assembled throughout a lifetime, at school, learned from adults and peers, and collected piecemeal into a system of describing, telling and expressing ourselves. Obviously, each one of us describes things differently, and some modes of description are more regulated or idiosyncratic than others. However, the encounter with war, what Weil calls Force or what Merleau-Ponty calls 'accident', compounds words with other unsettling meanings that get lost in the general use of the word. What do words like 'hose' or 'sleep' trigger for these returning soldiers? Similarly to the object to which they refer, those words stay the same, denoting the object used to wash out the remains of a comrade as well as to clean a suburban parked car. We could, of course, change the name so as to differentiate the 'war-hose' from the 'house-hose', or 'dead sleep' and 'real sleep', but we could also imagine that exercise implemented throughout language itself – a tagging of each word into pre- and post-war meanings. Language would become so idiosyncratic and personal, so often necessitating neologisms and stream-of-association meanings that it would fail at its main purpose: communication. Only the speaker, in other words, would understand his words, and hardly anyone else. What, then, can one do when the word changes without changing? How does one become different while staying the same? One paradigmatic moment of such a shock, one that also includes its linguistic causes and ramifications, can be seen in a story told by American linguist and anthropologist Benjamin Lee Whorf.

Serving for a time as an insurance claims agent, Whorf writes of a case in which a man who had avoided lighting a cigarette near barrels labelled as being filled with petrol lit one next to barrels empty of the liquid, even though they still contained highly flammable petrol fumes. The barrels exploded, taking the man by surprise. While this incident could be seen as yet another instance of learning ('next time, don't smoke next to any petrol barrels, whether empty or full'), it serves, as Whorf claims, to expose the extent to which language is complicit in our experience of reality. The case suffices to show, Whorf writes,

> how the cue to a certain line of behavior is often given by the analogies of the linguistic formula in which the situation is spoken of, and by which to some degree it is analyzed, classified, and allotted its place in the world.[25]

Thus, if the linguistic formula sets a full barrel as dangerous, that same formula leads one to believe that an empty barrel would be safe. In the wake of the ensuing explosion, according to Whorf, the man is struck not only by an explosion but also by the life-threatening repercussions of what should have been, ostensibly, a slip in language. A barrel full of dangerous liquid then becomes 'full of danger' and, thus, a barrel emptied of the liquid is one from which danger has been drained. If 'safety' is an empty barrel and 'danger' a full one, then the liquid comes to be confused with the abstract concept 'danger', somehow melding with it. The leap is from the physical state of disorder, or continuum, in which there exists another intermediate state of matter and non-matter, vapours, within the conceptual division of 'safe' and 'unsafe'. The man in Whorf's story, then, is not taught, or is not *just* taught, that 'empty' does not indicate 'safe' from a dictionary or a textbook, but is made to feel the physical ramifications such misunderstandings or misinterpretations may have for his own body. He was, so to speak, physically touched, made to react as an object would, in a manner that can be called, following Peirce, indexical. One result of this experience is, then, a lack of security in using language that stems at least in part from an inability to differentiate 'safe' and 'unsafe' words, or words associated with death, violence and wartime experiences from their other 'innocuous' meanings. Herein, at least part of what I call an injury to language can be glimpsed: the inability to use language confidently as a tool of communication.

The moment, event or prolonged exposure perceived by the individual to be responsible for such an undermining or undoing of a sense of security with using language is the 'accident' or 'surprise' that cannot be subsumed as yet another instance of learning. Information or content is not received, as the experience disrupts the very ability to process information, or to evaluate the relation between the experiencing body and either its temporal or its spatial context. In Freudian terms, at least in those fleshed out in *Beyond the Pleasure Principle*, this event could be described as bypassing systems of representation and meaning, and directly invading and subverting consciousness.[26] However, whether adhering to the Freudian narrative of trauma or not, the effect of this disruption is manifest in a difficulty to consolidate body and context, experience and language, or to perceive them as being possible at the same time and in the same place. A new diagram that would, indeed, allow for the inclusion of both at the same time is then needed: the poetic prosthesis.

The prosthesis of writing is a prop used to come to terms with the toll war takes on language and personality and, at the same time, to attempt a kind of description of war itself and of memorialising those who had died or, to use Weil's terminology, turned to objects. That task, however, is, more often than not, the lot of veterans who, to use Shay's formulation, had died in war, who appear alive and yet are dead, or what Weil dubs the 'compromise' between a man and a corpse. As Weil writes: 'The idea of a person's being a thing is a logical contradiction. Yet what is impossible in logic becomes true in life, and the contradiction lodged within the soul tears it to shreds.'[27] At the centre of one of this book's main thrusts, then, stands the torn-to-shreds, half-dead soldier, who appears whole and yet in some meaningful way is dead. That same veteran is moved to construct that mechanism or prosthesis that allows him back into life – poems and, in the case of *The White Donkey* discussed in Chapter 5, graphic novels. The role of writing is, again, not to describe, or not only to describe but also to provide a tool on which to lean in the attempt to limp back to life. And while the poetic aftermath of war can be detected in other, perhaps longer, forms of writing and art, poetry is, I would argue, that laboratory experiment with language that lends itself to the kind of almost philosophical investigation of communication and its shortcomings that is seen in much of soldier poetry. As Vietnam poet Bruce Weigl writes in his memoir, poetry replaces a former concept of 'life' with the artificial construct, the prosthesis, of poetry:

> The war took away my life and gave me poetry in return. The war taught me irony: that I instead of others would survive is ironic. All of my heroes are dead. The fate the world has given me is to struggle to write powerfully enough to draw others into the horror.[28]

Poetry uniquely marks the end of a former 'whole' and 'organic' conception of life and the beginning of a life marked by disability, by the uneasy and often painful limping that is poetic language.

Veterans' writing and poetry, then, rise from the pain of objecthood, from a point of having no language at all or of being at odds with it even being a language. As Elaine Scarry comments on the effect of pain on language: 'Physical pain does not simply resist language but actively destroys it, bringing about an immediate reversion to a state anterior to language, to the sounds and cries a human being makes before language is learned.'[29] It is from this void that poetic language emerges, a yelp of pain stylised into the form we recognise as poetry, a mode of speaking, as James Berger writes in *The Disarticulate*, that emerges out of the paralysing absence of language. Metaphor, Berger says, that foundational component of poetic and figurative language, is the mode of communication that 'emerges out of not-language'.[30] The work soldiers do after war, then, is to improvise a new way of speaking, using anything around them during war in order to secure their survival. They do not invent or create new words or meanings *ex nihilo*, but imperfectly complete what has been severed by war through improvisation, by using the tools already at hand, by using found material. A tool, again, is made to emerge out of the silence or non-language that, as World

War I veteran Rudolph Binding writes in his war diary, takes hold in the wake of war:

> Feeling deeply about it, one becomes less able to talk about it every day. Not because one understands it less each day, but because one grasps it better. But it is a silent teacher, and he who learns becomes silent too.[31]

The severed, uneasy, silent mode of existence and writing exposed in post-war poetry is contextualised in this book in terms of injury, solitude and, finally, disability. Poetry, then, for me was the most natural choice for this investigation, being that mode of artistic communication that is character-ised by the attempt to use words with known meanings who have, at war, lost their meaning, and twist them, wrangle them, in order to point them finally toward a new, more personal direction. It is a process similar or parallel to what Scarry describes as the 'human attempt to reverse the de-objectifying work of pain', one defined by 'forcing pain itself into avenues of objectification'.[32] The object in question is thus the poetic prosthesis: a prop made of words. But this initial discussion of the 'nuts and bolts' of what I call here the poetic prosthesis would not be complete without one significant artistic manifestation or narrativisation of both the need the post-war prosthesis is meant to fulfil and the manner in which it operates.

The work of the poetic prosthetic is, in light of these struggles, divided into two main parts: oscillation and disruption. By oscillation I mean the initiation of an ever-shifting field of meaning that warps commonly under-stood or abstract terms and concepts while, at the same time, pointing toward unsaid and perhaps unsayable meaning that is embedded in the concrete experience of traumatic events. This oscillation is key in these vet-erans' ability to regain a sense of humanity out of the 'limbo' or paralysis of post-war life, and it is such that marks the subjects, themes and modes that are unique to each prosthesis, with its unique modes of undermining and shifting meaning. However, even that field is marked by the ways in which the space is disrupted by the spectre of phantom pain, the violent, pain-ful and often uncontrollable recurrence of an index of pain and memory. As Wills writes in *Prosthesis* concerning his father's false leg, the prosthetic form of life, in its very essence, involves the missing organic part, the dis-comfort of the inorganic replacement and the experience of sudden pain:

> He is leaning on his elbows trying to decide whether to wait for another spasm, not that he has any choice, for it will come whether he waits or not; it is more a matter of deciding how to deal with it, in which position it would be preferable to receive it, so I am waiting too, pausing in mid-sentence when he

bends over, never sure whether to let his controlled yelp interrupt the flow of my prose, never knowing if I will still be able to resume along the same lines, indeed in the same language, once the phantom has made its wretched pass.[33]

The essence of the prosthetic mode of living is of 'deciding how to deal with it', one devoid of the option to 'ignore it', 'put up with it' or 'heal'.

War Index

The 'pinning down' of an external, general experience that pushes one to create a poetic prosthetic is not exclusively tied to veterans returning from war but is shared among all those who have felt similarly 'pinned down' by a violence or shocking life experience. This transformation of a traumatic event into text is described by philosopher and writer Susan Brison, herself the victim of a violent sexual assault, who compares the stark difference between the kind of text prompted by trauma against the type of rationalistic, abstract mode of philosophy typified by the Cartesian model:

> The 'accident of private history' that forced me to think about the 'personal' as philosophical was a near-fatal sexual assault and attempted murder. Unlike Descartes, who had 'to demolish everything completely and start again right from the foundations' in order to find any knowledge 'that was stable and likely to last,' I had my world demolished for me.[34]

There are, of course, important distinctions to be made between the experience and aftermath of a woman being assaulted in a domestic or urban context and near-death experiences by soldiers during war, far away from home – distinctions that will stand at the centre of Chapter 3, focusing on the war form of life. However, the idea of a compulsion from outside, an event that triggers what Brison calls the 'personal as philosophical' and that then pins down its survivor to the terror of its reality, seems to parallel the kind of linguistic investigations post-war poems undertake, along with the striking way in which Brison gives witness to her experience of becoming an object:

> When, after I 'woke up,' subsequent to being strangled into unconsciousness, and I realized that I was being treated as a corpse (my assailant was dragging me by my feet to a creek bed at the bottom of a steep ravine), I redescribed the event as 'a murder-in-progress'.[35]

The objectification, what Brison calls the 'accident of private history', results, in her case, in a work of philosophy, Brison's mode of investigating language in the wake of violence. In the case of those works written after war and that are at the heart of my discussion, that work is done through the no less investigatory mode of poetry, a reaction to a force being applied from without.

Thus, the compulsion outwards is as important to the understanding of these veterans' poems as the event that thrust them inwards, that need to break out of the objectifying, silent and painful life of the index of 'it' and address one's pain and experiences to others. Perhaps unsurprisingly, then, this is the work of reaching out, albeit hesitatingly: to utter general words used to communicate that which is most intrinsically tied with the communication of thoughts, emotions and experiences to others. This is one significant reason why the writings of philosopher Charles S. Peirce has become so important for me in my work on contemporary soldier poetry and writing. Peirce, who will be discussed at length in Chapter 1, offers an analysis of the main parts of any meaning-giving activity, one foundational assumption of which is that communication is not only possible – itself a bold statement compared to more contemporary works of philosophy and criticism that would cast serious doubts on that ability – but essential. And that, I find, is one important feature of the work soldiers do after war: the desperate need and, at times, desire both to communicate their wartime experiences to their home communities and families, and to find a way of bridging the gap between the extremity of war and, as Wool states, the ordinariness of everyday life.

Soldiers want to speak, need to speak, and often do so in the confines of very limited communities that share their experiences and fears.[36] The trouble is more often the fact that they do not know how to do so: not to the general public, to friends and family. They know how to speak, naturally, and can describe certain aspects of their wartime experiences or, conversely, ignore them entirely and speak the language of the home. A more pressing issue, however, becomes how to speak in a language that addresses both the extremity of wartime violence and death and the seeming ordinariness of everyday home life. I have experienced the gap between myself and others upon my return from up-close encounters with violence and death, and I have seen my words fall to the floor in futile attempts to capture one specific image lodged in my mind. But Peirce's theory of language presupposes one important aspect, important in my own story but also in the general narrative of veterans learning to speak again after war, and that is how the purpose of language and, by extension, poetry is communication.

However, this emphasis on communication, veterans' dire need to share with the people surrounding them, is one with implications that, naturally, range further than just the emotional needs and obstacles faced by the soldiers themselves. As I have argued, when soldiers struggle with life after war because of this communicational obstacle, then those immediately surrounding them – family, friends, partners and so on – are also made to carry much of that load. The deployment that tears soldiers from their surroundings, the growing alienation between families and their deployed loved ones during their tours of duty and the chasms that separate soldiers from their families upon their return are a source of strain for all involved, and cannot be considered solely in terms of 'helping the veteran'. In the context of this book they mean the work of soldiers writing their prostheses of language and of communities reading them, but also family members and partners writing, as I discuss later on, prostheses themselves, works that then require veterans to do some reading of their own. One cannot be separated from the other: the war and its aftermath, the soldier and his various support networks. As Kenneth T. MacLeish writes so beautifully of the complex of estrangement and pain in post-war life, 'to cast any unwanted excesses of war's violence as second order, peripheral, or "collateral" to its "necessary" violence is not only to misunderstand war but also to conspire in a confusion of its means and ends'.[37] To write after war is, then, also to untangle a complex web of pain and distance, of the extremity of the ordinary and the ordinariness of the extreme.

These poems, while straining communication by questioning the very possibility of communication, nonetheless also represent desperate attempts to communicate. The significance of that assertion is that the poetic act is to be understood not as an obtuse refusal to 'speak plainly' but as an attempt to speak that is so painful and difficult as to necessitate a whole new mode of language. While much work has been done regarding the apparent need felt by many victims to disclose their feelings and experiences in the wake of trauma, it has not always been clear what that work is, or what it resolves, and whether or not it performs the same 'work' for both men and women. Some studies, for instance, found men less willing to disclose positive emotion in the wake of trauma, as when they 'experience greater frustration and distress they disclose less, suggesting a possible male strategy of internalizing emotions when under pressure and becoming "strong and silent"'.[38] Peirce's philosophical analysis then aids in identifying the frustrating attempt to communicate detectable in post-war poetry, even if what is being transmitted is an unresolvable tension between experience and language. In some way, poems written by soldiers are able to function as prostheses, artificially replacing the 'natural' or 'organic' concept of teleological communication and language injured during war, by their very ability to contain two seemingly contradicting impulses – the need to stay silent in face of an inability to speak, and a necessity to speak as part of the desire to remain within community and, consequently, human life.

For the most part, the works this book discusses were written by men who had served in Iraq, Afghanistan and, in some cases, the Falklands War, with most of the entries coming from American veterans. What that choice highlights, I believe, is the American contemporary experience of war, one that is closer in a way to the American experience of the Second World War than, say, the British experience of the same conflict. American soldiers writing about contemporary war, like their mid-century counterparts, do so concerning a war that their home front knows little about, a home front that, unlike the blitzed citizens of 1940s Britain, is by and large protected from direct impact. As Susan Schweik writes, while 'that lonely masculine authority of experience – the bitter authority derived from direct exposure to violence, injury, and mechanized terror' – was rapidly dispersing among general populations of the British mid-twentieth century population, 'American culture was, obviously, characterized by far greater disjunctions between male and female "experience" of war than the British blitz society'[39] described by writers such as Robert Graves and others. And while the twenty-first century has seen an uptick in the extent to which women were exposed to combat, the gap, at least in terms of writing by men and women about their wartime experience, remains significant. What this amounts to is a much higher ratio of men who have experienced the violence of these wars as frontline soldiers, both because of the decreased participation of women in said militaries compared to men and because of the lack of American civilian involvement in the war.

This disparity, however, does present a few fruitful avenues for further investigations, two of which are touched upon in this book. The first is more of a conclusion this book seems to be hinting at, according to which the rhetoric of prosthesis that these pages enact, via the work of Peirce and Wills, is itself gendered. What I mean by that is a tendency, one that I associate with masculine post-traumatic or disabled experiences, to explain the breaking down of communication and the attempt to reconstruct that communication in mechanical terms. And this, as some may have already noticed, is my tendency as well, even in my own usage of terms like 'breaking down' and 'reconstruct' in the previous sentence: a tendency that may, for the time being, call my own ability to investigate that aspect of my work into question. It is an inclination that is noticeable in Peirce's division of signs, in Wills's usage of a term like 'prosthesis', which in many respects presents the foundation for my own thinking regarding that term in textual critique. This mechanical aspect could also be related to the mechanical nature of modern warfare, a theme I take up in Chapter 3. The second issue, one that I discuss more directly, is the gendered and ethnic disparity of what it means to 'experience' war in the contemporary military setting, a disparity laden with the same social issues plaguing society at large – racism, sexual harassment and assault, and others. I pick up on that aspect in several different places in this book: as part of Chapter 4's investigation of the wartime environment; as part of Chapter 5's discussion of the role post-war poetry plays in burial and memory; and as part of the concluding chapter's emphasis on the impact returning soldiers have on their home environments.

However, as a possible precursor to some of the issues mentioned above that are at least partially discussed in those sections, it is worthwhile raising one aspect that is related to the mechanical nature of war and, possibly, of one variety of reaction to war – the experience of the rigidity or mechanical nature of the post-war military support system. More specifically, what is the experience of non-male soldiers within the predominantly masculine institutional structures that attempt to rehabilitate veterans upon their return, such as the United States Department of Veterans Affairs (VA) in the American case, or the Office for Veterans' Affairs in the United Kingdom. If indeed, as I argue, veterans return from war dead while alive, devoid of communication, then what would be the experience of that linguistic and cultural gap with the added dimension of, for example, gender difference? One glimpse into that tension is provided by the writing of US veteran Chantelle Bateman, who returned from active duty in Iraq in 2005. In one of her poems, 'Lists and Scales', published online as part of the Warrior Writers project, Bateman relates the experience of a periodic meeting with a VA mental health professional in a manner that resembles an interrogation or perhaps torture, and, at times, sexual misconduct. These are the first three stanzas:

I hate being alone with him again
Even in my mind
Trapped in his looney bin of an office
Suffocated by these four walls
Padded in frames full of bullshit
His accolades for a job well done
From people who don't know how to do their damn jobs

I can feel him staring at me
Counting my tics, fidgets, and sweat beads
Sizing me up to see if I'm a good fit for crazy

Talking to me very slowly
With small words
About things bigger than he understands
Asking me questions
And only listening for answers from his lists
That tell him how far up I am
On the 'About to lose her shit' scale.[40]

Bateman's poem no doubt recounts a situation that should be familiar to returning veterans, that of having to fit experiences for which they may not have found words to a sliding scale of mental health or 'normality'. That gap, again, is seen in the manner that Bateman describes the therapist as embodying an institution that can only use, as the title suggests, lists and scales, with the VA representative described as counting 'tics, fidgets, and sweat beads' and using 'small words about things bigger than he understands'. The inadequacy and incompatibility of their two languages – that undone by war and that attempting to gauge said damage through 'counting' and 'small words' – are familiar and brilliantly represented here by Bateman. However, what the poem adds to this current discussion is her awareness of a gap not just in language but also in gender – of, in other words, being a woman in that situation: 'Trapped in his looney bin of an office', with the very opening line of the poem setting a firm gendered line between the two characters, one reminiscent perhaps of an abusive relationship: 'I hate being alone with him again.'

With that added stress in mind, other aspects of the poem – namely, the masculine gaze and measurement of the female body – gain even more force in this dual estrangement: civilian–soldier, man–woman. The counting of sweat beads, the seemingly stern observation, the compact physical setting: all enhance a sense of being probed not only with the 'wrong words' but in an explicitly gendered, objectifying and sexualised manner. This sense is enhanced later in the poem as the male character proceeds to 'go down the list' until reaching the category of sexual assault, and the female patient's identification of the very act of breaking down, objectification and classification of the therapist–patient encounter as such an assault:

Down the list
'Were you ever raped or sexually assaulted?'
Rape is sexual assault douche bag
And your question is reminiscent of the act
Penetrating and touching me without my consent

Whatever I tell you won't matter
I know you aren't here to help me find justice or peace
Where is the question that asks 'have you sexually assaulted anyone'
How many crazy points is that worth?
'Yes'
Up the scale[41]

Bateman's use of italicised internal dialogue highlights the gaping chasm that lies between her and her interlocutor. What he hears in response to his questions is 'yes', the only binary word available to her to express a frustration and shock of experience that, at least within the confines of this meeting, remains unsaid. Thus, the raging frustration from the probing, assaulting manner of his questioning is relegated to a silent internal storm. The questioning, no doubt meant to help the veteran demilitarise in complete mindfulness of the possibility of having experienced traumatic experiences during her service, only exacerbates that damage, the entire line of probing being experienced as retraumatising and aggressive.

We are, thus, presented with a paradox, one heightened as a result of just this short glimpse into the endless possibilities of investigating gender differences in the difficult task of returning home from war. That paradox lies in the fact that, in the very choice to address the effects of war on language as a 'breakdown' and in the act of talking of a 'reconstructing', a 'prosthesis', this book and its writer are engaged in the kind of rhetoric that mimics or follows the same cold, deconstructing, severe gaze of the therapist in Bateman's poem. In admitting as much, I am, I think, setting a limit to a kind of discourse that this book attempts to challenge but that it may also aid in perpetuating. However, despite this mechanical aspect of the wartime experience, further explored in Chapter 3, there is one possible way out of this paradox. It is one, I would argue, that runs through another, adjacent, paradox: that the undoing, breakdown or implosion of language in the wake of war may find an answer in an equivalent artistic implosion of any kind of mechanistic understanding of the work of meaning through the medium of the poetic prosthesis.

Chapter Outline

A discussion of veterans' writing and its prosthetic function intersects with several theoretical thrusts – military studies, literature, philosophy, gender studies, psychology, to name but a few – and thus the book itself is put together with the hope of initiating its own brand of movement between disparate poles. Chapter 1 begins that effort through a more thorough discussion of the nature of the movement and the significance of Peirce's category of 'dream' and of Wills's 'ghost' or 'phantom' to the reading of contemporary poems written by veterans. Chapter 2 will focus on the movement between 'reality' and prosthesis, and on the notion, already discussed here, that war is experienced as 'real' or 'realer' than life after war. The focus of this chapter will be my critique of the concept of post-war 'disillusionment' and my own emphasis on the alternative notion of post-war linguistic injury. The object created in order to initiate movement, the prosthetic text, will be discussed in terms of precisely refusing to pinpoint the 'location' of the event as either physical/mental or social, undermining our very ability to understand those concepts as hermetically distinct.

Chapter 3, however, will describe the 'form of life' or 'culture' that is war and the ways in which that culture affects the return home, as well as the need for a poetic prosthesis. In this chapter I shall focus on the ways in which war presents a distinct case of injury, through its symbolic, political, communal and cultural contexts. This section will also include a discussion of the variety of wartime experiences and the manner in which those experiences are shaped by persisting social issues such as sexual harassment, racism and others. The following chapter, Chapter 4, analyses the nature of that movement which the poetic prosthetic aims to resuscitate and its relation with a certain conception of irony. Here I address the tradition of viewing irony as something much more comprehensive and philosophically significant than a simple rhetorical device through the work of Friedrich Schlegel, Søren Kierkegaard and others.

Chapter 5, moreover, will centre on another function performed by the prosthetic text, that of providing a proper burial for those who were undone by force, who had become objectified, through either death or disability, beyond recognition as human. The act of burial, the ultimate return to the indexical past, is then conceived as performance, but of a specific kind: burial rite, elegy and mourning. The chapter will highlight the way in which post-war writing can be read in the context of the tradition of folk soldier commemoration, one that provides a proper burial for dead or lost comrades and that, as such, makes manifest an expression of care for the dead.

Next, in Chapter 6, I shall locate poetic prosthetics within the wider context of two seemingly competing theoretical narratives – trauma studies and disability studies – specifically in terms of what appears to be the opposition to representation in both fields. While naturally invested in trauma studies' focus on the kinds of event that produce stress, as well as representational or communicational impasse, the chapter will argue for the value of understanding wartime 'injury', as I refer to that event in this book, in terms also of disability.

Finally, the Conclusion will address some of the questions and limitations of the prosthesis theory I advance in this book through a discussion of the one text that I found resonated with my own post-war path back to society, Daniel Defoe's *Robinson Crusoe*. Stranded on a lonely island of injury, devoid of language and community, writers, through the kind of writing that both looks at the past and reimagines it as a moment of artistic agency, trace their way back into community. This chapter will also include one other aspect of care: the idea that the work of art is that which allows the audience or the reader to enter the experience of disability made manifest by the text. It will then progress to a brief discussion of the manner in which certain reception theories – namely, Wolfgang Iser's notion of the 'play of the text' – can further elucidate the manner in which the post-war text exposes readers to the interior landscape that is veterans' lives lived with invisible disability.

Notes

1. Meir Wieseltier, 'Seifa' [in Hebrew], in *Pnim Chutz* (Tel Aviv: Hakibbutz Hameuchad, 1977), translated by the author.
2. Eric J. Leed, *No Man's Land: Combat and Identity in World War I* (New York: Cambridge University Press, 1979), 3.
3. Herman Melville, *Moby-Dick*, edited by Hershel Parker and Harrison Hayford (New York: Norton, 1999), 192.
4. Zoe Wool, *After War: The Weight of Life at Walter Reed* (Durham, NC: Duke University Press, 2015), 5.
5. Ibid., 7.
6. Gerardo Mena, *The Shape of Our Faces No Longer Matters* (Cape Girardeau: Southeast Missouri University Press, 2014), 55.
7. There is more on this tool aspect of Mena's poetry in my essay 'A Good Coffin: The Iraq War Poetry of Gerardo Mena', in *Different Drummers: Military Culture and Its Discontents*, edited by Tad Tuleja (Salt Lake City: Utah University Press, 2020), 165–76.
8. Mena, *The Shape of Our Faces*, 55.
9. Nil Santiáñez, *The Literature of Absolute War: Transnationalism and World War II* (Cambridge: Cambridge University Press, 2020), 156–7.
10. Mena, *The Shape of Our Faces*, 55.
11. Jonathan Shay, *Achilles in Vietnam: Combat Trauma and the Undoing of Character* (New York: Simon and Schuster, 1995), 51–2.
12. Edward Tick, *War and the Soul: Healing Our Nation's Veterans* (Wheaton, IL: Quest Books, 2005), 12.
13. Leed, *No Man's Land*, 21.

14. Graham W. Lea, 'Annotated Playscript', in *Contact! Unload: Military Veterans, Trauma, and Research-Based Theatre*, edited by George Belliveau and Graham W. Lea (Vancouver: University of British Columbia Press, 2020), 44.
15. Maurice Merleau-Ponty, 'Eye and Mind', in *The Merleau-Ponty Aesthetics Reader: Philosophy and Painting*, edited by Galen A. Johnson (Evanston, IL: Northwestern University Press, 1996), 125.
16. Wool, *After War*, 3.
17. Sarah Hautzinger and Jean Scandlyn, *Beyond Post-Traumatic Stress: Homefront Struggles with the Wars on Terror* (New York: Routledge, 2016), 120.
18. Simone Weil, 'The *Iliad*, or the Poem of Force', *Chicago Review* 18, no. 2 (1965): 6.
19. Ibid., 5.
20. Wool, *After War*, 11.
21. 'PTSD Checklist for DSM-5', *U.S. Department of Veterans Affairs* website. Available at: <https://www.ptsd.va.gov/professional/assessment/adult-sr/ptsd-checklist.asp>; 'Exhibit 1.3-4 DSM-5 Diagnostic Criteria for PTSD', *National Center for Biotechnology Information* website. Available at: <https://www.ncbi.nlm.nih.gov/books/NBK207191/box/part1_ch3.box16/ (both last accessed 25 February 2022).
22. Randall Jarrell, *The Complete Poems* (New York: Farrar, Straus, and Giroux, 1981), 144.
23. Merleau-Ponty, 'Eye and Mind', 124–5.
24. John Limon, *Writing after War: American War Fiction from Realism to Postmodernism* (New York: Oxford University Press, 1994), 38.
25. Benjamin Lee Whorf, *Language, Thought, and Reality*, edited by John B. Carroll (Cambridge, MA: MIT Press, 1956), 137.
26. Sigmund Freud, *Beyond the Pleasure Principle*, translated by James Strachey (New York: Norton, 1961), 22–7.
27. Weil, 'The *Iliad*', 9.
28. Bruce Weigl, *The Circle of Hahn* (New York: Grove Press, 2001), 5–6.
29. Elaine Scarry, *The Body in Pain: The Making and Unmaking of the World* (New York: Oxford University Press, 1985), 4.
30. James Berger, *The Disarticulate* (New York: New York University Press, 2014), 11.
31. Rudolph Binding, *A Fatalist at War*, translated by Ian F. D. Morrow (London: George Allen & Unwin, 1929), 60.
32. Scarry, *The Body in Pain*, 6.
33. David Wills, *Prosthesis* (Stanford: Stanford University Press, 1994), 7.
34. Susan Brison, *Aftermath: Violence and the Remaking of Self* (Princeton: Princeton University Press, 2003), 25.
35. Ibid., 32.
36. See Charles A. Braithwaite, '"Were *You* There?"': A Ritual of Legitimacy Among Vietnam Veterans', *Western Journal of Communication* 61, no. 4 (Fall 1997): 423–47; Holly A. Wheeler, 'Veterans' Transitions to Community College: A Case Study', *Community College Journal of Research and Practice* 36 (2012): 783–5; Tatiana Prorokova, '"I Don't Belong Here Anymore": Homeland as an Uncomfortable Space

for War Veterans in Irwin Winkler's *Home of the Brave*', in *Conflict Veterans: Discourses and Living Contexts of an Emerging Social Group*, edited by Michael Daxner, Marion Näser-Lather and Silvia Nicola (Cambridge: Cambridge Scholars Publishing, 2018), 170; and Philip Held, Brian J. Klassen, Joanne M. Hall, Tanya R. Friese, Marcel M. Bertsch-Gout, Alyson K. Zalta and Mark H. Pollack, '"I Knew It Was Wrong the Moment I Got the Order": A Narrative Thematic Analysis of Moral Injury in Combat Veterans', *Psychological Trauma: Theory, Research, Practice, and Policy* 11, no. 4 (2019): 402.

37. Kenneth T. MacLeish, *Making War at Fort Hood: Life and Uncertainty in a Military Community* (Princeton: Princeton University Press, 2013), 10.

38. David G. Purves and Philip G. Erwin, 'Post-Traumatic Stress and Self-Disclosure', *The Journal of Psychology* 138, no. 1 (2004): 30; and Lawrence B. Stein and Stanley L. Brodsky, 'When Infants Wail: Frustration and Gender as Variables in Distress Disclosure', *The Journal of General Psychology* 122 (1995): 19–27.

39. Susan Schweik, 'Writing War Poetry Like a Woman', *Critical Inquiry* 13, no. 3 (Spring 1987): 534.

40. Chantelle Bateman, 'Lists and Scales', *Warrior Poets* website. Available at: <https://www.warriorwriters.org/artists/chantelle.html> (last accessed 22 February 2022).

41. Ibid.

CHAPTER 1

Index, Ghost, Dream

Yes, I only have one language, yet it is not mine.

— Jacques Derrida[1]

Prostheses are fabricated in order to replace limbs or organs and are made of parts – metal rods, connectors, elastic bands, an artificial skin – that come together to mimic the structure and function of a lost original. One central aspect of the prosthetic 'experience' is an eerie relationship between the organic body and the assemblage of inanimate objects made to supplement what had been severed from the organic. On the one hand, it is, as I shall discuss later in this chapter, a tool of survival, a thing or prop. On the other, it is the kind of prop used to mimic the organic, and as a result one that also foregrounds the inanimate features of the 'living' or 'organic' body. Rods are rods, indeed, but so are bones, and the ways in which the inanimate enters the realm of the living body and thus also confuses those very terms funnel into one general concept – 'unease'. In David Wills's depiction of his father's false leg given in the Introduction, he provides an essential moment of such unease, describing the manner with which his father, who uses a prosthetic leg, is painfully and uncontrollably reminded of his artificial limb. It is the scene of a shooting pain that highlights not only the artificiality and falsity of the prop, or the missing organic part it is meant to replace, but his own objecthood, as he is rendered, for a moment, helpless with pain:

> He is leaning on his elbows trying to decide whether to wait for another
> spasm, not that he has any choice, for it will come whether he waits or not; it
> is more a matter of deciding how to deal with it, in which position it would
> be preferable to receive it, so I am waiting too, pausing in mid-sentence

when he bends over, never sure whether to let his controlled yelp interrupt the flow of my prose, never knowing if I will still be able to resume along the same lines, indeed in the same language, once the phantom has made its wretched pass.[2]

Wills's recollection of the discomfort of his father's phantom pain, along with the role that unease plays in Wills's own experience of that pain, that which stands at the centre of his text, is an essential aspect of the prosthesis's resistance, as well as the nature of that resistance. The prosthesis resists, by its very existence, the fantasy of wholeness, of a return to a lost original, or of a complete 'healing'. Wills's father can undoubtedly walk but is nonetheless abruptly reminded of the fact that a part of his body has been irrecoverably severed. The resistance his father faces is not epistemological or theoretical – there is little doubt that his father would rather do away with his pain – but ontological and 'real': the leg is gone and an artificial replacement is fitted in its stead. And yet to understand the complex movement of the prosthetic is also to situate it vis-à-vis two ways of describing the narrative of injury, one in which war leads to injury and another in which injury returns one back to war. War did happen, for if it did not one would not have been injured. And yet *how* war happened or how to describe its effect proves more elusive.

One could, if one wished, think of the prosthesis, as the designator itself perhaps invites, as being just one link in a causal chain of events: a certain event or experience takes place during soldiers' experience in war or elsewhere in their military service that then injures their concept of language, necessitating the prosthesis. And this notion of causality seems to be, involuntarily if not intuitively, encouraged from my own use of medical and mechanical terminology in referring to what could be called here the 'phases' of injury and irony after war, such as 'injury', 'prosthesis', 'event' and 'amputation', which I have at least partly discussed in the Introduction. It would be easy to claim that the prosthetic leg used by an amputee war veteran lies at the end of the causal chain that was set off by his injury, for instance. But while this line of causality is easy enough to conjure, I would nonetheless urge readers to resist that aspect as well, for two reasons. The first is that I, the writer of these words, am also in many ways linked to both the subject matter discussed in it and the modes of analysis presented in the attempt to delineate it. I do not state this as a way of skirting the issue, but to say that entirely resisting what I sense as the allure of a conception of a quite straightforward chain (war–injury–prosthesis) is all but impossible. With this remark I return to the one I made in the Introduction, regarding the appeal of mechanical references in post-war writing and the possible gendered component they may have. This is another way of saying that I too had felt the persuasive power of this depiction and in no way can I altogether dismiss it. In fact, it would not be far from the truth to say that the persuasive power of this depiction is very much in effect during the writing of these very lines, a predicament I shall address further in the concluding chapter. However, as a point of emphasis, resisting should not be read as meaning 'annihilating' or 'cancelling'. Instead, it means just that – resistance, a maintaining of a tension between whatever pole this factual, causal strain represents and one other, just as important and not as easily succumbed to.

On the other side of that simple causal chain lies the view of wartime trauma as obliterating any sense of narrative whatsoever. This version of narrative, in which the 'story' is recreated after the fact, for instance, bears the mark of Freud's *Nachträglichkeit*, or 'belatedness',[3] in which knowledge of an event only arrives after the fact: that there is a kind of insight or analysis that one performs backwards, and that constructs or reconstructs something like a causal chain of events. A more extreme version of this thought in dealing with post-traumatic texts such as those under discussion in his book would be to say that the poetry after war *invents* or fabricates not only the ironic gap between real-life events and the manner in which they are communicated, but also, to an extent, the breakdown itself. 'Fabricates' may seem a harsh word, for it implies deceitfulness and yet it means only what it denotes – that the story of one's encounter with war or violence can be constructed only after the fact, to the point of, again, 'fabricating' the story itself – for until that point it had not been a story at all, just shrapnel of memory and pain. However, this view, I am compelled to say, we must resist – almost successfully – as well, since while it may be true that, for instance, soldiers 'fabricate', create stories and texts that in turn recreate a kind of reality, it is very important in the post-traumatic context to assert the 'realness' of that originary moment. It is this 'realness' that causes so much pain in its unexpressed, unprocessed form, and a realness that motivates the very act of writing of the prosthesis, even if, eventually, that reality is transposed from the event to the text motivated by said event.

The above sentiment, that an event did take place in 'reality', is, I think, central to what I have been describing as the experience of the prosthesis and also to the function that prosthesis can be said to have for returning veterans. On the most basic of levels, veterans attempt in their poetry and writing to communicate events that had, until that point, been experienced as incommunicable and perhaps even unfathomable, and yet real. At the heart of that effort lies the belief, one embedded in their moral position as witnesses to others' pain, that *something did in fact happen*, and that the only issue is *how* to describe that something in a way that would resist the many obstacles that stand in the way. This issue is pressed again by the appeal to Peirce's semiotics, which, while very influential on structuralist and post-structuralist thinkers such as linguist Roman Jakobson and psychoanalyst Jacques Lacan, was decidedly pre-Saussurean in its use of 'reality' as an axis along which to gauge the different types of signs. When discussing the shooting, unpredictable agony that is phantom pain or the unease of prosthesis, whether in physical or linguistic terms, whatever is happening, *that* – namely, the pain – seems to serve as an anchor of sorts to 'reality'. The mall, the very present physical reality that engulfs veteran Tim, in his stirring monologue presented in the Introduction, is 'fake', while the war, a distant, almost unbelievable event, is 'real'. The prosthesis in its very artificiality, in its being made, seems to highlight, then, not just the loss of the 'real' leg but the fact that soldiers also suspect the category of real itself, especially as it is expressed by their home communities. The steel rod that had replaced the bone, in other words, had turned the bone into something of a steel rod.

One example of the kind of complication or paradox that may occur when taking either route too literally is a testimony mentioned in the introduction to Dori Laub and Shoshana Felman's *Testimony*. In it, Laub and Felman famously describe a Holocaust survivor as she details her experience of the explosion of the crematoriums in Auschwitz during the Jewish revolt in the death camp, but in a manner that seems not to fit with all of the known historical facts regarding the events of the revolt.[4] On the one hand, the survivor's story is regarded as unreliable by historians, as 'fake'; on the other, the emotional and psychological impact of the event seems to explain what could be considered a deviation from the historical event. The merit in Laub and Felman's approach, however, is in establishing what it is that has taken place for the survivor precisely through gauging the tension between what historians say happened and what it is that the survivor describes or remembers: in other words, not discounting the story as fiction, while not accepting it as historical fact *per se*. Thus, as is the case with many aspects of the poetry written by veterans under discussion in this book, we return to the most basic structure – a tension that cannot be resolved between distinct poles. On one hand, it would be too simplistic to buy into the idea of a causal chain of events after war, one having to do with injury and the construction of 'prosthesis'. On the other, a total reliance on a backward-creating gaze calls into question the reality of events that, as far as the veterans are concerned, did happen. So, if indeed we are to resist both poles while still recognising the validity or draw of both, how are we to address the poems themselves, the real-life, physically evident prostheses? How does one construct a poem, an object, that makes use of the 'stuff of life', as well as warping that same material into the realm of personal expression or art? One way to understand this paradoxical position would be through the concept of irony, to which I shall return through the discussion of the prostheses' mode of operation, or what makes them 'work'. Another concept, as important, in my eyes, to an understanding of what kind of life is lived while constantly rejecting both reality and artifice, is one that is not unfamiliar to those who use prostheses – unease.

An interesting instance of artistic or poetic unease in the wake of war, and one that complicates the two temporal narratives at play here, is provided by the many well-known examples of trench art created following several twentieth-century wars[5] but most notably during and after the First World War. Using cannon shells, bullet casings and other materials, often in violation of military regulations,[6] soldiers took the very source of wartime violence and remade it in their own modes of artistic expression and commemoration. By taking, quite literally, the 'real' materials of experience and fashioning them into a differ-ent kind of object – artistic, testimonial, memento – First World War soldiers were effectively demonstrating the tension that war brought about between the living and the dead, all while creating a new kind of connection between war and their own experience and bodies. This was not just a description or a narrative, though a description in its own way, but also a new set of relations, a means of expressing one's relation to war through, quite literally, reshaping pieces of war. As Nicholas J. Saunders writes:

> Paintings and memorials represented war from a distance, spatially and tem-porally. They connected through impressions, possessing little or no sensuous or tactile immediacy. By contrast, metal Trench Art was made from the *waste of war*, its varied forms incorporating the agents of death and mutilation directly. Anonymously responsible for untold suffering and bereavement, expended shells, bullets and shrapnel were worked into a variety of forms, engaging visual, olfactory, tactile, and sometimes auditory senses, as well as memory.[7]

While poetry written by veterans after war is not as tactile as a crucifix made of bullets, poems fashioned in the aftermath of war are similar to Saunders's characterisation of trench art, in that they are in themselves twisted, carved-out linguistic structures made of the bricks and mortar of the now fallen communicational structure. And while the 'waste of war' in the above excerpt is the literal waste of war – cartridges, casings, bullets – the waste of war for soldier poets is made up of the signs of language itself, at once the only means they have to communicate and, by virtue of their perceived failure, a threat. As those carving out spent tank shells, as well as those used to demonstrating the failing of words, deal directly with their most immediate threats, they do so as a means of gaining what they have lost: talking about or describing their experiences. Thus, while attempting to sabotage commonly held beliefs concerning such key concepts such as 'life', 'death' or 'war', veterans' post-war art works as a mediator, a bridge between soldiers and their environments. The indexical pronoun 'I', which opens all but one line in the online poem 'Coward', written by a veteran identified only as 'Ex-Officer', should represent a living and consequently whole speaker, and yet that speaker senses a lack which 'I' fails to denote. The index 'I', in other words, points us, anchors us to a concrete speaker, and yet that concrete speaker's experience is coloured by the 'un-concrete', ambiguous nature of his own identity and the equally elusive source of his unseen pain. Here are the poem's closing lines:

I stand in the shower physically whole
I touch what they have lost yet
I cannot touch what I have lost
I do not know exactly what it is or where it was
I move among the people eyes down
I feel a coward.[8]

Communicating not exactly what it is the speaker has lost, since he cannot place it, an undoing of his whole, complete, alive 'I', is nonetheless a communication of a new state of affairs. The result, in the case of this specific post-war prosthesis, is a sense of moral failing – guilt, shame or failure around the fact of being physically unscathed while others have lost life and limb. Shame is felt for the importance that seeing and aesthetics have in determining the extent of one's pain. This unease, a gap between perception and reality, serves as an important component or perhaps pre-condition to what makes prostheses 'move'. And, like similar, tension-based rhetorical devices, it allows us to say something about something by saying something else. But far from it being just a rhetorical device used to circumvent communication, the unease or irony it generates becomes an index of communication itself, one enabling soldiers to consider both a life and a future under the ever-present spectre of death. In that way, too, these poems' irony is similar to that detectable in pieces of metal trench art. As Saunders again writes:

> Rich in symbolism and irony, metal Trench Art is a complex kind of material culture, whose physicality and nature make it a unique mediator between men and women, soldier and civilian, individual and industrialized society, the nations which fought the war, and, perhaps most of all, between the living and the dead.[9]

This notion of communicating, or keeping vigil, with the dead or with death is a topic I will attend to more extensively later on, notably in Chapter 5 and in the Conclusion. But even this paying tribute to the dead is like the steel rod that props the artificial construct of the prosthesis up, and a central aspect of the confusion that brings those prostheses about, as well as their own makeup. It is, in short, the incorporation of death – as in dead objects, such as those used to construct prostheses – into the everyday work of life.

Prosthesis as Tool

For veterans, the introduction of death into life is a feature of prosthesis making or, more generally, tool making, and serves as the general of poetic production. Life becomes paralysed and unliveable without the slow introduction of death, or at least the kind of death that prosthesis represents – inanimate things used to sustain the animate. Poetry is, in other words, that space in which elements that seem completely disparate are made to be present, and must be present, pulling at each other through their semiotic stand-ins in the form of indices and symbols. If there is an answer to be found to the question of the prosthesis, then an important stepping-stone en route to that answer is, again, the tool and that is because the prosthesis's main function is to serve as an artificial replacement of what was once organic, or of the kind of form of life in which concepts such as 'alive' and 'organic' have a clear, stable and distinct meaning. Now I would like to explore the idea of the prosthesis as a tool: specifically, the technical or mechanical side, the foundations for which I have laid with Peirce's semiotics, that exists in every prosthesis, including the linguistic variety, as well as the kind of knowhow required to construct a tool, as opposed to using one.

* * *

The middle of the twentieth century saw the rise of a debate concerning the role tools have in human life, and the way in which tools define the human as such, especially within the confines of mid-century continental linguistics, philosophy of language and aesthetics. At the heart of this renewed interest was a move to regard tools, language perhaps being the prime example, not as products of human intelligence but part and parcel of the human. Taking an anthropological and archaeological approach, André Leroi-Gourhan, in his *Gesture and Speech*, traces the first documented use of tools as a watershed mark in the development of *Homo sapiens*. Leroi-Gourhan argues that, far from being ingeniously devised objects, the product of human intelligence, tools were themselves external manifestations of human intelligence:

> We perceive our intelligence as being a single entity and our tools as the noble fruit of our thought, whereas the Australanthropians, by contrast, seem to have possessed their tools in much the same way as an animal has claws. They appear to have acquired them, not through some flash of genius which, one fine day, led them to pick up a sharp-edged pebble and use it as an extension of their fist (an infantile hypothesis well-beloved of many works of popularization), but as if their brains and their bodies had gradually exuded them.[10]

For Leroi-Gourhan, the notion of tools as part of human evolution was true not only of hammers and spears but also of language and the symbolic system more generally, with both types of tool – physical and symbolic, linked to the same 'equipment in the brain' – leading him to conclude 'not only that language is characteristic of humans as are tools, but also that both are the expression of the same intrinsically human property'.[11] Tools in general, then, and language specifically are an expression of human intelligence. That externalised part of human intelligence, moreover, changes and is perfected over time. Leroi-Gourhan's take on language as a central tool in the human bag of tricks can also be seen in the work of Emile Benveniste, who emphasises the specific role pronouns have in the work the linguistic tool can do. In his 1971 *Problems in General Linguistics*, Benveniste continues what could be called Leroi-Gourhan's anthropological approach, asserting, however, that language cannot be aligned with the other 'material' tools constructed by humans. Tools such as the 'pick, the arrow, the wheel' are 'fabrications', according to Benveniste, while language 'is in the nature of man':

> We can never get back to man separated from language and we shall never see him inventing it. We shall never get back to man reduced to himself and

exercising his wits to conceive of the existence of another. It is a speaking man whom we find in the world, a man speaking to another man, and language provides the very definition of man.[12]

While, again, seemingly disagreeing with placing language along with the other tools – created, as is stated, by the 'same equipment in the brain' – Benveniste retains a general empiricist tone. His assertion is, in other words, based on what is 'found in the world', similar to what Leroi-Gourhan described as 'found in the prehistoric evidence'.

If I may be forgiven for this slight foray into anthropology, I believe the value of these comments lies in explaining, at least partially, that the issue at hand for soldiers devoid of an ability to community after war is more than simply linguistic or symbolic. It is not, in other words, just that they find themselves unable to translate their wartime experiences but that the injury to their way of speaking is one that strikes deep into their own self-perception as human and, as we have seen, being alive. As Elaine Scarry writes in her reading of Marx:

> What differentiates men and women from other creatures is neither the natural acuity of our sentience nor the natural frailty of the organic tissue in which it resides but instead the fact that ours is, to a vastly greater degree than that of any other animal, objectified in language and material objects and is thus fundamentally transformed to be communicable and endlessly sharable.[13]

To lose that ability, as Scarry argues in her study of the obliteration of language under physical pain, is to lose one's humanity. And to build that tool again, by inference, the impossible task of recreating language, is to extent what the poems veterans write after war attempt to achieve – to return to humanity and then also perhaps to a sense of belonging and community. However, one other value in this quick foray into the language of cavemen and women is another aspect of Benveniste's work, particularly the role a special class of symbols or words has in the creation of individual subjectivity – pronouns. Creating a two-fold link between man and language, the French linguist argues that language would be impossible if it were not for the 'setting up' of subjects. Conversely, one's subjectivity is not 'set up' until this is done in language. The pronoun 'I', for instance – 'I am physically whole' – plays a central role in the assertion of one's self and one's own existence:

> Language is possible only because each speaker sets himself up as a *subject* by referring to himself as *I* in his discourse. Because of this, *I* posits

another person, the one who, being, as he is, completely exterior to 'me', becomes my echo to whom I say *you* and who says *you* to me. This polarity of persons is the fundamental condition in language, of which the process of communication, in which we share, is only a mere pragmatic consequence . . . If we seek a parallel to this, we will not find it. The condition of man in language is unique.[14]

Later in his essay, Benveniste adds that it is 'in a dialectic reality that will incorporate the two terms and define them by mutual relationship that the linguistic basis of subjectivity is discovered'.[15] Thus, language, as per Benveniste, is transformative and to an extent subject-forming, but it is a special class of signs that performs that task, one that could be aligned with Peirce's index: namely, pronouns.

However, as I have stated earlier, while the role and function of the prosthesis are indeed to enable life, the experience of the prosthesis is that of resistance and unease. And so one mode of resistance relevant here is resisting the idea of tools as enhancing, extending, empowering, in the sense that has become ingrained in certain strands of post-human thought. Writing of what he calls 'technics' in his *Technics and Time*, thinker Bernard Stiegler addresses the existence of tools throughout human history not as proof of human intelligence, but as an inherent part of whatever it is that we call 'human' and an important agent in the 'evolution' of that form of life. Following earlier works dealing with the place of the tool and the prosthetic, such as those by Freud and Derrida, Stiegler situates the tool and the advancement of the tool as markers of the human: not human in what could be called an exclusively organic way, but by the very involvement with tools and their production, both organic and inorganic. Stiegler's discussion, in other words, is geared toward breaking the organic/inorganic dichotomy through the prosthetic. Technics, as he writes in his *Technics and Time*, 'is the pursuit of life by means other than life'.[16]

It is worthwhile lingering on Stiegler's use of the complementary concepts of 'life' and 'other than life' in relation to the prosthetic movement that stands at the heart of this book. Indices anchor that artificial or 'lifeless' part of the ironic tension. On the other hand, symbols, much like the word 'life' itself, provide the semantic content or meaning – it is a general, abstract word we just use because we think we know what it means, without the need for a thorough investigation, much as we do not need to know why a basketball is orange to play basketball. Thus, to return to Geraldo Mena's poem 'So I Was a Coffin', discussed earlier, Mena's 'I', the indexical pronoun that, per Benveniste, discovers and creates subjectivity, is attached to a series of lifeless symbols, creating, in Stiegler's words, 'life by means other than life'. Once the line has been read or uttered, the tension or oscillation between the prostheses' constituent parts alters the indexicality of the 'I', along with its ability to denote a specific, living speaker, as well as changing the meaning of the symbol 'life'. Life, as it is now experienced through Mena's poem, is not an organic, whole or 'causal' use of the word, nor a new figurative meaning of it, but a new set of relations: one that includes death. It is these which Stiegler refers to as 'a third genre of beings': namely, 'inorganic organized beings'.[17]

However, later in *Technics and Time*, Stiegler describes, through Leroi-Gourhan's conception of the human's essential attachment to the tool, the transformation that he claims takes place through the 'pursuit of life by means other than life':

> Interior and exterior are consequently constituted in a movement that invents both one and the other: a moment in which they invent each other respectively, as if there were a technological maieutic of what is called humanity. The interior and the exterior are the same thing, the inside is the outside, since man (the interior) is essentially defined by a tool (the exterior).[18]

It would not be difficult to find parallels in the motion described in this excerpt and what I call the poetic prosthetic. The transformation taking place in the space between the man and his tool thus resembles the motion enacted within the prosthesis itself, one which imitates the function of a lost confidence in language and yet cannot escape the discomfort or unease of that loss, one that, again, resurfaces through the prosthesis itself, for which it serves as a constant reminder. However, as Stiegler goes on to argue, it is a discomfort destined to be forgotten, slipping into what he calls the 'illusion of succession' in which man precedes and dominates tools. The origin of that illusion is

> an originary forgetting, *ēpimētheia* as delay, the fault of Epimetheus. This becomes meaningful only in the melancholy of Prometheus, as anticipation of death, where the facticity of the already-there that equipment is for the person born into the world signifies the end: this is a Promethean structure of being-for-death, a structure in which concern is not the simple covering-over of *Eigentlichkeit*. This is the question of time.[19]

As opposed to Stiegler's argument here, I would claim that the prosthesis, which precisely sets it apart as a special case of the tool, of which the flint seems to be Stiegler's prime example, is a tool of resisting the illusion cited above. Not that it is incapable of slipping into that illusion – as I have stated, this is something I often do myself when I speak of prosthetics and movement. However, the tool does not lose its separation, its otherness, its peculiarity in the experience of its use. It is a supplement attached to the body that reminds one of its artificiality, of the loss of 'life', a reminder that can come with the grind of everyday life after war or more dramatically with the violent appearance of phantom pain or flashbacks. To assume otherwise, to pin a sense of 'healing' on the slow process of limping with a prosthesis, is, to me, an unethical position.

Ethics, as defined in this book, refers to a persistent unease, the chafing of prosthesis and living tissue and the sudden onset of phantom pain, neither of which can be undone even by the work of the prosthesis itself: an ethics of foregrounding – to use Jan Mukařovskýs term[20] – the tension between impossible and necessary communication, as well the act of suspension. In that way, the prosthetic is nothing but the construction of a mechanism that posits both necessary and impossible, both indexical and symbolic, at one and the same time, in such a manner that none can be resolved completely. Wills writes of this lack of resolution as inherent to the prosthetic, saying that: 'Prosthesis is about nothing if it is not about measuring distance – that of the necessary separation and unavoidable complication between animate and inanimate form, between natural and artificial.'[21] The function of measuring distance and, thus, transmitting that distance to others is one of the uses that the tool is constructed to perform and is the essence of prosthesis. However, to claim that this function does not in fact measure distance, or, as Stiegler writes, is 'not a "means" for the human but its end', means closing the same gap that the prosthesis tests, measures and transmits. If the ironic tool is understood as exposing or revealing, whether philosophically, archaeologically, theoretically or anthropologically, a 'true' or 'essential' human nature, then that tool ceases to fulfil one major function – the sustaining of the ironic gap. In other words, the creation of a post-human and, to an extent, post-modernist reinscribing of the human through the definition of the tool-user – or cyborg, to use a post-humanist term – amounts to yet another metaphysical glossing over, this time over a main facet of the prosthesis experience: a nagging discomfort or pain that cannot, ontologically speaking, go away. While the framing of the prosthetic in terms of not addition but *telos* presents an intriguing intellectual challenge, finally, it cannot and does not address the phantom pain so vividly described in Wills's description.

One case in point is 'Burying the Dead', a poem posted online by Falklands War veteran Trace Currall in 2009. The poem presents a soldier's internal monologue as he frustratingly deals with the demand to 'get over' what he had experienced in war, focusing on one key idiomatic phrase – that he should 'bury his dead'. For the speaker here, the crux of the matter is precisely the uneducated, insensitive use of a phrase that means 'continue with your life' or 'forget and move on' but literally points to the issue at hand – that those demanding he bury his dead do not know of the dead he has buried, both symbolically and literally. In fact, the poem's opening line itself reads as perhaps the most sweeping attempt to gloss over the gap the speaker insists upon: 'Burying the dead is a metaphor.' But placing the problematic phrase into a new framework does not, for lack of a better term, 'work' for the speaker, who, in keeping with the poem's title, 'digs' until reaching bedrock – the reality of the wartime dead:

Burying the dead is a metaphor.
They don't literally mean bury the dead
Try not to think too much about it
They mean put things to rest
Pull your socks up
Stop harping on
Get on with it
Let things lie
Get a grip
Forget.

They've never buried the dead.

Literally.[22]

Currall's speaker is measuring distance: namely, that between himself and those, 'they', who use the same words to mean completely different things. They mean 'get on with it'; he means burying the dead, 'literally'. And in exposing that gap the speaker demonstrates his great skill in 'getting it', in ostensibly being able to understand and respond – he knows, in other words, what he is being asked to do. This is similar, I would add, to a soldier who knows what he is 'supposed to do' with bullets and shells in the wake of war, and yet chooses to use them in order to create art. And yet the unease, the pain, the personal duty of the dead, of Wills's 'ghost' mentioned in the Introduction interrupt that ability, a spasm not unlike that which rippled through the missing leg of Wills's father. The work of the prosthesis is indeed, as so vividly demonstrated in 'Burying the Dead', a measuring, and in some way also a contacting, a sending out and a receiving.

In a different moment of measuring through the technology of poetry, American poet and former Predator drone operator Lynn Hill repeatedly makes use of the measurement of time in her work. Primarily a fiction writer, Hill had contributed segments of spoken poetry to *Holding it Down: The Veterans' Dream Project*, a collaboration between musicians Vijay Iyer and Mike Ladd aimed at highlighting the wartime experiences of army veterans of colour. One such act of measuring can be found in the third track, a poem-song by the name of 'Capacity', in which Hill time and again counts off her two years' participation in the Predator programme, a relatively novel form of warfare that, despite its detachment from a physical battleground, can bring about harrowing trauma in its wake.[23] This is a mode of war invested less in the mechanics of space, for space has all but been imploded in the drone operator's notion of war, but with a keen investment in time:

I have a capacity for war. I have a capacity for hate. I have a capacity for insanity. For anger. For lies. 525,600 minutes times two, before I break into an explosion of thoughts, of insurgents and soft kills, and career moves. Capacity for destruction. Capacity for loss. Capacity for death, violence, nothingness. Twenty-four months of pain and disgust. Actions of my hands accuse me. Guilty, charge. Unclear clear details and shaky intel, but still I pull the trigger. There's a limit to madness. Gague clocks out at two years, but they serve up poison like entrees at Blueberry Hill. Crazy with a side of numb. It took 63,720,000 seconds to go from me to somebody else. To change.[24]

While 'Burying the Dead' explores the space between the speaker and those surrounding him, and between his life after war and his wartime experiences, 'Capacity' uses time in order to gauge both the duration of the experience – two years – and its effect. Two years are, then, both the period in question and a limit beyond which Hill could not pass – the 'limit to madness' following 'Twenty-four months of pain and disgust'. Hill's case is interesting when compared to Currall's in that respect because of her unique position as a drone operator, engaged in war in Iraq and Afghanistan while sitting in an operator's booth in Nevada. Her main concern, one different from, say, that of Currall, is not the space of language or idiom but that of time, having directly to do with the fact that, as opposed to Currall, Hill had been 'at home' and 'at war' at the very same time. She did not 'go' to war, in other words, but was at war and at home simultaneously, going to war and then coming back home in time 'for the six-o'clock news', as Hill states in another of the project's poems, 'Dreams'.[25] And thus perhaps it is that aspect – time – which becomes the focus of her own mode of measuring. The quantifying of 'madness' or 'guilt' at the 'actions of my hands' may seem impossible, and yet within the poetic space Hill creates it is at least calculable: 'twenty-four months', '525,600 minutes' and '63,720,000 seconds to go from me to somebody else'. However, despite the stark differences in the context of Currall's and Hill's poems – period, type of warfare, gender, ethnicity, nationality, to name but a few – in both cases I would argue that the measuring of distance does not amount to a new, enhanced whole, but a new kind of composite, one which, as 'Burying the Dead' seems to suggest, is covered up by the everyday use of idioms or metaphors. In what respect, however, does the notion of prosthesis offer another, difference-erasing type of metaphor?

Cultural theorist and amputee Vivian Sobchack writes about the dangers of appealing to metaphor when addressing what could be called prosthetic relations, even when thinking about what she claims has become the metaphor of the prosthesis itself as it is used in post-human thought. The 'scandal of the metaphor', Sobchack says,

> is that it has become a fetishized and 'unfleshed out' catchword that functions vaguely as the ungrounded and 'floating signifier' for a broad and variegated critical discourse on technoculture that includes little of these prosthetic realities. That is, the metaphor (and imagination) is too often less expansive than it is reductive, and its figuration is less complex and dynamic in aspect and function than the object and relations from whence it was – dare I say – amputated.[26]

To go back from Sobchack's discussion of the prosthesis in post-human academic discourse to my discussion of the prosthesis in soldier poetry, or perhaps to weld the two together, the poetic prosthesis is meant precisely to point out, at least in part, the failings of a blanket metaphorical understanding of the soldier's post-war position regarding language. What for the speaker in Currall's poem has become amputated, to use Sobchack's terms, is the phrase 'burying the dead' in the literal sense and that same phrase meaning only 'leaving your past behind'. The amputation is made that much more complex and painful by the fact that the two phrases are identical, much in the same way that a whole-looking, human-looking war veteran looks identical to the person they were before leaving their home communities. In the same way, moreover, Hill's 'time' at war is identical to her 'time' at home, necessitating the distinctly poetic work of clarification, of prying the two apart. And the way in which that is achieved, as I argue throughout, is the assemblage not of a metaphorical prosthesis, of the kind I suspect Sobchack disapproves, but of an ironic object, prosthesis, tool of words, constructed to make invisible injuries – such as the amputation of two identical-looking instances of 'burying the dead' or 'hose' – visible, seen. In Currall's example, specifically, the indices, perhaps like the surprise appearance of Sobchack's 'I' at the tail end of the above quotation, are used at one and the same time for anchoring abstract, often trite statements uttered by those who cannot or do not wish to experience the gap the speaker refers to, and as stand-ins for the unsaid experience. Examples include the use of 'they' as a marker for people who do not see the gap in question, as well as a recurrent use of 'it' when pointing toward that gap. To assume that a redefinition of the human via the post-human takes away that tension, in other words, is to imagine a new, technically informed utopian theory that fails those who use tools for a *living*.

The poetic function of indices such as 'I' or 'it' parallels, to an extent, the analysis Jakobson was to initiate in the following century concerning what was first defined by Otto Jespersen as 'shifters'. Shifters in language, as their name may imply, are those signs or words that shift deictic centres of the communication – person, place and time.[27] Like indices, shifters are signs that require context, common symbols, in order to have any definite meaning. In his seminal 'Shifters, Verbal Categories, and the Russian Verb', Jakobson links Jesperson's concept to Peirce's index,[28] while distancing the two somewhat by categorising 'shifters' as 'indexical symbols'. In other words, shifters, the first-person pronoun being the prime example ('I' and 'we'), are as anchored to existential experience as to social agreement, an agreement of the kind that would make a pointing index finger mean 'look there' as opposed to 'look at my finger'. Ultimately, however, Jakobson's analysis also recognises the dual use made possible by the shifting nature of indices, similar to the one foregrounded by the ironic tensions discussed here. As Jakobson writes: 'The indexical symbols, and in particular the personal pronouns, which the Humboldtian tradition conceives as the most elementary and primitive stratum of language, are, on the contrary, a complex category where code and message overlap.'[29] This foregrounding of the overlapping in the nature of indices is key, I would argue, to the effect of the ironic tension, along with what could be called the emphasis on indexicality or arbitrariness, in socially accepted symbols.

Constructing a Dream

Poetry is the act of fashioning a space where one *can* outline the gap between what can and what cannot be said, in a fabricated, wrought product made from the very material it undermines. It is a machine utilising symbols generating movement or momentum, based on their known, socially determined meaning, and indices acting as the pulleys that, following Jakobson's term, shift that movement elsewhere. The product, ultimately, is a material, individual, functioning model of a new way of speaking, built from the scraps and loose ends of the now destabilised view of language. What that machine produces or makes manifest is irony: not irony as a material instance, but as a kind of relation between types of objects or signs, one that hovers, as Kierkegaard indicates, and as I shall relate in the chapter on prosthetic irony, above and within the machine, and not in any one place. As Kierkegaard writes in *The Concept of Irony*: 'Irony is not present at some particular point in the poem but omnipresent in it, so that the visible irony in the poem is in turn ironically mastered.'[30] Thus what I have so far discussed as 'unease', the phantom pain tearing through Wills's father, renders both the poem and the poet free, masters over what Kierkegaard calls 'irony', or constant tension.[31] The poem, thus, allows for the creation of what I shall refer to, using Peirce's terms, as a 'diagram' or 'dream'. To return momentarily to Elaine Scarry's brilliant analysis of the undoing of language under physical pain, the work of initiating that ironic tension, of building an organ of language, is, in some way, physical, internal, 'real' prosthetic work, what she refers to as the 'process of self-artifice'. As Scarry writes, it is a task or process embedded in the fact of the profound intertwining of the social and linguistic with the physical. Human beings, she writes,

> project their bodily powers and frailties into external objects such as telephones, chairs, gods, poems, medicine, institutions, and political forms, and then those objects in turn become the object of perceptions that are taken back into the interior of human consciousness where they now reside as part of the mind or soul, and this revised conception of oneself – as a creature relatively untroubled by the problem of weight (chair), as one able to hear voices coming from the other side of a continent (telephone), as one who has direct access to an unlimited principle of creating (prayer) – is now actually 'felt' to be located inside the boundaries of one's own skin where one is in immediate contact with an elaborate constellation of interior cultural fragments that seem to have displaced the dense molecules of physical matter.[32]

To write, and to write poetry, then, if I am to pivot slightly from Scarry's 'self-artifice', is that dream of a resumed connection between experience and language, between the physical reality of one's body and the socialisation into which it is embedded. The task, as this chapter has argued, is never truly complete, constantly interrupted or moored by phantom pain, by the context of necessity, interrupted by the harassing experience of a loss that cannot be retrieved, of an awareness of the very artificiality of the form, what I have called thus far 'discomfort'.

One noted advantage, then, of addressing poems posted online by independent authors, as this book attempts, is the ability to see not only those prostheses that succeed in projecting this basic sense of discomfort or irony, but also those in which that tool, at least in terms of creating the oscillating tension that marks the poetic prosthesis, is not yet complete. An example of what could be seen as a semi-constructed prosthesis, or one that is realised in stages, is 'Warm Dusky Nights' by James Love, a Falklands War veteran who writes of a scene of battle that, while being distant in both temporal and spatial senses, remains imminent:

On warm dusky nights,
where now only the weeds stand guard
watched over by the same moon and stars
men once fought and died.

On ground scorched by fire,
grass now grows,
while in the silent moonlit nights
misty grey figures rise, ready for battle
carrying on a war long ended.

No rattling gun or scream of shells,
no cries from wounded or the dying.
The fit have gone home now.
The dead lie where they've fallen.[33]

The tension or unease referred to by the speaker in the poem is centered around the issues raised by the passage of time, that between what once was and the way things are 'now'. The 'weeds' and 'grass' symbols that 'now' grow on what was once a battleground are juxtaposed with the vivid battle scene, the 'rattling gun or scream of shells' and 'cries from wounded or the dying'. Moreover, the 'grass' and 'weeds' are defined anew within the poem via a negation of the battle environment: 'No rattling gun or scream of shells, no cries from wounded or the dying.' But as present as temporal indices are in 'On Dusky Nights', indices that would point at a sense of first-hand experience, such as pronouns, as well as a limited presence of any spatial indices, are noticeably missing. Nor do we see indices serving as stand-ins for the wartime experience, as is often the case with 'it' or 'that'. What we have instead is an attempt to describe war to those who had not experienced it, to paint the scene, as it were, of an abstracted war. That missing indexical reference, however, does make its appearance, albeit in the area reserved for the writer's comments following each poem that was present in its original site of publication. Thus, following the poem's apparent final verse, came the following addition:

James Love
Author's Comments on 'Warm Dusky Nights'

I've seen them.[34]

The poem's exclusion of 'I've seen them', a statement attaching the body of the text, so to speak, to the body of the writer, is the exclusion of the personal subject, including the author's, the personal pronoun from the realm of 'poetry', and relegating it to the area reserved for 'non-poetic' notes. The format of online poetry here allows for a visual experience of what could be called the discomfort of the prosthesis, functioning, as it were, as kind of appendage to the appendage, one, I would argue, intimately tied to the 'disillusionment' model of addressing post-war veterans – that by supplanting a lost world of content with another, the injury is 'healed'. Thus, the speaker – though in this instance we can confidently say 'the writer' – feels that the 'I' cannot be a part of his poetry since his poetry is meant not to construct a new reality following war, decades after war in fact, but 'describe' or 'narrate' war in order, as Currall writes, to 'move on'. This desire is, of course, not only society's but also one the veterans themselves feel as part of what psychoanalyst John P. Muller describes as the pressure to 'heal' from trauma. However, that pressure may have, Muller writes, disastrous results:

Patients themselves pressure us to think of them as victims. Such one-way thinking sees the patient as developmentally arrested by trauma and such thinking lends itself to one-way solutions: young, non-analytically trained

therapists, cheaper to enroll in 'preferred provider' organizations, read-
ily take over the assignment of doing something to or for the patient to
compensate for the developmental deficit, the traumatization of the patient
by someone else . . . Such non-analytic practice deletes the 'I' of the patient
as distinctive subject, brackets the meaning of unconscious repetition, and
manages the treatment in the ways one might manage a business.[35]

James Love's poem sheds light, I believe, on the somewhat paradoxical
tension of constantly reliving the past while attempting to disentangle
oneself from that past's oppressive presence. What Love's poem and,
moreover, the poem's online setting allow us to see is that the prosthesis as envisioned by Love is incomplete as a result of the absence of the
index 'I', perhaps triggered by the sense that indexical experience and
symbolic communication are mutually exclusive, forever severed. Only
once the 'I' that designates the speaker is inserted into the space of the
poem is the prosthesis finally constructed, as a diagram that measures
space between the poles of the above-mentioned gap in communication and the writer. To see the prosthetic operation of Love's poem we
must, then, go against his own wishes or his own definitions of 'poetry',
including the author's comments as part of a new prosthetic whole: 'The
dead lie where they've fallen / I've seen them.'
    As in war, one's successful use of objects does not rely on how those
things were meant to be used, but on them achieving their goal. The
only thing that matters, in other words, is that it 'works', much in the
way that a building works as shelter from gunfire; a signpost works as
a support for a broken leg; a hose, as in Jarrell's 'The Death of the Ball
Turret Gunner', works for washing out human remains. Poetry, in this
way, 'works' as it allows a path back into language, into a different kind
of language, since, first and foremost, it is in itself a kind of space that
allows, perhaps even requires, the tension I have addressed as irony.
While visual art and music could also be seen as addressing issues of
communication, or at least the various kinds of communication, poetry
as verbal art is essentially involved in that issue since its building blocks
are the exact ones used for communication (be that communication in
everyday, scientific, academic, military or any other use). Like trench art,
as I have argued above, it represents the construction of a new linguistic
apparatus made of the bits and pieces that used to make up one's now
subverted notions of complete or accurate communication.
    Ultimately, poems written by veterans in the aftermath of war
are discussed here as attempts to forge what Peirce calls the 'icon' or
'diagram' – a sign which, much like any prosthesis, serves as a stand-in

for a lost function, as well as one that operates by determining the necessary relations and tensions that allow for that functioning. This is achieved by demonstrating the kind of poetic words and meanings they have *now*, after war, as opposed to the kind of relationship they had in their previous life. What this new set of relations brings about, through the very act of writing, through the desperate attempt to communicate, is the reinitiation of movement, of play. One example of that can be seen in the Mena poem described above, 'So I Was a Coffin'. While the repetition of the death scene highlights the biographical and moral urgency of that indexical moment through its repetition, that repetition also becomes a moment of artistic agency and performance. The helplessness of the biographical moment, the failure to save a friend's life, is transformed to the control of the poet describing that same event, again and again. Control and lack thereof, subjugation to the past and an overcoming or transformation of that past, coexist in the same space of the prosthesis. Thus, an emblem of the split is itself created, one that, ironically, functions as a stand-in or diagram for an entire worldview, and in which the split remains unresolved and can be addressed only through use of the poetic prosthesis, what Frederik Stjernfelt calls in his discussion of Peirce's work 'a moment of fiction'.[36] To reiterate: this does not mean the tension is 'resolved' through the creation of narrative; nor does this refer to the catharsis of 'telling', only the objectification, the making real, of the tension itself. This notion also aligns itself quite well with what Kelly Oliver refers to as the core of the double movement of what she defines as 'witnessing' and also her notion of subject creation: 'that the subject is constituted by virtue of a tension between finite historical contexts that constitute subject position on the one hand and the structure of infinite addressability and response-ability of subjectivity on the other'.[37] This is the movement that poetic prosthesis imitates, the constant oscillation that restores subjectivity into the dead-yet-living state of post-war life. As Anne Freadman writes in *The Machinery of Talk*,

> All signs have the touch of the tramp; but they can be pinned down awhile. This is the task of the special class of signs called the index, which is the kind of sign that transforms qualities and relations into 'matters of fact' by connecting them to experience.[38]

Peirce's division of signs then allows the mapping out of the forces at work in each prosthesis as well as pointing at the undoing of those poles, the constant oscillation and transfer that take place in the act of reading itself: the creation of a 'good failure', as opposed to the traumatic, painful perceived failures of the past – the failure to save a friend's life, the failure, at times, to die at war.

Art, and specifically, in discussing veterans' poetry, verbal art, is that artificial space of 'diagram' or 'dream', a tension between veterans' personal experience and communal communication that allows the discussion of the middle stance in regard to language: one, as in the case of the poems discussed here, brought on by the onset of personal pain. The literary text allows for a simultaneous move away from both 'reality' or 'fantasy' in the attempt to create a new space in which signs and meaning are something with which one can play. In the new diagram of relations between words and things, between real and unreal or between real and impossible, a prosthetic space of distance is created, producing a mode of communication that also serves as a comment on the limits of communication in the face of overwhelming experience. This work of both reality or pain, the index of 'then' and 'there', and the communality of the symbol, of 'death' and 'life', morphs into the kind of text that reveals a structure, what Peirce calls 'diagram' and, subsequently, 'dream'. The poem is a new diagram between indices of concrete place and time and general symbols of communication, one that measures the distance between the severed parts. In that way, the effect of these poems for those writing them is similar to what Peirce calls 'dream' in his discussion of the third type of sign: the icon. Writing of the function of the icon, and specifically that of the geometric diagram – the abstract measuring of actual distance – Peirce has this to say:

> A diagram, indeed, so far as it has a general signification, is not a pure icon; but in the middle part of our reasoning we forget that abstractness in great measure, and the diagram is for us the very thing. So in contemplating a painting, there is a moment when we lose the consciousness that it is not the thing, the distinction of the real and the copy disappears, and it is for a moment a pure dream, – not any particular existence, and yet not general. At that moment we are contemplating an *icon*.[39]

The icon, in the Peircean articulation, is that space between absolute experience (index) and absolute abstraction, or communication (symbol), one that is anchored to both to a certain degree, and yet which enables the kind of interaction that is somewhat of the order of forgetting, of 'dream'. I would argue that this dream-like effect of the icon, the product not of something being there or being missing but of an ironic tension between presence and communication, is also echoed in Merleau-Ponty's discussion of the tension that is immanent to painting. Merleau-Ponty, in his discussion of the cave paintings at Lascaux, refers to a visibility 'to the second power':

> The animals painted on the walls of Lascaux are not there in the same way as are the fissures and limestone formations. Nor are they *elsewhere*. Pushed forward here, held back there, supported by the wall's mass they use so adroitly, they radiate about the wall without ever breaking their elusive moorings. I would be hard pressed to say *where* the painting is I am looking at. For I do not look at it as one looks at a thing, fixing it in its place. My gaze wanders in it as in the halos of a Being. Rather than seeing it, I see according to, or with it.[40]

As in the icon, the tension created by it being fixed, or 'moored' as Merleau-Ponty puts it, and at the same time 'unmoored', is that of experiencing the dream of a way of life. In the context of the prosthesis, it is the experience of the form of life of prosthesis, of the very need for an artificial replacement of the link with language and the world. Poetry is that dream of a connection with experience and language, one constantly interrupted or moored by phantom pain, by the past and by the context of necessity: interrupted by the harassing experience of a loss that cannot be retrieved, of an awareness of the very artificiality of the form, of its artfulness, artifice, performativity and, finally, personal agency.

The division of signs was born out of Peirce's effort to break down components of communication and representation in order to unify the sciences into a coherent structure of language, one that relies on the successful implementation of all three types of sign. In effect, this means that any attempt to address and use semiotic systems has to include all of the signs Peirce denotes – iconic, indexical and symbolic – in order for the system to convey successfully not just facts, but facts as they are in a given situation, setting or experience and the tension produced as a result between the communal and the personal. This is the basis of Peirce's pragmatism: that human interaction – the ability to read signs and communicate with others – is the ground from which the investigation begins, as well as its *telos*. Peirce's analysis effectively serves, as Freadman writes and as Brison expresses, as a criticism of the Cartesian effort to expose the foundations of knowledge and language through a solitary intellectual and sceptical effort, instead opting to see the basic elements of language and communication as inherently interpersonal. Peirce rejected an early bent toward nominalism and a complete Cartesian doubt since, Freadman writes,

complete doubt is a form of self-delusion, possible only in the absolute solitude of the 'individual consciousness,' and since no consciousness is absolutely singular but is always divided by its condition in time and history, the
postulate of the solitary and absolutely autonomous mind, able to clean the
slate and start *ab origo*, is itself a delusion.[41]

This 'delusion', I would argue, serves as part of the background of poetry
written after war, part of the destabilised notion of language, since, perhaps like Benveniste's rejection of a 'man without language', they were
compelled into forming a bridge back to life as a result of a fear of falling
into death. As Peirce writes in 1896, decades after his first exposition of
the division in 'On a New List of Categories',[42]

> When an assertion is made, there really is some speaker, writer, or other sign-
> maker who delivers it; and he supposes there is, or will be, some hearer,
> reader, or other interpreter who will receive it. It may be a stranger upon a
> different planet, an aeon later; or it may be that very same man as he will be a
> second after. In any case, the deliverer makes signals to the receiver.[43]

As the above excerpt stresses, signs, as per Peirce, are uttered in an
attempt to convey, and are seen or understood within the attempt to
interpret or understand. The difference between the types of sign, then,
is in *how* messages are conveyed and what that communication assumes
about the possibility of transmitting as such. However, to what degree is
it even appropriate to discuss a semiotic analysis with regard to poetry
or art in general, where the very notion of communication is, at best, a
contested term?

Poetry as Personal Prosthesis

Poetry is, then, that site where language is made to work and as a result
that place where its cracks are most visible. In this way, poetry for veterans is also like a prosthesis, in that it is the broken speech and unortho-
dox phrasing that marks one as disabled: a fact that may, at times, widen
the gap between veterans and their home communities as a result of the
stigma and shame associated with disability. However, what I tried to
show in the somewhat theoretical section above is that poetry is also a
tool-making exercise, the consequences of which are the construction of
a tool for a new mode of post-war thinking and speaking, for if language
is an essential tool for our own understanding of what passes as human,
then a failure to construct that tool means a failure to do just that: to be

human. In this way, poetry, like any prosthesis, is also the scar that marks the injured as well as a tool that breaks open their path from solitude back into society, a tool of oscillating tension that creates the effect of a dream or diagram, a machine of meaning-blurring irony. Irony, then, the 'spirit' in the poetic machine, is a non-systematic way of thinking, an untethered philosophy as, Rudiger Bubner writes, arguing that 'poetry is correspondingly capable of rising to the level of philosophical speculation through the medium of irony'.[44]

So, if irony or unease and duality (organic–mechanical, alive–dead, mobile–immobile, human–object and so on) are read as the subversion of meaning production in everyday language, then poetry is that physical space in which that subverting takes place: not, again, as a mode of annihilating communication or of making it more difficult but as creating the diagram, the prosthesis, that would allow the measuring of distance, and thus subversion of both poles – realistic and arbitrary. Writing in a manner similar to this dual oscillation as an inherent property of poetry, Roman Jakobson argues that the power of the poetic lies precisely in creating ambiguity, that same shifting cloud of meaning that enables soldiers to break out of their silence and begin to build a new kind of language, all without untethering the all-important anchor to their private and painful past. As Jakobson writes, the

> supremacy of the poetic function over the referential function does not obliterate the reference but makes it ambiguous. The double-sensed message finds correspondence in a split addresser, in a split addressee, as well as in a split reference, as is cogently exposed in the preambles to fairy tales of various peoples, for instance, in the usual exordium of the Majorca storytellers: 'Aixo era y no era'.[45]

'Aixo era y no era', or 'it was and it was not', Jakobson's paradigm of what he calls a 'supremacy of the poetic function' that 'does not obliterate the reference', could be seen in itself as an instance of index–symbol irony. As in Peirce's index, which is never a pure index, meaning it always necessitates a certain degree of social acceptance, 'it was and it was not', a statement using indices only, makes it ambiguous and defamiliarises both 'it' and 'was'. As with Merleau-Ponty's cave paintings, it is both the work of fiction and one embedded into the index of reality. As Christopher Collins writes of Jakobson's analysis:

> 'Aixo era y no era' is not quite the same as 'fictionality': it does not simply mean that something is acknowledged to be untrue and need not be literally

believed. It means that something *is* true and *not* true simultaneously. Denying absolute negativity, it affirms the possibility that contraries can coexist in matters of propositional truth.[46]

As in the working of the prosthesis, as well as the 'moored' and 'unmoored' cave paintings in Merleau-Ponty's analysis presented earlier, and the Peircean 'dream', the oscillation that characterises the poetic – 'So I was a coffin' or 'I've seen them' – gestures at something that cannot be communicated and that has, in a way, been communicated. According to Collins, this reciprocal action and influence take place in the reader as a reaction to the text,[47] conjuring up what German philosopher Friedrich Schlegel, in his discussion of irony – which will feature prominently in the chapter on irony – refers to as 'conversation': here, a conversation between text and reader, as opposed to an outright, accurate or descriptive communication, such as the language of military orders and reports, the language of the Western fantasy of stability and clarity.[48]

And just as Peirce makes sure to stress that the division into index, symbol and icon is one of degree and not of absolute categories, so does Jakobson emphasise that poetry is the site in which what he calls the poetic function of language is given predominance, not absolute dominance. The poetic function exists in other forms of speech, perhaps including everyday communication, but by being accented or foregrounded in poetry, it is precisely that function that bolsters these soldiers' attempt to map out their post-war relation to other objects, humans and language itself. As Jakobson writes, the poetic function, 'by promoting the palpability of signs, deepens the fundamental dichotomy of signs and objects'.[49] However, at the same time, as Derek Attridge writes, for Jakobson, far from

> being seen as held apart, signifier and signified ... are seen as unusually tied in poetry; the 'palpability' of poetic language has been transferred from the independence of signs from their referents to the inherent connection between sound and meaning.[50]

Thus, they are separated from most forms of language use and more concretely connected, defined or demarcated and yet, at the same time, anchored together – 'it was and it was not' – to form the newly constructed poetic prostheses.

Irony in poetry, to repeat, serves as the ghost in the machine of the index–symbol tension, through which veterans construct their personalised version of language – the prosthesis. An object has been made, one that has a direct, personal relationship to a violent past and yet one in which meaning cannot be pinned down, bringing to mind Wills's statement regarding the impossibility 'to determine rigorously when and where transfer from one mode to the other is supposed to have taken place'.[51] What is created, under this idea of *poesis*, is not a loyal representation of facts; nor is it a disloyal representation of facts (or a lie) but a new relation or 'dream'. This creation is the poetic machine, constructed of both facts and a deep distrust as to the ability to communicate them. The product of this effort, I would argue, is something akin to the discussion raised by literary critic Wolfgang Iser regarding text, in general, as 'something that had not existed before', in which author, text and reader are closely interconnected:

> In the Aristotelian sense, the function of representation is twofold: to render the constitutive forms of nature perceivable; and to complete what nature has left incomplete. In either case mimesis, though of paramount importance, cannot be confined to mere imitation of what is, since the processes of elucidation and of completion both require a performative activity if apparent absences are to be moved into presence.[52]

While I discuss Iser's conceptualisation of 'play' and its relationship to the reception of post-war literature in the Conclusion, I will say now, however, that he considers this push to include the reader in the meaning-making of the text to be a shift in the classic notion of mimesis as words depicting reality, a mirror to nature. It is one that, I would argue, goes a long way towards describing the system of references set up by those injured in war: words, said otherwise, no longer label things, or do not *just* label things.

However, poetry does more for soldiers than allow for the index–symbol tension to take place, to take material form, but the form also lends itself to the creation of individual, customised prostheses. While the ironic tension, and the way in which it influences the reading and function of both indices and symbols, is a constant aspect of the various prostheses, the constructions themselves differ according to personal need. Thus, a poem like 'On Issue War Stock', posted online by Falklands War veteran Nigel 'Bernie' Bruen, creates an almost disembodied irony, never referring to the body or pronoun in question but centring exclusively on the ironic subverting of the concept of survival. The machine or prosthesis constructed, in other words, is less about the irony of personal experience than about the way in which the irony of wartime experience as a whole distorts words, pulls at meaning:

> Slashed Survival-suits
> Survived as slashed suits, not as
> Suits/(slash)/Survival;
>
> But a slashed Suit (survival)
> As a Survival-suit (slashed)
> Survives suitably
> To splash below parachutes.[53]

The repeated use of two main symbols, 'survival' and 'suits', renders the meaning of both all but ridiculous in the space of two short verses. For most of the poem, the indexical anchors are not necessarily spatial–temporal indices or pronouns, but the punctuation itself, using 'slash' – both word and graphic sign – and parentheses as ways to elucidate further and, consequently, disintegrate the various ways in which both symbols are employed. Ultimately, however, the almost linguistic or theoretical treatment of these symbols, through their repeated use, culminates in a closing couplet that brings in both sound elements and a strong indexical temporal anchor, creating a specific time and place – the paratrooper dropping into the sea – while using the same repeated sound that has characterised the poem, imitating the sound of a paratrooper splashing into the sea. The aftermath is, as with the image of the 'limp' I have time and again pointed to as a way of understanding post-war life lived with the assistance of the prosthesis, is one lived 'suitably'.

There is a way, moreover, that Bruen's poem, as with several other of the pieces discussed here, demonstrates in its tension and subversion the very act of tension and subversion that brings about what I have called an experience of injury to language. That the 'fall' from a worldview in which words are used mostly to name and signify to one in which words have a problematic, almost arbitrary, relation to objects is in a way similar to the 'drop' of a dead paratrooper, his survival suit failing him, only to disappear under the sea. In other words, a fear of losing language is a fear of losing one's life, one's distinction as an individual life and a disappearance in a boundless body of water. A similar notion can be detected in the middle of 'When the Men Came Back', a poem written not by a veteran but by Cesca Croft, a close friend of

Falklands War veterans who had observed their behaviour upon their return. The speaker in Croft's poem describes how exploding fireworks send one of them back into a warplane over the Atlantic during the Falklands War:

> We could be dead soon,
> we could plunge to the icy sea,
> disappear under the Atlantic,
> never to be found again.
> 'Lost at sea'
> R.I.P.[54]

This is the sea that threatens war veterans with isolation, the same that surrounds the island trapping Robinson Crusoe's island, which I shall discuss in the Conclusion, a snare of silence and fragmentation.

However, while this descent into the sea can be detected in other poems, the manner in which indices and symbols are employed differs radically, as do the kinds of indices and symbols used, allowing for a personal poetic expression of injury to language. A case in point is Currall's poem, in which the idiom 'burying the dead' is investigated and subverted parallel to what could be seen as an actual act of digging, exhuming what, for the speaker, stands as the 'burying the dead' buried under that idiom. The way in which that descent is achieved is by highlighting the juxtaposition between the indexical 'they' and the supposed casual or unethical use 'they' make of the idiom. Thus, the poem begins and ends with the same line, having gone through the machinations of subverting what the idiom means through the index–symbol. Another example, again of the movement of the ironic tension being depicted in the poem as one of descent, is Mena's 'So I Was a Coffin', in which the speaker, as discussed above, identifies himself as a series of objects ('so I was a spear', 'so I was a flag', 'so I was a bandage') until finally identifying himself as both a speaking, acting agent and a coffin being lowered into the earth.

Prosthesis, then, in the manner formulated and discussed in this book, is not tantamount or equivalent to an experience of 'health', 'repair' or 'return', at least not in non-ironic, dogmatic uses of those terms. Instead, the form of life glimpsed in these poems, and to a large extent created by them – to repeat Merleau-Ponty, not 'seeing it' but 'according to, or with it' – is one of managing discomfort, of a rejection of the ability to form a distinct, reliable and constant safe/unsafe division, or a division between natural or unnatural. This is a diagram propelled by and resulting in irony, which reflects only relation, not fact. As Wills writes: 'By means of prosthesis the relation to the other becomes precisely and necessarily a relation to otherness, the otherness, for example, artificially attached to or found within the natural.'[55] An object or event no longer 'fits', and specifically 'naturally' so, but is tied to other objects only by virtue of an inherently artificial relation.

In language, particularly in the language of veterans, this means that even figures of speech, ostensibly tied to a specific meaning, can also be torn away from that meaning and made to interact with a different set of relations. This phenomenon, again visible in Currall's detaching and reattaching of the idioms 'burying the dead' or 'get on with it', as well as in Bruen's detachment of and subsequent play with 'survival', Ex-Officer's 'whole' and even Mena's 'I', is used to refer to a series of objects. If a living 'Being', as capitalised by Merleau-Ponty, can turn into an object, can be propelled and leaned against, then its 'Being-ness' is not inherent to it, but a product, again, of a certain set of relations or movements. That point of view, or way of life, is one of assemblage and artifice, characteristics that transfer to the manner with which words and idioms are used to create the ironic set of relations, or the icon. As Wills writes:

> Prosthesis reads this possibility from the following point of view: if an utterance, such as a figure in the center of a painting, can be grafted onto another context, this means that it has no 'natural' place, never did have, and that the relations it forms with subsequent contexts inevitably reinscribe that fall out of naturalness.[56]

The 'fall out of naturalness', again, does not result in a glorified, new and improved mode of being, but in a sense of imperfect, fragile survival through the formation of the ironic prosthesis. As Wills later adds, prosthesis is, ultimately, 'a figure for which the term "figure" is no longer appropriate, for it betokens a writing that obeys a whole other dynamism, that of constantly shifting relations'.[57] That tension and dynamism are, then, the new mode of communication, and to an extent, thinking veterans construct these for themselves after war.

Notes

1. Jacques Derrida, *Monolingualism of the Other; or, The Prosthesis of Origin*, translated by Patrick Mensah (Stanford: Stanford University Press, 1998), 2.
2. Wills, *Prosthesis*, 7.
3. Sigmud Freud, 'Project for a Scientific Psychology', in *Standard Edition of the Complete Psychological Works of Sigmund Freud*, vol. 1, edited and translated by J. Strachey (London: The Hogarth Press, 1975), 283–397.

4. Shoshana Felman and Dori Laub, *Testimony: Crisis of Witnessing in Literature, Psychoanalysis, and History* (New York: Routledge, 1992), 59–62.

5. Nicholas J. Saunders, *Trench Art: Materialities and Memories of War* (New York: Berg, 2003), 199–208.

6. Ibid., 41.

7. Nicholas J. Saunders, 'Bodies of Metal, Shells of Memory: "Trench Art," and the Great War', *Journal of Material Culture* 5, no. 1 (2000): 46; emphasis added.

8. An Ex-Officer, 'Coward', originally posted on the *War Poetry Website*. Now available at: <https://war-poetry.livejournal.com/852459.html> (last accessed 22 February 2022).

9. Saunders, 'Bodies of Metal, Shells of Memory', 46.

10. André Leroi-Gourhan, *Gesture and Speech*, translated by Anna Bostock Berger (Boston: MIT Press, 1993), 106.

11. Ibid., 113–14.

12. Emile Benveniste, 'Subjectivity in Language', in *Problems in General Linguistics*, translated by Mary Elizabeth Meek (Coral Gables: University of Miami Press, 1971), 223–4.

13. Scarry, *The Body in Pain*, 255.

14. Benveniste, 'Subjectivity in Language', 225.

15. Ibid.

16. Bernard Stiegler, *Technics and Time, Vol. I: The Fault of Epimetheus*, translated by Richard Beardsworth and George Collins (Stanford: Stanford University Press, 1998), 17.

17. Ibid.

18. Ibid., 141–2.

19. Ibid., 142.

20. Jan Mukařovský, 'Standard Language and Poetic Language', in *Essays on the Language of Literature*, edited by Seymour Chatman and S. R. Levin (New York: Houghton Mifflin, 1967), 241–9.

21. Wills, *Prosthesis*, 42.

22. Trace Currall, 'Burying the Dead', *Voices Compassionate Education* official website. Available at: <https://voiceseducation.wordpress.com/2009/04/15/poetry-from-a-falklands-conflict-veteran/> (last accessed 22 February 2022).

23. See, for example, Wayne Chappelle, Tanya Goodman, Laura Reardon and Lillian Prince, 'Combat and Operational Risk Factors for Post-Traumatic Stress Disorder Symptom Criteria among United States Air Force Remotely Piloted Aircraft "Drone" Warfighters', *Journal of Anxiety Disorders* 62 (March 2019): 86–93; and Amit Pinchevsky, 'Screen Trauma: Visual Media and Post-Traumatic Stress Disorder', *Theory, Culture & Society* 33, no. 4 (2016): 51–75.

24. Lynn Hill, Mike Ladd and Vijay Iyer, 'Capacity', track 3 on *Holding it Down: The Veterans' Dream Project*, 2013, digital. Available at: <https://vijayiyer.bandcamp.com/album/holding-it-down-the-veterans-dreams-project> (last accessed 22 February 2022).

25. Ibid., 'Dreams', track 16.

26. Vivian Sobchack, 'A Leg to Stand On', in *The Prosthetic Impulse: From a Posthuman Present to a Bioculture Future*, edited by Marquard Smith and Joanne Morra (Cambridge, MA: MIT Press, 2006), 20.

27. Monika Fludernik, 'Shifters and Deixis: Some Reflections on Jakobson, Jespersen, and Reference', *Semiotica* 86, no. 3–4 (1991): 193–230.

28. Roman Jakobson, 'Shifters, Verbal Categories, and the Russian Verb', in *Russian and Slavic Grammar: Studies 1931-1981*, edited by Linda R. Waugh and Morris Malle (The Hague: De Gruyter Mouton, 1984), 42–3.

29. Ibid., 43.

30. Søren Kierkegaard, *The Concept of Irony with Constant Reference to Socrates*, translated by Lee M. Chapel (Bloomington: Indiana University Press, 1965), 324.

31. Ibid., 336.

32. Scarry, *The Body in Pain*, 256.

33. James Love, 'On Warm Dusky Nights', *War Poetry Website*. As with other examples found here, the original version that includes the author's notes has since been removed from the *War Poetry Website*. The poem itself can be found on *The War Poetry LiveJournal* website. Available at: <https://war-poetry.livejournal.com/734115.html> (last accessed 25 February 2022).

34. Ibid.

35. John P. Muller, *Beyond the Psychoanalytic Dyad: Developmental Semiotics in Freud, Peirce, and Lacan* (New York: Routledge, 1996), 72.

36. Frederik Stjernfelt, *Diagrammatology: An Investigation on the Borderlines of Phenomenology, Ontology, and Semiotics* (Dordrecht, Netherlands: Springer, 2007), 112.

37. Kelly Oliver, 'Witnessing and Testimony', *Parallax* 10, no. 1 (2004): 80.

38. Anne Freadman, *The Machinery of Talk: Charles Peirce and the Sign Hypothesis* (Stanford: Stanford University Press, 2004), 105.

39. Charles S. Peirce, *The Writings of Charles S. Peirce: A Chronological Edition*, vol. 5 (Bloomington: Indiana University Press, 1993), 163.

40. Merleau-Ponty, 'Eye and Mind', 126.

41. Freadman, *The Machinery of Talk*, xxv.

42. Charles S. Peirce, 'On a New List of Categories', in *Charles Sanders Peirce – The Collected Papers Vol. I: Principles of Philosophy*, edited by Charles Hartshorne and Paul Weiss (Cambridge, MA: Harvard University Press, 1931), 335, 558.

43. Charles S. Peirce, 'The Regenerated Logic', *The Monist* 7, no. 1 (October 1896): 19–40.

44. Rudiger Bubner, *The Innovations of Idealism*, translated by Nicholas Walker (Cambridge: Cambridge University Press, 2003), 201.

45. Roman Jakobson, 'Linguistics and Poetics', in *Language in Literature*, edited by Krystyna Pomorska and Stephen Rudy (Cambridge, MA: Harvard University Press, 1987), 85–6.

46. Christopher Collins, *The Poetics of the Mind's Eye: Literature and the Psychology of Imagination* (Philadelphia: University of Pennsylvania Press, 1991), 52.

47. Ibid.

48. Daniel Dahlstrom, 'Play and Irony: Schiller and Schlegel on the Liberating Prospects of Aesthetics', *The History of Continental Philosophy, Volume I*, edited by Alan Schrift (Chicago: University of Chicago Press, 2011), 108.

49. Jakobson, 'Linguistics and Poetics', 70.

50. Derek Attridge. *Peculiar Language: Literature as Difference from the Renaissance to James Joyce* (London: Routledge, 1988), 132.

51. Wills, *Prosthesis*, 16.

52. Wolfgang Iser, 'Play of the Text', in *Realism*, edited by Lillan R. Furst (New York: Longman, 1992), 206.

53. Nigel 'Bernie' Bruen, 'On Issue War Stock', *Free Verse from Forgotten Men* (self-published, 2016), 12–13.

54. Cesca M. Croft, 'When the Men Came Back.' Originally posted on the *War Poetry Website* but since taken down. Now available at: <https://war-poetry.livejournal.com/731314.html> (last accessed 22 February 2022).

55. Wills, *Prosthesis*, 44.

56. Ibid., 45.

57. Ibid., 249.

CHAPTER 2

Reality, Disillusionment, Play

If the work of the prosthesis is to create a new, ironic space of oscillation, one that posits both the indexical and symbolic poles in order to implode them ultimately into the space play, then one of the functions of that space is, among others, to cast doubt on the notion of a stable, objective reality. However, to undermine the 'reality' of wartime experiences would seem to go against at least part of the gist of the previous chapter: the pull of the past never lets up, the phantom pain never gives fair warning, and the weight of speaking for others is unrelenting. Thus, given the central-ity of the reality of the past in the poetics this book puts forth, it would stand to reason that that reality is never called into question. And to a large degree that is indeed the case: the past never is called into question – Mena never doubts whether or not Kyle died in his arms, nor does Currall wonder whether or not he had indeed buried the dead. The past, then, is not a dream – 'it', to use the indexical, really happened. However, the reality that the past presents plays the *role of reality* in what would become the prosthetic text created in the wake of these events. Thus, at one and the same time, the past is the event that is so certain that it anchors the entire poetic machine, the index that makes concrete any generalised talk of 'war', and the past is that which is artistically transformed in the pros-thetic act itself. I have already tackled this central function of the prosthe-sis, that it posits the index as the concrete time and place of events as well as transforming it into performance. What I did not yet state, however, is that the impact of that gesture toward the past can be understood only once we underline the central role the concept of reality has had in the discussion of war and of writing after war in the last century or so.

Reality has taken on several different shapes throughout the history of our conversation about war. The first, as already stated, is the function of the event as 'real' in the minds of post-war writers – that a specific event must be communicated, and that it be communicated truthfully or correctly. Secondly, there is the notion of the trauma of war as real or as resisting representation, an aspect I shall discuss at length in Chapter 6. Thirdly, there is the traditional role of war as an event 'realer' than most any other human experience, and the related notion that violence is in some way the ultimate index of reality for its power to touch the human body in the same way Peirce's paradigmatic index – the weather vane – is touched by the wind ('It's not real. Afghanistan's real. It's something. When I'm there, I'm something'). However, ultimately, and importantly in terms of this current chapter, war has been marked as real in a tradition going back at least to the Great War, in that depictions of war since that dramatic event have been read as exposing the *reality* of war and, to some extent, modern life in the West. And that act of exposing has taken on the name of 'disillusionment': the individual soldier encounters the reality of war, is educated by it, and then proceeds to educate the reading public regarding those realities. My goal in the next few pages is double: to investigate the possible theoretical sources that could have led to the early twentieth-century understanding of war as exposing reality, and to show the ways in which poetic prosthetics run counter to the concept of 'disillusionment'. In short, the goal of the poetic prosthesis is not to expose the reality of war but to address the reality of surviving it, one which is touched in more than one way by the seemingly unreal.

Disillusionment and the Act of Unveiling

A generation that had gone to school on a horse-drawn streetcar now stood under the open sky in a countryside in which nothing remained unchanged but the clouds, and beneath these clouds, in a field of force of destructive torrents and explosions, was the tiny, fragile human body.

— Walter Benjamin, 'The Storyteller'[1]

There seems to be little doubt as to the influence of the poetry written by a group of World War I soldiers – the Trench Poets – on our modern understanding of soldier poetry, the re-emergence of soldier poetry as a distinct genre at the beginning of the twentieth century, and its role as dissenter against the falsities of power.[2] However, despite that centrality, the Great War poets did not come up with the concept of poetry about war *per se*, or even the concept of lyric poetry concerning warfare, a trend also traceable to the American Civil War, to name just one precursor in the English-speaking world.[3] War and poetry have been linked from the onset of the Western poetic tradition, with such prominent examples as Homer's *Iliad* and *Odyssey*, Latin texts such as the *Aeneid* and northern European epics such as *The Saga of the Volsungs* and *Beowulf*. As Robin Norris writes, the link between poetry and war in the West is one that uncovers a unique aspect of the human response to such a grand-scale violent event as war:

> Transmitting sorrow through the technology of poetry is an experience unique to human beings, to being human, and reading such texts subjects us to a contagious mourning that allows us to weep for individuals we've never met, and who may have never even existed.[4]

As James Tatum writes in his introduction to *The Mourner's Song*, the *Iliad* and, I would add, the Western tradition of war poetry '[speak] to the way we think about war, because the one impulse that has proved as enduring as human beings' urge to make wars is their need to make sense of them'.[5] Thus, the significance of Great War poetry lies not only in the dramatic increase in soldier writing and in the prominence those writings received but in the stress on the reception of war poetry as a realistic depiction of modern warfare.

The traditional link between war and poetry could be said to indicate the enduring effect that violence and the fear of death, as such, have on language. However, that claim, also made in Giambattista Vico's *The New Science* and illustrated by the manner in which Vico links the creation of poetic language with the fear of the thunderclap,[6] far exceeds the goals and breadth of this chapter. What could be said, however, is that there has been a well-documented shift in the manner in which war and poetry have aligned in the last century or so – namely, in the disappearance, if not critical rejection, of the epic mode of war poetry – and a shift too, if not ideological emergence, of first-person poetry written not by bards but by the soldiers themselves.[7] In other words, not only has the standard for war poems shifted into the sphere of first-person privileged writers, privileged for having experienced war, but the seemingly structural shift could bear ideological weight as well: the privileging of first-person accounts of war represents a move away from metaphysical elucidations of violence and into the realm of the 'accurate', 'authentic' and 'real.' Thus, perhaps in keeping with Norris's claim that tragedy is made more accessible through individual suffering,[8] the rise of lyric, first-person soldier poetry in the twentieth century proved a watershed moment in modern culture, the most visible and influential examples being the poems coming out of the trenches of World War I. Spearheaded by such writers as Siegfried Sassoon, Wilfred Owen and Isaac Rosenberg, Great War poetry fused the image of the soldier and the poet, rejecting an omniscient, Homeric, classical and, to some extent, metaphysical[9] view of battle and valour, and introducing a detailed, often graphic, rendition of their own personal encounter with violence. And while prominent writers in both poetry and prose who participated in and wrote about the war – Sassoon, Ernest Hemingway, e. e. Cummings, to name but a few – differed in style, genre and subject matter, the rejection of what could be called metaphysical language concerning war is nonetheless visible, albeit on different levels. Following the Great War and the outpouring of soldier poetry, the various forms of what was seen as a rejection of Homeric ideals in favour of a brutal realism came to be understood as 'disillusionment'.

Fundamentally, disillusionment, entering the critical and cultural discourse concerning the experience and writing of soldiers during and after combat following the Great War, is the experience of having been shocked into realising the mistake of a former view of the world, one described by terms such as 'naïve', 'idyllic' or 'classical', and the attempt to criticise and correct those mistakes. One common error, perhaps the most noted, is that of chauvinistic language or modes of speech, understood as being the tools of propagating violence via romantic euphemisms and Homeric values such as 'valour', 'glory' and 'homeland'. As Daniel Tobman writes, perhaps articulating the leading interpretation of the British Great War experience, an understanding that would go on to fashion the basis of how Western culture views the soldier's experience to the present day:

> A generation of eager young Britons joined up to fight a war they didn't understand. They marched off to France and Flanders, leaving behind an idyllic Edwardian age that would never be recaptured. Once there, they fell under the command of incompetent commanders . . . Time and again they were thrown forward in ill-conceived assaults that achieved nothing . . . The pitiful survivors who returned to Britain were silenced by the trauma of their experiences – only the words of a tiny band of warrior poets could communicate the truth of what they had been through.[10]

What those poets communicated, the 'truth' they brought to bear, was, again, to a large extent available due to the failure of a former set of beliefs, ideologies and modes of speech to describe what was perceived as the 'reality' of war. Thus, under this understanding of disillusionment, soldier poets and writers, such as Sassoon, Owen, Erich Maria Remarque and many more, were, and still are, understood, at least in the most vocal interpretations of the most renowned poets,[11] as having encountered a grim reality that shattered any illusion concerning a classical or mythological view of war, a revelation that is understood as taking place chiefly in language. One such literary moment, which became a symbol for the disillusionment model of the soldier's experience, is found in Ernest Hemingway's *A Farewell to Arms*,[12] written following Hemingway's own experiences as a volunteer ambulance driver on the Italian front in World War I:

> I was always embarrassed by the words sacred, glorious, and sacrifice and the expression in vain. We had heard them, sometimes standing in the rain almost out of earshot, so that only the shouted words came through, and had read them, on proclamations that were slapped up by billposters over other proclamations, now for a long time, and I had seen nothing sacred, and the things that were glorious had no glory and the sacrifices were like the stockyards at Chicago if nothing was done with the meat except to bury it.[13]

The experience of words not fitting the emotional impact of 'losing one's words in the face of terror' is translated into an effort to eject those elements of language seen as most 'dangerous' to the 'true' understanding of war. According to Hemingway, war was not 'glorious', but was in fact closer to the 'stockyards at Chicago', a reference to the city's infamous slaughterhouses, as the traditional glorious death in war is reduced to 'meat'. What was supposed to be 'glorious', or what has been described as 'glorious', turned out to be a bloody mess, and thus, from a moral standpoint, one *ought* to describe war as a slaughterhouse, as opposed to the scene of Homeric valour. To be disillusioned, therefore, is to be shocked into the realisation that one was duped, so to speak, by a verbal sleight of hand that hid senseless violence behind patriotic hyperbole, a mistake leading to the attempt to cleanse one's language, and poetry as a category of language, of such pitfalls. Writing of Siegfried Sassoon, perhaps the paragon of the 'disillusioned' soldier poet, James Anderson Winn explains:

> Chivalric myth is no longer an adequate motive for combat, and reaching into the dream world of fairy tales is no longer an adequate purpose for poetry. Brutalized by combat and disillusioned with knightly honor, he now takes pleasure in lust and senseless hatred. Poetry, which once served to glorify combat, is now a way of seeking absolution.[14]

Along the same lines, John Silkin describes Owen's 'Dulce et Decorum est', perhaps the most celebrated work in this tradition, as the expression of an experience that

> cancers the innocent flesh of the victims, so the thoughtless retelling of the story to children, and to adults, corrupts their imagination; and this, quite apart from the distortion of the suffering. Had the chauvinist been a participant, it is implied, he would not be perpetrating the old Lie that it is sweet and fitting to die for one's country, whatever the death.[15]

Echoing this idea of a truth in an almost ontological, referential way, while referring to Owen's 'Anthem for a Doomed Youth', Mary Ann Gillies and Aurelea Denise Mahood write: 'There is no anthem, only "the stuttering rifles' rapid battle" and the "shrill, demented choirs of wailing shells",'[16] adding that the 'sonnet anchors grief in the actual experience of death instead of in empty language and hollow rituals'.[17] As Randall Stevenson writes, the 'new and almost unimaginable experience of war also profoundly challenged the capacities of conventional literary forms, and ultimately of language itself, to represent the life and death of the times'.[18]

However, as noted in the decades-long scholarship concerning modern war poetry, graphic, often gory, depictions of violence, in themselves, are not necessarily a novelty, even in those classical sources supposedly used to deceive twentieth-century soldiers as to the 'true' nature of war. In the earliest examples of war poetry, the effort to highlight, to varying degrees, the indexical or immanent has always had a prominent role. While the designation 'epic poetry', associated perhaps above all with works concerned with war, invokes a bird's-eye view of battle and its horrors, these works were not without their focus on individual lives undone by random violence. One example is the way in which the text relates to the seemingly random, violent death of the Trojan Ilioneus, in a section I will also discuss briefly elsewhere:

> This man's father was Phorbas, whom Hermes loved
> More than any other Trojan and who had the flocks
> And wealth to prove it, but only one child,
> Ilioneus. Peneleos' spear
> Went through his eye socket, gauging out the eyeball,
> And going clear through the nape of the neck.[19]

The depiction of Ilioneus's death, as in several other cases in the *Iliad*, not only includes graphic detail but also refers to the wider familial context of the now brutally killed Ilioneus, making visible, in this case, the only child of a man otherwise favoured by fortune, allowing the reader to imagine the effect that the news of his son's death would have on Phorbas. Thus, while omniscient and omnipresent, Homer's narrator, framing war and the merciless, often random violence it presents in an overtly religious framework, speaks not only of nations and gods but also of a very concrete brand of violence and death along with a very personal grief and mourning.[20] In other words, the innovation of the Trench Poets coming out of the First World War, and, as a result, twentieth-century soldier poetry in general up until the present day, may not have necessarily been an attempt to punch holes in the religious or metaphysical rhetoric concerning war – or at least not only that, but also, in a more general sense, the removal of violence and the encounter with violence from a metaphysical framework, as such. A rude awakening, no doubt, but one that bears its own brand of metaphysical rewards.

Seen as providing a kind of template or manifesto for this effort to cleanse language of its abstract or senseless impurities and to move toward greater 'realism', Owen, famously killed a week before the 1918 armistice, calls in the intended preface for his collection of poems for what could be named a linguistic purging, one that would expel what he labels 'Poetry' with a capital 'p', ushering in 'poetry' instead:

> This book is not about heroes. English Poetry is not yet fit to speak of them. Nor is it about deeds, or lands, nor anything about glory, honour, might, majesty, dominion, or power, except war. Above all I am not concerned with poetry. My subject is War and the pity of War. The Poetry is in the pity. Yet these elegies are to this generation in no sense consolatory. They may be to the next. All a poet can do today is warn. That is why the true Poets must be truthful.[21]

Evident in this preface, or, at the very least, in the way the preface has been read in the years since its publication, is Owen's attempt to draw a limit, set a border, to what he thinks 'English poetry' can and cannot speak of. For Owen, first and foremost, the best way to convey his take on poetry is to list the things it cannot include – 'heroes', 'deeds', 'lands', 'glory', 'honour', 'might', 'majesty', 'dominion' or 'power' – even going as far as to say that his poetry 'above all . . . [is] not concerned with poetry'. A stripped-down depiction of war is, according to the preface, the most 'truthful' way in which a poet can speak of it. Owen's preface serves as a kind of manifesto for what has become the paradigmatic twentieth-century poetic reaction to war, characterised by an attempt to reconstruct one's link to words and language not necessarily through the construction of a poetic tension with reality but via a rejection of non-realistic pollutants, a language suitable to a world divested of classical or Victorian ideals. It is a call to arms that finds echoes in other works of contemporary poets and thinkers, one somewhat parallel to a general interest in language in the early twentieth century. In fact, another preface, written by Ludwig Wittgenstein, himself a World War I veteran, for his *Tractatus Logico-Philosophicus*, published just a few years after Owen's death and written during Wittgenstein's time as a prisoner of war, calls for a similar kind of limit on language, one that would aim to eject the same kinds of words:

> The book deals with the problems of philosophy, and shows, I believe, that the reasons these problems are posed is that the logic of our language is misunderstood. The whole sense of the book might be summed up in the following words: what can be said at all can be said clearly, and what we cannot talk about we must pass over in silence.
>
> Thus the aim of the book is to draw a limit to thought, or rather – not to thought, but to the expression of thoughts: for in order to be able to draw a limit to language, we would have to find both sides of the limit thinkable (i.e. we should have to be able to think what cannot be thought).[22]

Both Owen and Wittgenstein, as I have argued elsewhere,[23] seek to purge speech of the pitfalls of language, whether their source is in what Owen calls 'Poetry' with a capital 'p' or in what Wittgenstein dubs 'metaphysics'. As Marjorie Perloff suggests, one could read the entirety of the famously enigmatic *Tractatus* as a kind of war poem, itself 'a critique of "heroism in the wrong place"'.[24]

While it would seem jarring to couple Owen's and Wittgenstein's prefaces, despite Perloff's suggested reading, both men's post-war attempt to achieve a clearer, less obfuscating way of speaking is one that can be understood as part of an influential trend in the humanities of the earlier part of the previous century: namely, the discussion of the role of language not only in describing the world but in taking an active role in world-creating. In what has come to be known as the 'linguistic turn' in Western philosophy, thinkers and writers such as Wittgenstein, influenced by Immanuel Kant's philosophical work – at least early on in his career, as seen in the preface to his *Tractatus* quoted above – sought to gauge the relationship between language, philosophy and experience, with many seeking to create the 'perfect language' or, at the very least, study language's pitfalls as part of the goal of creating a way of talking about science and philosophy

that was as scientific, so to speak, as the science itself. Thus, at least historically or culturally speaking, it is not impossible to speak of a much
wider cultural revolution of 'disillusionment' taking place in the Western
tradition in general, one in which post-war disillusionment has a central,
moral role. In other words, war in general, but the Great War specifically,
is seen as a kind of cautionary tale regarding what it is that goes wrong
when words are allowed to mislead and conceal instead of detail, expose
and reveal.

Thus, disillusionment, in and of itself, beyond denoting a perceived
process of being stripped of one set of rigid cultural ideals or ideology,
has also served as the marker for a transition from a period of cultural
and political naïveté to an austere form of an almost scientific realism.
To be disillusioned, in other words, is to mark oneself as having passed
from a cultural moment of a mistaken 'fairy tale' worldview – Georgian
chivalry, in the British context – to a world devoid of illusions and
consequently more realistic and precisely scientific. Writing of this shift
in terms of Western culture's changing relationship with death, Lorrie
Goldensohn references the modern phenomenon of the war lyric as a
move away from sentimentalism, arguing that

> the war lyric shares in the cultural aftermath of the change in rituals identified
> by Jahan Ramazani, that took death out of our houses and brought it to hos-
> pitals and funeral 'homes' in the late nineteenth and early twentieth century,
> thereby creating the expressive need for the anti-sentimental, the anti-elegiac,
> and, ultimately, the anti-heroic and anti-war.[25]

This sober realism, or perceived lack of sentiment, was achieved through
a kind of semantic realism, via the aspiration, if not moral demand,
for a brutal accuracy when it comes to describing scenes of war – graphic
details of violence, the afore-mentioned cleansing of 'Poetry' and
'metaphysics' – and through what could be called a structural realism –
in other words, how the chaos and 'reality' of war are such that language
itself must become just as chaotic. While the discussion of the latter has
been dominated by the sense of disillusionment as a cleansing exercise,
the former is understood as having a central, if perhaps not formative,
place in the formation of what came to be known as Modernism in
the arts – the rearranging of objects and words so as to better mirror
the uncertainty of reality. And while the debate continues regarding the
extent to which World War I helped shape this former kind of structural
realism – the two sides of the argument broadly represented by Paul
Fussell, who argues that the irony emanating from the trenches was

essential to Modernism, and Modris Eksteins, who sees the Great War as the Modernistic *par excellence*,[26] or others who view them as completely separate movements[27] – one common thread remains: that the disillusionment coming out of the war either triggered or participated in a cultural shift toward a more honest, brutal and realistic view of the world. As Ramazani writes of the new poetry that arises, not necessarily from the fronts, to befit this new age of the realistic and non-metaphysical: 'Yeats, Eliot, and Pound insistently describe modern poetry as "hard," "cold," "dry," "austere," and "impersonal," sharply distinguishing it from the poetry of "sentiment and sentimental sadness," of "moaning or whining," of "effeminacy" and "emotional slither."'[28] Using somewhat more explicit language, Eric J. Leed writes of the links between this idea of disillusionment and spiritual advancement, a link also associated with the social class of those claiming to have been stripped by illusion. As he writes: 'at least in Christian doctrine, disillusionment has been regarded as a positive experience. It was a painful but necessary awakening from the enchantment experienced by material and sensual realities, an awakening from the world of mere appearances.'[29]

I would not claim, perhaps to clarify, that what has come to be called disillusionment is unrelated to the experiences of soldiers during the Great War; nor is the experience of being stripped of the ability to speak regarding one's personal encounters with violence unrelated to the concept of injury and prosthesis this book offers. I would argue, however, that the concept of disillusionment was bolstered by contemporary and later readers and critics as part of what has been recognised as a cultural, perhaps spiritual, shift away from the mythological, sentimental, perhaps religious aspects of classical culture and toward a greater stress on what would appear to be the era's newly emerged cultural ideals – accuracy and realism. In other words, the critical reception of the Trench Poets' work as an 'unveiling' of reality should be understood in the context of two major points: the first, as mentioned above, that the notion of making a more perfect way of speaking should be read amid broader trends of the same ilk during the early twentieth century in Western culture; and the second, that the concepts of 'stripping down' or 'real' should be understood as ideological concepts in and of themselves, as opposed to 'anti-ideological' or 'realistic' in any kind of ontological way. As Richard Rorty writes in his introduction to *The Linguistic Turn*, concerning the early twentieth-century attempt to revolutionise and perfect language:

The revolutionaries were found to have presupposed, both in their criticisms of their predecessors and in their directives for the future, the truth of certain substantive and controversial philosophical theses. The new method which each proposed was one which, in good conscience, could be adopted only by those who subscribed to those theories.[30]

Disillusionment, then, both in the general cultural sense and in the specific case of soldiers returning from war, was not the hoped-for extra-ideological leap, but the terra firma on which the leaper has already landed. The twin concepts of wartime injury and post-war prosthesis are focused less on the ideological shifts that war can and does at times bring about and more on an understanding about what it is that happens to individual soldiers during war that warrants such a leap and why the leap itself can be communicated, partially at that, only via the mechanism of the poetic prosthesis. In other words, it centred on the ability of soldiers' writings after war, regardless of the character of the various ideological responses to war – to demonstrate the rattling that precedes its ideological conclusions.

The Poetic Real: Poetry as History

The impact of the cultural shift into a realism of facts and away from what could be called a realism of the abstract that takes place at the turn of the century and gains force with the fallout of the Great War cannot be overestimated. This, as I have argued above, is all but obvious in cultural, philosophical, scientific and literary terms, as the West moves, first with nineteenth-century realism and later with the 'realities' of the early twentieth century, away from Homeric and Romantic 'fairy tales' and toward a world of 'facts', 'austerity', 'exactitude' and 'logic'. However, the force of this paradigm shift has been equally sensed in our understanding of war and in the manner in which poetry by soldiers has been read both in the twentieth century and, in some ways, all the way up to the present day. One sign of this enduring impact is the fact that, despite the dramatic changes that have taken place during last century in both war and how we have come to view it, I would argue that war is still contemplated through the lens of the post-World War I 'unveiling' of its true nature via the apparatus of realism and the 'real'. The changes to war itself include, to name but a few, a continued mechanisation of warfare, the impetus for which stemmed from significant advances in military technology, some of which saw their first use during the Great War[31]; a consequent shift away from ground combat and hand-to-hand engagements to the use of aerial, long-range and even remotely operated weapons[32]; and a shift in the demographic makeup of the American and British militaries with the rise of a largely voluntary force in both the USA and the UK. In terms of the public's relationship with war, the last century has also seen the marked rise of photographic and televised journalism, a significant part of which is broadcast either as events unfold or soon after they have transpired, in addition to the advent of the internet and social media, who have made both access and its instantaneous nature even more accented, having a significant impact on the war experience of soldiers and their families.[33] However, and despite major political, military, sociological, linguistic and philosophical changes, two constants dominate the writing and reading of war writings to this day: the fact that war writing, specifically poetry, is produced and continues to be produced in the wake of every armed conflict in the twentieth and twenty-first centuries; and that poems written by soldiers are almost never read as poems, as artistic expressions or, as I read them here, as poetic prostheses that use poetry to remake language after war, and are instead used as documents or evidence as to the 'real' war.

The first of these claims is a fairly easy one to demonstrate since poetry, as stated in the previous section, has in fact been produced during and following the many conflicts that the twentieth century would come to produce – the Second World War, the Korean War, the Vietnam War and the Falklands War, as well as wars in Iraq, Afghanistan, the Balkans and Africa. This includes certain non-canonical brands of poetry, such as the writing of military nurses,[34] journals and letters by civilians, and that seen in Santanu Das's seminal study of poems recited and written by sepoy soldiers in German captivity during World War I.[35] Naturally, poems continue to be written about every other human phenomenon in that period, such as those focusing on love, society at large, family, parenting and any other aspect of human life. Where I would argue that soldier poetry differs from these, however, is in the habit of reading that poetry as an authentic document about the *realities* of war: a reading, as I will expand upon in the second constant point, that has not changed since the work of the luminaries of Great War writing, such as Owen, Sassoon and, to a much lesser extent, Rosenberg. The poems about war written during and after the war, whether for historical, aesthetical or sociological reasons, in other words, remain the paragon of how a twenty-first-century audience thinks and feels about the human encounter with war, a claim we would not so quickly ascribe to the effect of poetry on love, life in the city, entertainment and so on, and this despite the above-mentioned changes and passage of time. As Goldensohn writes: 'Even in the dialogue of wars shared between generations of English soldiers, the Great War poets continued their overshadowing mark.'[36] Why is it, then, that the shock of encountering a whole new and barbaric way of making war, a theme that dominates World War I poetry, remains a leading, if not dominant, cultural factor in how we think about and view war today?

There is, naturally, one way in which the effect that Owen and Sassoon had on the field of soldier poetry is very tangible and noticeable – and for good reason. After all, despite the US Civil War's status as the first mechanised modern war in the West, the Great War is perhaps the site in both space and time where the now clichéd ideological and liberal West used its force with the utmost brutality, linked to the ideological discharge with which it is related. Thus, to a large extent, the shock of the First World War, which, in the eyes of the main body of research, found its way into the so-called Trench Poets' work, is one that could not be replicated by any other subsequent armed conflict. This shock, which finds parallel expression in the term 'disillusionment', could perhaps be said to taper off as wars raged on, until becoming either non-existent or self-explanatory in the present day. As Giorgio Agamben argues, channelling Walter Benjamin whose words open this chapter, the kind of unsettling encounter experienced in the trenches of the First World War has, in highly industrial, post-modern societies, been subsumed into everyday modern life and has become part of the very definition of modern experience: 'Today . . . we know that the destruction of experience no longer necessitates a catastrophe, and that humdrum daily life in any city will suffice. For modern man's average day contains virtually nothing that can still be translated into experience.'[37] And so, one could argue, there has not been a conflict like the Great War in the last century; consequently, in the same span there has not been a poetry of war that is as important.

However, I would argue that, even when considering the cultural shifts that have certainly taken place in the last century, the Trench Poets' legacy remains as dominant as it is not only because of the apparent shock of mechanised violence and the 'disillusionment' that violence caused, but because the poems written by Owen, Sassoon and Rosenberg, as well as many others, were never read as poems. Instead, their writings were, and still are, read, whether by detractors or supporters of their purported message, as 'real' documents of the reality of human suffering in war, at that moment of grand awakening to the brutal 'reality' of war. They are not read as poems in the same way that Keats's 'Ode to a Grecian Urn' is read, as the *Iliad* is treated or as a personalised, personal prosthesis, but as a statement of universal, physical, moral fact, with each reader interpreting that fact in every possible way: the heroics of war or the horrors of war. And this, again, is true, almost regardless of the interpretational stance taken: whether they are said to adopt an 'anti-war' or 'pacifist' tone, as they have been widely read, or as documenting human 'bravery' in the face of violence.

One paradigmatic reaction to the supposed realness that I claim these poems were and are associated with, is demonstrated by W. B. Yeats's exclusion of the widely popular Trench Poets from his 1936 *Oxford Book of Modern Verse*. Writing in his introduction to the collection, Yeats, hinting at poets such as Owen and Sassoon without referring to them directly, explains:

> I have a distaste for certain poems written in the midst of the great war; they are all in anthologies, but I have substituted Herbert Read's 'End of the War' written long after. The writers of these poems were invariably officers of exceptional courage and capacity, one a man constantly selected for dangerous work, all, I think, had the Military Cross; their letters are vivid and humorous, they were not without joy – for all skill is joyful – but felt bound, in the words of the best known, to plead the suffering of their men. In poems that had for a time considerable fame, written in the first person, they made that suffering their own. I have rejected these poems for the same reason that made Arnold withdraw his 'Empedocles on Etna' from circulation; passive suffering is not a theme for poetry. In all the great tragedies, tragedy is a joy to the man who dies; in Greece the tragic chorus danced.[38]

The response to Yeats's now infamous comments was an equally well-documented backlash[39] from several contemporary critics. Yeats, however, continued to stand by his original decision, writing later that year:

> My anthology continues to sell and the critics get more and more angry. When I excluded Wilfred Owen, whom I consider unworthy of the poets' corner of a country newspaper, I did not know I was excluding a revered sandwich-board Man of the revolution and that some body has put his worst and most famous poem in a glass case in the British Museum – however, if I had known it I would have excluded him just the same. He is all blood, dirt and sucked sugar stick (look at the selection in Faber's Anthology – he calls poets 'bards,' a girl a 'maid,' and talks about 'Titanic wars.') There is every excuse for him but none for those who like him.[40]

While decades have passed since Yeats wrote his diatribe against Owen's poetry, it remains at the focal point of continuing academic discourse concerning war poetry in general, and that written after war specifically.

Joseph Cohen sees the exclusion as a reaction to Owen's assault on his own view of how poetry should depict war:

> Yeats was apparently always attracted to the view ... that the only valid military theme for poetry was the *joy of battle* theme, i.e., the ancient, Romantic, exhalant glorification by the combatant of his strength in arms and his willingness to sacrifice all, whatever the cause.[41]

Hermann Peschmann, moreover, dismisses Yeats's exclusion, by arguing that Owen's poetry was not passive because of the very fact that it included an extra-poetic effort, a 'selfless plea on behalf of suffering humanity'.[42]

However, Yeats's decision to exclude the Trench Poets sheds light on two other issues. Firstly, as a prominent literary figure, he has the power to edit out that which he deems unpoetic, a fact that will become more significant as this book shifts its focus to amateur, unedited online soldier poetry. Secondly, there is the very reason for that exclusion: Yeats did not consider Owen's poetry to be poetry – not because of the passivity it displays, but rather because it marks suffering in war, as opposed to what could be called an active act of rejoicing in the face of death, and also, in the terms of the current discussion, because it was 'too real'. It provides the 'sugar stick' the masses seem to require in their poetry; after all, even Yeats could not and did not ignore Owen's popularity, which he sarcastically refers to in discussing Owen's 'glass case in the British Museum' – and thus performs little by way of eliciting poetry or tragedy. For the public, to put it another way, Owen's words were a way of expressing the futility and pain of war, thus disregarding it as a work of literature – one that involves a tension between the real and unreal, truth and fiction – while Yeats wrote them off as poetic failures, precisely, as I argue, because of this same 'realness'. And that, ultimately, may be the legacy of Great War poetry and the scope of its influence in the preceding century – not the first time that soldiers write of war, but the first time that poetry and war have been divorced in such a fashion as to negate the poems' representational status or their irony.

Thus, a tradition of reading soldier poetry begins, and to a degree, ends, with the Trench Poets, whose poems are read not as plays on index and symbol, vis-à-vis Peirce's terminology, but as one of many 'real' forms of text: manifestos, historical documents, psychological case studies, works of social commentary and brain imaging scans, all seen as proving what has come to be known as the disillusionment of the soldier in war. An example of one such reading of war poetry can be seen in Janis Stout's expansive work on soldier poetry, *Coming Out of War*, in which she argues that the majority of war poetry written in the first half of the twentieth century is decidedly 'anti-war' or 'anti-military':

> Most of the poetry I discuss – indeed, most of the poetry that emerged from the two world wars – is antimilitary in impulse. And most of *that* reflects an antiwar impetus. The two are not necessarily the same. 'Antimilitary' indicates a dislike of the culture of military organizations. 'Antiwar' – a term that often taxes our definitional abilities, with its variance from narrow to general meaning – designates a powerful distaste for and opposition to either a specific war or, more sweepingly, war in general. Being antiwar does not necessarily mean being pacifist, any more than opponents of, say, the 2003 war in Iraq are necessarily pacifists.[43]

Notwithstanding Stout's perceptive distinction between anti-war and anti-military, her categorisation of all war poetry as being anti-military, whether accurate or not, is one that, I would argue, stems from the standard reading of war poems as 'real': as having, in other words, a clear 'message', the same type of clear-cut message gleaned from historical reports and journalistic articles. Stout's work, it should be said, is not singular in this respect, and manifests a larger trend in the reading and understanding of soldier poetry as expressing 'real' pain, 'real' messages, both having to do, I believe, with the realness that readers and writers ascribe to the encounter with violence. The violence, as we have seen in Tim's stirring monologue, is real, and thus, by proxy or infection, any description of violence is, or perhaps *ought* to be, real as well, written in the furnace of violence's reality.

There are many contemporary instances that demonstrate not only the lasting influence of the Great War poets, but also the enduring, persistent inclination to associate soldier poetry with reality. One such example is a 2011 article in the British *Telegraph* newspaper, discussing contemporary soldier poetry, including several works discussed in this book. Following a brief description of the historical importance of soldier poetry via the obligatory mention of Owen, Sassoon and Rupert Brooke, the article goes on to quote Lord Baker, editor of *The Faber Book of War Poetry*, as saying: 'When someone reads a war poem, they get the most vivid impression of what war is like – much more so than any report on television.'[44] Poetry written by a soldier, in other words, not only is definitively 'real', but it provides a *realer* view of war than journalistic reports. A more recent *New Yorker* article discussing contemporary war writing refers to these newer works' lesser reliance on context, going on to say:

Fragments are perhaps the most honest literary form available to writers who fought so recently. Their work lacks context, but it gets closer to the lived experience of war than almost any journalism. It deals in particulars, which is where the heightened alertness of combatants has to remain, and it's more likely to notice things. To most foreign observers, the landscape of Iraq is relentlessly empty and ugly, like a physical extension of the country's trauma. But in the poetry and the prose of soldiers and marines the desert comes to life with birdsong and other noises, the moonlit sand breeds dreams and hallucinations.[45]

In this instance, the point of comparison is again between war poets and journalists in terms of 'honesty' and 'closeness to lived experience'. Reality, as this book claims, or its linguistic stand-in in the form of the indexical, obviously has a significant role in the poems under discussion here, not in the form of a message but in the form of a challenge: not 'this is real' but 'what is real any more?' What is real beyond a doubt, then, is not the world as it is revealed through the encounter with war or through the reading of soldier poetry, but the absolute destruction of the personality and of one's humanity in the face of violence, and the desperate attempt to dig oneself out of the grave.

In any analysis of this concept of 'realness', as I have already discussed, and specifically in the exploration of the indexical aspect of the poems, we must admit that the concept of 'realness' serves as an essential point of reference in the poems themselves. The speaker in 'Burying the Dead', for one, seems to be very much involved with what is real and what is not: which 'burying the dead' is a figure of speech, say, and which is 'literally' burying someone who has died. Likewise, in his poem 'A Soldier's Winter', one soldier poet who identifies as 'Chris from Kandahar' is puzzled by his inability to detect the real from the unreal, reaching, as we can see in this excerpt, the point of not being able to discern whether his own body is there:

I see trees, I see sky, I see clouds,
All winter white,
Can I reach upward to touch the falling flake?
I try but never seem to connect,

And as I lay there staring at the sky
Is my body cold?
As I lay I hope I am not forgotten
But here I am alone.
I close my eyes and try to think of home
Is this really happening to me?[46]

Elsewhere, Gerardo Mena's 'So I Was a Coffin' shifts and manipulates reality, changing form after form, until it is no longer at all clear what is more real: his existence as a soldier, a bandage or a coffin. Perhaps going even further than that, it is not uncommon for the poems themselves to profess to having access to a level of reality that is inaccessible to those who 'were not there', Currall's poem being at least one example of that tendency as well. One other example would be 'Acknowledgements' by British Iraq veteran Danny Martin.

In Martin's poem, the speaker attacks the mainstays of his own culture – Hollywood films, recruitment ads, parents – in a manner reminiscent of Owen's rejection of heroic rhetoric, for misleading him about what he now considers to be the true nature of violence. And by going down that route, by opting in a way into the post-Owen tradition of poetry as doing away with platitudes and fantasy, or received as such, the poem also points toward its ability to access unmediated reality, one inherently intertwined with the index of war's violence:

My thanks to Hollywood
When you showed me John Rambo
Stitching up his arm with no anaesthetic
And giving them 'a war they won't believe'
I knew then my calling, the job for me

Thanks also to the recruitment adverts
For showing me soldiers whizzing around on skis
And for sending sergeants to our school
To tell us of the laughs, the great food, the pay
The camaraderie

I am, dear taxpayer, forever in your debt
You paid for my all-inclusive pilgrimage
One year basking in the Garden of Eden
(I haven't quite left yet)

Thanks to Mum and thanks to Dad
Fuck it,
Thanks to every parent
Flushing with pride for their brave young lads
Buying young siblings toy guns and toy tanks
Waiting at the airport
Waving their flags.[47]

Martin's poem assaults the many misrepresentations of war, attesting to his ability to see war for what it is: not *Rambo* or recruitment ads but, one would think, a state of affairs much closer to what Hemingway describes as the 'stockyards at Chicago'. However, while deploying its disingenuous 'seeing beyond' rhetoric, 'Acknowledgements' never points to what could be considered the real of the war scene. There are no bodies or dying comrades, no blood and smoke to point indexically at the unspoken horrors of combat. Instead, the only reference to the scene itself is as the 'Garden of Eden', itself a symbolic stand-in for the geographical area in which Martin was stationed – Iraq. Thus Martin does not attempt to unveil war, only to punch through the platitudes that, according to the poem, have misled people as to its nature. That nature, however, remains shrouded in symbolism. In such a way, then, we can read Martin's poem as not exposing anything but the sense of injury to communication that the encounter with violence has brought on, one in which reality, far from being an absolute anchor of fact, is no longer certain, and in which the war does not seem to be able to stay in the war and returns home with the returning soldiers. This 'realness' is tested, played with, as opposed to being the be-all-and-end-all measure by which these poems are and should be read. Not that their 'poemness' is completely ignored, but that quality itself is enlisted, so to speak, as a way of indicating the reality it ostensibly describes. It should be said, then, that this notion of a poem describing something or appealing to the real is not one which can be banished altogether; in fact, it occupies most of what it is that the poets themselves seem to be trying to articulate or construct.

Nevertheless, what separates these poetic discussions of the real from the 'real' of reports and documentation is the fact that the poetic prosthesis reacts to, is confounded by and questions reality, treating it as an oppressive agent that must, to an extent, be resisted. Currall's speaker is not necessarily interested in ending a discussion of language and its fuzzy edges by appealing to the 'real', or by arguing that there is only one true 'burying the dead' that supplants all others – or at least not interested *only* in that. Far from making an attempt to cleanse language, as seen in Owen and Wittgenstein, Currall's speaker is forced to deal with both 'realities' at the very same time: that those around him mean 'bury the dead' one way and that he *also* understands it in another way. There is no ideological push here to supplant one real with the other, or any decisive conclusion along the lines of 'their "burying the dead" is wrong, the soldier's is right'. Instead, the poem points toward a gap in language, a difference in the way words are said and understood, between a collective 'they' and a suffering 'I'. Understanding Currall's speaker as 'disillusioned' is tantamount to glossing over that gap, since the term seems to refer to a process in which he who undergoes it sees things 'as they really are'. I would argue that disillusionment essentially exacerbates that gap, since the knowledge that certain soldiers return from war 'disillusioned', as I have argued, is just another way of effacing individual experiences by arranging them under an abstract concept, even if that concept is seemingly constructed around a 'real' or 'individual' idea. Thus, a soldier encounters an idiom – 'burying the dead' – and explains to himself what it is that 'they' mean by using it: a metaphor, with many possible denotations, all having to do with moving on from the soldier's persistent suffering. The manner with which that need is expressed forms an ironic tension between not only the speaker and a misunderstanding audience, but also, perhaps despite what he seems to say, between what is real and what is unreal. Thus, to read those poems as 'real', or to disregard their role as objects of play between real and unreal, is to strip them of their prosthetic nature, to cease viewing them as objects made by specific human beings in order to advance specific ends or needs – poems: to stop seeing them as emanating from specific human suffering, culminating, I would argue, in the disappearance of their individual, self-constructed subjectivity. All of this only enhances the sense of death, the arresting of the same motion the prosthesis aims to initiate.

The Real Right Now

If, as I have argued, there has not been any significant change in the way in which we have addressed soldier poetry in the last century or so, to the extent that 100-year-old poems still define our view of war, what is it, after all, that has changed, at least in terms of the reality or 'real' in question? There is a way in which this claim of historical consistency or continuity exists in my own claims: namely, that soldiers have constructed and are forced to construct poetic prostheses following war. But, while the effort to outline or fabricate a new speaking organ remains, the content that organ deals with, or the cultural environment in which it is asked to mediate, has changed radically. Said otherwise, the content of 'realness' these poems incorporate, while persistent in soldier poems across the ages, has changed. What, then, we could ask, is the difference, if any, between the reading and writing of soldier poetry now, of the kind this book discusses, and that published following the Great War? This is, of course, a significant question, and involves a century's worth of technological, sociological, tactical, literary and philosophical changes and research concerning those changes. And, for the most part, a soldier's attempt to stab at the fog that prevents his own experience from coming through, whether that fog is national chauvinism or stark realism, seems one clear constant. Despite these inescapable limitations, I would like, by way of leading up to a more thorough discussion of the poems themselves, to touch upon on what I see as the two most important changes in terms of this discussion of the persistent 'realness' that has been ascribed to soldier poetry from its very inception in the modern age: that is, the manner in which we have learned about the 'reality' of war – namely, the media through which that information is received; and, just as importantly, the manner in which we now address the way that reality affects the psychology or 'reality' of the soldier, both inner and outer.

One major development is the many different ways in which information about war is provided to both prospective soldiers and the public, including photographic and televised material coming out of the various war zones, a process that has reached its apex in the current state of twenty-four-hour news cycles, internet news sources and social media. Thus, while First World War audiences would construct their images of the war mainly through text (news articles, poems) and, to a lesser degree, through images and film,[48] the modern public is kept informed 'live', meaning as things occur, as well as receiving that information in a much more image-oriented form or, at least, up-to-the-moment fashion. The image, whether a picture, a video insert on the news or an amateur clip on YouTube, has become the main tool of communicating war to non-combatants, a tool that, in and of itself, has an epistemological effect on our understanding of war. Writing in *Regarding the Pain of Others*, Susan Sontag explores this epistemological effect in her discussion of Virginia Woolf's correspondence with an acquaintance concerning the war, one documented in Woolf's *Three Guineas*. In *Three Guineas*, Woolf, as she is filtered through Sontag's reading, argues that men and women understand war differently, going on to say that war, perhaps following Charlotte Smith's damning of the wars of 'Man',[49] is an essentially a masculine activity, and yet seemingly lets go of any idea of subjective or gender-based difference when discussing a newspaper war photograph. Woolf's tacit argument, via Sontag, is that 'photographs of the victims of war are themselves a species of rhetoric. They reiterate. They simplify. They agitate. They create the illusion of consensus.' Sontag goes on to say 'Invoking this hypothetical shared experience ("we are seeing the same dead bodies, the same ruined houses"), Woolf professes to believe that the shock of such pictures cannot fail to unite people of good will.'[50] Woolf, in other words, through Sontag's analysis, gives voice to a larger human tendency to view pictures and film as providing objective information concerning war, which is especially true, I would add, regarding pictures of violence and victims of violence. Woolf also describes how those images, in turn, form our perception or idea of those events, but ultimately create a sense of infallibility or realness – my notions concerning those images are both ironclad and shared by all 'people of good will'.

Stated in the terms I have been using thus far, the assumed moored or indexical quality of photographic images brings about a sense that they, as means of communication, communicate or describe war in a more accurate and, ultimately, real way – so real, if we follow Sontag's critique of Woolf, as seemingly to make the social norms and means of communication necessary for the deciphering of the purported message entirely redundant. In terms of the warfare involving American and British troops in the last century or so, this shift from a mostly written account of war to a largely photographic one is most notably associated with the Vietnam and Falklands Wars, respectively. These conflicts were televised to such a point, in fact, that a discussion existed, and still remains, around whether or not the US government, for example, should have censored media reports from Southeast Asia,[51] given the impact of the images making their way to the American public. From that point on, war has been and is a primarily televised and photographed event, with Operation Iraqi Freedom, colloquially known as the Iraq War, making new headway in the complex relationship between war, journalism and reality with the advent of what has come to be called 'embedded journalism', by which the military allowed reporters to join fighting units. Amid a growing concern with 'authenticity' and 'reality', images of violence are no longer 'real enough': in other words, they necessitate the assimilation of media members into the fighting units as a means of obtaining the 'realest', unmediated images. This notion of reality is taken to task throughout this study, but it is important to add that the ability of embedded journalists to gain objective facts is controversial as well, despite or perhaps because of the unlimited access they gained.[52] Ultimately, it is these images that, as Sontag argues, create

a perch for a particular conflict in the consciousness of viewers exposed to dramas from everywhere [which] requires the daily diffusion of snippets of footage about the conflict. The understanding of war among people who have not experienced war is now chiefly a product of the impact of those images.[53]

Later, Sontag adds: 'The ultra-familiar, ultra-celebrated image – of an agony, of ruin – is an unavoidable feature of our camera-mediated knowledge of war.'[54]

However, this drastic shift in how we experience war and learn of its 'realities' is not limited to the way we learn of war but has, of course, much to do with the contemporary mode of war itself – elusive invisibility. Thus the media through which we experience war are indeed instant and electronic, and yet that is also what modern war has become. Long gone are the dramatic landscape-shifting trenches and the ominous weapons of mass destruction, replaced, ironically perhaps, with the search for unfound, unseen weapons of mass destruction and a war front that seems more and more like no front at all. With conflicts dominated by drones, 'smart' weaponry, electronic and remotely operated weapons, the ability to see war for what it is has become one other obstacle en route to its description: not just the unspeakability of trauma, then, but the double bind that is the invisibility and unilaterality of violence. Writing in his seminal series of essays, published before, during and after the Gulf War, Jean Baudrillard writes of this new unseen, unfelt mode of war as a war that 'does not take place'. As Baudrillard writes in the third and final essay of the series, 'The Gulf War Did Not Take Place'; war itself had to go 'underground in order to survive':

> In this forum of war which is the Gulf, everything is hidden: the planes are hidden, the tanks are buried, Israel plays dead, the images are censored and all information is blockaded in the desert: only TV functions as a medium without a message, giving at last the image of pure television. Like an animal, the war goes to ground. It hides in the sand, it hides in the sky. It is the Iraqi planes: it knows that it has no chance if it surfaces. It awaits its hour . . . which will never come.[55]

The war, as well as any epistemological evidence of its violence, then, not only is no longer in sole possession of the returning soldier; in one way, too, that visible, accessible war is not even there to be seen. The act of witnessing required of veterans upon their return, in other words, relates to an event that, to some, may not have even taken place. As Baudrillard later adds: 'War stripped of its passions, its phantasms, its finery, its veils, its violence, its images; war stripped bare by its technicians even, and then reclothed by them with all the artifices of electronics.'[56] How does one return from war if the war was not even there?

One other significant shift I shall discuss briefly here can be described as the attempt to come to medically 'real' terms with the psychological effects of war on soldiers and civilians. This process has leapfrogged from 'windage' following the US Civil War[57] to shell shock during and after World War I[58] and, finally, the contemporary category of post-traumatic stress disorder (PTSD) following the Vietnam War.[59] And even today, PTSD, as a diagnosable category, continues to shift, with the publication of the fifth edition of the *Diagnostic and Statistical Manual* in 2013 broadening an already quite wide, and controversial,[60] set of criteria and symptoms, described in the previous version published in 1994 and updated in 2000. In other words, whereas the British and American publics were shaken, and remain so, by the images of war as put forth by the so-called Trench Poets, readers today, and to an extent Western culture in general, have come to expect the psychologically wounded soldier as a result of war, on a par, perhaps, with ruined streets and grieving families. PTSD, as Hautzlinger and Scandlyn write, shifted from the background of post-war experience to something like a buzzword: 'Journalists invoked untreated PTSD to explain domestic violence, reckless driving, and other distress veterans displayed following deployments. Stories about PTSD and its effects have filled radio, television, and newspapers throughout the wars.'[61] And as Kenneth T. MacLeish adds in the beautiful prologue to *Making War at Fort Hood*, almost every aspect of veterans' life is in some way predetermined by a known, rigid narrative: 'the noble hero, the burned-out victim, the unrepentant killer, and the crazy, dangerous war vet who rages equally against foreign enemies, oblivious civilians, and the indifferent Army'.[62] Thus, soldiers, as a cohesive, non-differential unit, return from war 'damaged', an image supported by myriad films and novels after Vietnam and, later, the Gulf and Iraq Wars, such as *Born on the 4th of July* and *Rambo*, depicting what could only be called, again, the 'real' version of disillusionment. The result of these changes in how Western society understands soldiers returning from war is, thus, what could be seen as a convergence of the slowly changing medical and psychological categories ('windage', shell shock, PTSD and so on) and the concept of disillusionment – and that soldiers' disillusionment is now defined also, if not predominantly so, by medical, and thus physical or *real*, categories. The realness of war's internal effects, to reiterate, got 'realer', for want of a better term.

The conclusion of these two significant shifts, I would argue, is that, along with the persistent idea of war and wartime experiences as bearing a special mode of reality, even if it is expressed through art such as poetry, soldiers returning from war at the beginning of the twenty-first century have the added experience of seeing this concreteness or realness replaced by media reports and medical analysis. Put otherwise, the cultures to which they return from war have a very real, very professional and precisely predetermined image of both war and its assumed personal after-effects that seems to make the personal experience of war either expected or redundant. This is not to say, obviously, that the medical categories themselves preclude personal, non-categorised treatment of these veterans, or that the images of war made public on TV and YouTube prevent civilians from empathising with a particular soldier or even with the possibility of individual suffering. Only that they make those actions more difficult. It is more difficult, perhaps, or at least difficult in a completely different manner, than the experience of those soldiers returning home from war in 1918, 1945 or 1969. Thus, I would argue, while war poetry has indeed continued to be produced in the previous century, the role of the soldier as harbinger or agent of the 'reality' of battle has diminished considerably, as audiences at home – that home, in the cases discussed in this book, being the United States and Britain – receive up-to-date information, images and statistics regarding the violence taking place thousands of miles away, as well as diagnostic categories and statistics around the mental effect of those images on the soldiers' bodies and minds. Moreover, the wars in question take place vast distances away from the soldiers' homes, often in radically different cultural environments – be that culture a civilian or religious society or the culture of war as such. And yet that physical distance has been traversed more and more swiftly as the century has progressed, whether through constant contact via social media/Skype/FaceTime, as I shall discuss further in the following chapter, or through the sheer speed with which soldiers return from the front. Writing of what he sees as the effect of faster travel on the twentieth-century soldier, Howard Dean says this of Vietnam veterans:

> When the Vietnam veteran returned to the United States, he did not come back slowly on a troop ship with his comrades (as had been the practice in World War II, allowing time to unwind, 'decompress,' and assimilate the experience), but was flown back quickly by himself, moving from the blood and gore of the combat zone to his hometown in the space of twenty-four hours. Once at home again and trying to deal with the shocking transition, he was either totally ignored by the civilian population or, worse, spit upon and blamed for losing the unpopular war.[63]

While Dean's emphasis on how the manner in which Vietnam veterans were treated differently from soldiers returning from earlier wars (lack of parades, the 'G.I. Bill' and so on) contributed to the growing PTSD diagnosis is controversial, his point regarding the shortening distances between war and home is a salient one. It is all the more so, I would argue, with today's veterans, who are deployed and released from battle zones at greater and greater speed, without any real change to the 'speed' of their readjustment from a culture of war and the linguistic injury that may bring about. That injury, as I claim, never truly goes away, and yet the relative ease with which family members and friends receive both news of their loved ones and their loved ones themselves may drive an even larger wedge between the home environment and the returning soldier. Writing of British soldiers of the First World War, Paul Fussell refers to the 'ridiculous proximity'[64] of the trenches to the soldiers' home, and the tension between violence and death at the trenches and the regular arrival of packages and letters from family and loved ones. One would have to assume that the existence of tools such as social media (Facebook, Twitter, Skype, FaceTime, SnapChat and more) and televised journalism could have the power of ratcheting up that tension ever further.

In service to those forced to fashion art in the wake of their encounter with disaster, violence and war, I would like, for a moment, to withdraw from the hyper-digital realism of our contemporary age and move to mid-nineteenth-century America: specifically to Herman Melville's Ishmael, floating to safety or, at least, back to life on land, on the ornate coffin fashioned by fellow seaman Queequeg – the object of death, the object that by its very objecthood *is* death, that allows for a return to life:

> Buoyed up by that coffin, for almost one whole day and night, I floated on a soft and dirge-like main. The unharming sharks, they glided by as if with padlocks on their mouths; the savage sea-hawks sailed with sheathed beaks. On the second day, a sail drew near, nearer, and picked me up at last. It was the devious-cruising Rachel, that in her retracting search after her missing children, only found another orphan.[65]

Confounded by an indistinguishable mass of realness, one that, as I have discussed above, overtakes both the soldier's physical surroundings and the ability to communicate personal and particular experience, soldiers are at risk of what can only be called drowning. Unable to reattach securely what has been detached by war – a secure relation between symbol and referent and, as a result, to differentiate securely between that which is dangerous and that which is safe – veterans are surrounded by letters, words and sounds, unable to separate out specific, personal uses in order to communicate their own unique experience to their community.

There seems to be something about the very event of war, about the nature of violence, which perceives even the most preliminary attempt at gaining a foothold amid this linguistic chaos as a 'real' or 'journalistic' account of both violence and its effect on one's psyche. Hence, finally, the use of the prosthetic: the attachment not only of that which is dead, but, often, that which is death itself to the living body in order to regain an elusive sense of having communicated something, of humanity and communal belonging. The indexical, the object, the shifter and, ultimately, the constructed, artfully made poem – the coffin – saves, albeit uncomfortably and without any true sense of absolute safety, the drowning soldier from disappearing below the sea of undifferentiated danger and insecurity. It is the coffin, the return to agency via the work of art, which 'padlocks' the sharks' mouth as they swim harmlessly alongside Ishmael. In several instances it is these objects of death that appear again and again as a means of warding off a homogenous mass of realness. Such is the case in Currall's 'Burying the Dead', in which the very act of burying is discussed in conjunction with modes of speaking and writing ('burying the dead is a metaphor'); in Croft's 'When the Men Came Back', with its speaker fearing the possibility that he would 'disappear under the Atlantic'; Chris from Kandahar's 'A Soldier's Winter' and the terror of the homogeneously white snow covering reality; and, most notably perhaps, in Mena's 'So I Was a Coffin'. The attempt to resist the oncoming mass that aims to drown, bury and colour the individual experience of one soldier, who struggles, as Goldensohn writes of Wilfred Owen's language, 'to keep faith with the unburiable'.[66] Not only do they sort out the mangled bodies of their dead comrades and past lives, thus saving their friends from oblivion, but, in the very act of fashioning poems and coffins, save themselves from that same unbounded expanse of reality.

* * *

To return to the point with which I began this chapter, these concepts of reality as it pertains to war have dominated not only the age-old relation to war as real and violence as an index of reality, but also, in the past century or so, the discourse concerning representations of war. And it is precisely this tendency, one that has been cemented, as I have attempted to show, in a tradition of receiving soldier writing as realer than other forms of literature, that highlights just how difficult and transformative is the task of, so to speak, flipping the index. By flipping, I mean transforming it into a tool for play and performance, while, as in Merleau-Ponty's discussion of the cave paintings and Peirce's iconic diagram or 'dream', retaining its indexical function, both as grounder or anchor and as reminder or memorial of the past. And that is not to say that soldier writers would not like perhaps to envision a complete fantasy, in which the war was a dream from which they could wake up. However, as I have discussed, that dream is always interrupted, whether by the onset of sudden phantom pain or by the persistent debt to those who had died at war, and whose stories the poet is seemingly fated to tell. It is this combination of personal reality, social circumstance and the inherent symbolic nature of military service that I shall address in the next chapter.

Notes

1. Walter Benjamin, 'The Storyteller', in *Illuminations*, translated by Harry Zohn (Glasgow: Fontana, 1973). Cited in Giorgio Agamben, *Infancy and History: Essays on the Destruction of Experience*, translated by Liz Heron (New York: Verso, 1993), 13.

2. David Reynolds, *The Long Shadow: The Legacies of the Great War in the Twentieth Century* (London: Norton and Company, 2014), 183–93; Jay Winter, 'Beyond Glory: First World War Poetry and Cultural Memory', in *The Cambridge Companion to the Poetry of the First World War*, edited by Santanu Das (Cambridge: Cambridge University Press, 2013), 242–57; and Jay Winter, 'Introduction', in Paul Fussell, *The Great War and Modern Memory* (Oxford: Oxford University Press, 2013).

3. Faith Barrett, *To Fight Aloud is Very Brave: American Poetry and the Civil War* (Amherst: University of Massachusetts Press, 2012), 73; Alice Fahs, *The Imagined Civil War: Popular Literature of the North and South, 1861–1865* (Chapel Hill: University of North Carolina Press, 2001), 93–120.

4. Robin Norris, 'Mourning Rights: Beowulf, the Iliad, and the War in Iraq', *Journal of Narrative Theory* 37, no. 2 (Summer 2007): 277.

5. James Tatum, *The Mourner's Song: War and Remembrance from the Iliad to Vietnam* (Chicago: University of Chicago Press, 2003), xi.

6. Giambattista Vico, *The New Science*, translated by Dave Marsh (London: Penguin, 2000), 146.

7. Brian Murdoch, *Fighting Songs and Warring Words: Popular Lyrics of Two World Wars* (New York: Routledge, 1990), 3–6.

8. Norris, 'Mourning Rights', 276–7.

9. Wolfgang Kulman, 'Gods and Men in the Iliad and the Odyssey', *Harvard Studies in Classical Philology* 89 (1985): 6–7.

10. Daniel Todman, *The Great War: Myth and Memory* (London: Hambledon and London, 2005), x–xii.

11. Elizabeth Vandiver, 'Homer in British World War One Poetry', in *A Companion to Classical Receptions*, edited by Lorna Hardwick and Christopher Stray (Oxford: Blackwell, 2008), 454.

12. Kenneth S. Lynn, *Hemingway* (Cambridge, MA: Harvard University Press, 1995), 385; Fussell, *The Great War and Modern Memory*, 21; Charles Hatten, 'The Crisis of Masculinity, Reified Desire, and Catherine Barkley in *A Farewell to Arms*', *Journal of the History of Sexuality* 4, no. 1 (July 1993): 97.

13. Ernest Hemingway, *Farewell to Arms* (New York: Scribner, 2012), 161.

14. James Anderson Winn, *The Poetry of War* (Cambridge: Cambridge University Press, 2008), 18.

15. John Silkin, *Out of Battle: The Poetry of the Great War* (London: Oxford University Press, 1972), 221.

16. Mary Ann Gillies and Aurelea Denise Mahood, *Modernist Literature: An Introduction* (Edinburgh: Edinburgh University Press, 2007), 87.

17. Ibid., 88.

18. Randall Stevenson, *Literature and the Great War: 1914–1918* (Oxford: Oxford University Press, 2013), xi.

19. Homer, *Iliad*, translated by Stanley Lombardo (Indianapolis: Hackett, 1997), lines 502–7.

20. Tatum, *The Mourner's Song*, 117; Winn, *The Poetry of War*, 52.

21. Wilfred Owen, 'Wilfred Owen's Preface', in *The Collected Poems of Wilfred Owen*, edited by C. Day Lewis (New York: New Directions, 1963), 31.

22. Ludwig Wittgenstein, *Tractatus Logico-Philosophicus*, translated by David Francis Pears and Brian McGuiness (New York: Routledge, 1974), 3.

23. Ron Ben-Tovim, 'Owen, Wittgenstein, and the Postwar Battle with Language', *Philosophy and Literature* 42, no. 2 (October 2018): 344–60.

24. Marjorie Perloff, *Wittgenstein's Ladder: Poetic Language and the Strangeness of the Ordinary* (Chicago: University of Chicago Press, 1999), 40.

25. Jahan Ramazani, *Poetry of Mourning: The Modern Elegy from Hardy to Heaney* (Chicago: University of Chicago Press, 1994), 21. Cited in Lorrie Goldensohn, *Dismantling Glory: Twentieth-Century Soldier Poetry* (New York: Columbia University Press, 2003), 2.

26. Modris Eksteins, *Rites of Spring: The Great War and the Birth of the Modern Age* (New York: Doubleday, 1990), 146.

27. Vincent Sherry, *The Great War and the Language of Modernism* (New York: Oxford University Press, 2003), 7–8.

28. Ramazani, *Poetry of Mourning*, 21.

29. Leed, *No Man's Land*, 81. Elsewhere Leed also makes an interesting equivalent between the idea of 'disillusionment' and social class – see, for example, 75–6.

30. Richard Rorty, 'Introduction: Metaphysical Difficulties of Linguistic Philosophy', in *The Linguistic Turn: Essays in Philosophical Method*, edited by Richard Rorty (Chicago: University of Chicago Press, 1992), 1.

31. See, for example, Alan Kramer, *Dynamics of Destruction: Culture and Mass Killing in the First World* War (Oxford: Oxford University Press, 2007); Barton C. Hacker, 'The Machines of War: Western Military Technology 1850–2000', *History and Technology* 21, no. 3 (2005): 255–300.

32. See, for example, Michael W. Lewis, 'Drones and the Boundaries of the Battlefield', *Texas International Law Journal* 47 (2011): 294–314; Derek Gregory,

'From a View to a Kill: Drones and Late Modern War', *Theory, Culture, and Society* 28, no. 7–8 (2011): 188–215; and Christian Enemark, *Armed Drones and the Ethics of War: Military Virtue in a Post-Heroic Age* (Abingdon: Routledge, 2014).

33. See, for example, Pat Matthews-Juarez, Paul D. Juarez and Roosevelt T. Faulkner, 'Social Media and Military Families: A Perspective', *Journal of Human Behavior in the Social Environment* 23 (2013): 769–76; and Sarah Maltby and Helen Thornham, 'The Digital Mundane: Social Media and the Military', *Media, Culture & Society* 38, no. 8 (2016): 1119–35.

34. Mary Borden and Ellen Newbold La Motte (eds), *Nurses at the Front: Writing the Wounds of the Great War* (Boston: Northeastern University Press, 2001); Christine E. Hallett, *Nurse Writers of the Great War* (Manchester: Manchester University Press, 2016); and Margaret Higonnet, *Lines of Fire. Women Writers of World War I* (Harmondsworth: Penguin, 1999).

35. Santanu Das, *India, Empire, and First World War Culture* (Cambridge: Cambridge University Press, 2018).

36. Goldensohn, *Dismantling Glory*, 33.

37. Agamben, *History and Infancy*, 13.

38. W. B. Yeats, 'Introduction', in *The Oxford Book of Modern Verse: 1892–1935*, edited by W. B. Yeats (London: Oxford University Press, 1941), xxxiv.

39. Joseph Cohen, 'In Memory of W. B. Yeats – and Wilfred Owen', *The Journal of English and Germanic Philology* 58, no. 4 (October 1959): 637–49; Jonathan Allison, 'War, Passive Suffering, and the Poet', *The Sewanee Review* 114, no. 2 (Spring 2006): 209.

40. From a letter of 26 December 1936, in *Letters on Poetry from W. B. Yeats to Dorothy Wellesley* (Oxford: Oxford University Press, 1964), 113.

41. Joseph Cohen, 'In Memory of W. B. Yeats', 643.

42. Hermann Peschmann, 'Yeats and the Poetry of War', *English* 15 (1965): 183.

43. Janis P. Stout, *Coming Out of War: Poetry, Grieving, and the Culture of the World Wars* (Tuscaloosa: University of Alabama Press, 2005), xv.

44. 'Modern War Poetry: British Soldiers Explore Afghanistan and Iraq Wars in Verse', *The Telegraph*, last modified 17 April 2011. Available at: <http://www.telegraph.co.uk/culture/culturenews/8455677/Modern-war-poetry-British-soldiers-explore-Afghanistan-and-Iraq-wars-in-verse.html> (last accessed 23 February 2022).

45. George Packer, 'Home Fires', *New Yorker*, last modified 7 April 2014. Available at: <http://www.newyorker.com/magazine/2014/04/07/home-fires-2> (last accessed 23 February 2022).

46. Chris from Kandahar, 'A Soldier's Winter', originally on the *War Poetry Website*, now deleted. Available in several other locations, such as: <http://sckelleyartist.weebly.com/heroes/a-soldiers-winter> (last accessed 23 February 2022).

47. Danny Martin, 'Acknowledgments', *ForcesWatch*. Available at: <https://www.forceswatch.net/comment/war-poems> (last accessed 23 February 2022).

48. One noted example is the propaganda film *The Battle of the Somme*, which included crude footage of the notorious battle and was shown to British audiences in 1916.

49. Writing of the fallout from the French Revolution, Smith repeatedly refers to war as a masculine activity, assigning femininity to 'mercy' and 'justice'. One statement reads: 'Yet Man, misguided Man, / Mars the fair work that he was bid enjoy, / and makes himself the evil he deplores.' *The Emigrants* (London, 1793), 3. For further discussion of Smith's gendered critique of war and violence, see, for example, Susan J. Wolfson, *Romantic Interactions: Social Being and the Turns of Literary Action* (Baltimore: Johns Hopkins University Press, 2010), 47. For a detailed look at the tradition of feminist response to war vis-à-vis 'cosmopolitanism', see Tonne Brekke, '"Citizen of the World": Feminist Cosmopolitanism and Collective and Affective Languages of Citizenship in the 1790s', in *Beyond Citizenship?: Feminism and the Transformation of Belonging*, edited by Sasha Roseneil (Basingstoke: Palgrave McMillan, 2013), 39–65.

50. Susan Sontag, *Regarding the Pain of Others* (London: Penguin, 2003), 5–6.

51. Daniel C. Hallin, *The Uncensored War: The Media and Vietnam* (London: University of California Press, 1989), 211–17.

52. Shahira Fahmy and Thomas J. Johnson, 'Embedded Versus Unilateral Perspectives on Iraq War', *Newspaper Research Journal* 28, no. 3 (Summer 2007): 98–114.

53. Sontag, *Regarding the Pain of Others*, 19.

54. Ibid., 21.

55. Jean Baudrillard, 'The Gulf War Did Not Take Place', in *The Gulf War Did Not Take Place*, translated by Paul Patton (Bloomington: Indiana University Press, 1995), 63.

56. Ibid., 64.

57. Anthony Babington, *Shell Shock: A History of the Changing Attitudes to War Neurosis* (London: Leo Cooper, 1997), 17.

58. Stephen McVeigh and Nicola Cooper, 'Introduction: Men After War', in *Men After War*, edited by Stephen McVeigh and Nicola Cooper (London: Routledge, 2013), 6.

59. Eric T. Dean, *Shook Over Hell: Post-Traumatic Stress, Vietnam, and the Civil War* (Cambridge, MA: Harvard University Press, 1997), 14.

60. Robert L. Spitzer, Michael B. First and Jerome C. Wakefield, 'Saving PTSD from Itself in DSM V', *Journal of Anxiety Disorders* 21 (2007): 233–4.

61. Hautzinger and Scandlyn, *Beyond Post-Traumatic Stress*, 17.

62. MacLeish, *Making War at Fort Hood*, 5.

63. Dean, *Shook Over Hell*, 7–8.

64. Fussell, *The Great War and Modern Memory*, 64.

65. Herman Melville, *Moby Dick, or The Whale* (New York: Norton, 2002), 427.

66. Goldensohn, *Dismantling Glory*, 82.

CHAPTER 3

War Life, Life as War

Language is a dialect with an army and navy.

— Max Weinreich[1]

War serves as a unique encounter with violence, one which triggers an equally unique linguistic response or injury and, consequently, necessitates its own type of poetic prosthesis. This is not because the kind of linguistic injury I describe is unique to war or soldiers, as evident, for example, in Susan Brison's discussion of linguistic scepticism or injury in the wake of sexual assault, and in decades of trauma discourse concerning anything from familial abuse to genocide, torture and natural disasters. War, however, as both event and social symbol, is indeed set apart through the unique form of life that makes up the wartime experiences, one that must be recognised by those who attempt to reach past the isolation and frustration of returning veterans. War is, then, a form of life, a culture, a setting, the discussion of which is inseparable from any analysis of the kind of devastation war brings upon its veterans. Speaking of the importance of clinical professionals gaining information regarding military culture and the war form of life, Amanda Roberts-Lewis, a social work professor aiding care takers to understand veterans' wartime experiences, claims that 'in order to provide good mental health services to the military folks who are coming home, you must understand the culture of this group. Understanding the culture will assist you in becoming a better clinician.'[2] As this chapter will discuss, however, beyond the everyday social realities of military culture, it is also, and importantly in terms of the unique struggle with language after war, a symbolic form of life.

War is symbolic as a result of it being a form of life, at least in the context of modern warfare in the English-speaking West, dominated by overt symbolism – soldiers are fashioned, trained, taught to function as identical, transparent signifiers in the grand symbolic exchange that is war. As such, war exerts a particular kind of strain on the two poles which, in this book, serve as the starting point of a kind of linguistic injury: the communal (symbolic), referring to the community of which soldiers are symbols, as well as to the symbolic interplay of war and the symbolic interplay of the home in addition to the community the soldiers themselves form during their military service; and the extremely personal, unspoken, painful, and unsymbolic nature of violent events (indexical). It is, however, a community that suffers and perhaps even enhances some of the structural and institutional flaws evident in its 'home' or larger community, a fact of military and wartime life that can compound wartime trauma with the persistent influence, for instance, of sexual violence, racism and more.

War as a Form of Life

The experience of losing one's ability to communicate and the necessity to write about that experience in order to regain even a partial confidence in using language is one that could be said to exist not only after war, but following a variety of other kinds of experiences too. All of these, as Brison writes concerning her experience of attack, and whom I have already quoted in the previous chapter, could be said to result in the same kind of 'uneasy paralysis. *I can't go, I can't stay.*'[3] In this section, however, I will try to focus on the specificities of the English-speaking military, perhaps Western, war environment, with an emphasis on its component parts in an effort ultimately to link what I see as its inherent symbolism and mechanical, segmented nature and what could be called the ironic, oscillating nature of the soldiers' mode of poetic response. It should be added, before I proceed, that there is a fundamental complication in trying to understand not only the ways that war is different from other kinds of encounter with violence but the fact that war is a generalisable event or environment at all. As military scholars have argued, while battles and war have been a constant presence in the Western world, the attempt to say something about 'war' as a concept or as a social symbol, especially when relating to the manner in which individuals experience war, should be resisted. Wars belong to 'finite moments in history', as John Keegan writes, 'to the societies which raise the armies which fight them, to the economies and technologies which those societies sustain'.[4] So, in attempting to address, in general terms, an encounter with violence and its effects on language, my aim is not to make a general statement on war as such. Instead, I hope to link what I see as certain structural aspects of the military experience, a notably Western and relatively modern one, and associated with the wars waged in the latter part of the twentieth century and the beginning of the twenty-first century, to what I see as a crisis with language that takes place during and after war. It would be far beyond the scope of even this relatively large study to perform a comparative analysis of the nuances that each war and each culture represents, no doubt a subject of fruitful future research. However, what I will focus on are those elements in modern Western warfare that seem to parallel some of the ideas I have already discussed: the presumed stability of language in its 'organic' state and the surprise or accident of its instability in the wake of war. In this part I shall attempt to mirror that discussion through a similar duality in Western military life: the stability and rigidity of military training and military symbolism, and the manner in which those characteristics are undermined by the theatre of war.

Military life during peacetime or during training, taking place in remote, isolated and mostly rural areas,[5] is regulated to such a degree as to create automatic connections between the soldier's person and his surroundings (chain of command, orders and reports, arms and ammunition, equipment and so on). It is regulated, in fact, to the point, as Rachel Woodward argues regarding contemporary British military practices, of constructing a specific kind of rural masculinity: 'In this process, individuals must be shaped and molded according to a uniform template for appearance, behavior, and attitude.'[6] However, while this austerity remains a kind of overarching ideal or framework, it is to a large degree undone by the realities of war through the experience of sudden, violent and unpredictable situations over a protracted period of time. War, in other words, is the site of an intense branding of the soldier's body with communal values, as well as the site of their possible collapse as a result of that duration. Whereas in peacetime, as Elaine Scarry writes, the 'nation may ordinarily be registered in his limbs in a particular kind of handshake or salutation performed for a few seconds each day', the protracted violence of war imprints the nation on the body in a dramatically more pronounced manner, as 'the same arms and legs lent out to the state for seconds or minutes and then reclaimed may in war be permanently loaned in injured and amputated limbs'.[7] The result of this contrast, of the ordered ideology and aesthetics of the state and the violence and chaos of the wartime event, is the double character of a Western soldier's experience of war – on one hand regulation, uniformity, repetition and discipline, and on the other violence, disorder, improvisation, assemblage, supply shortages, chaotic radio chatter, friendly fire, and so on. It is a duality that will be stressed throughout the portion dealing with what is called here the military or wartime form of life, one stressed also in an attempt to steer away from generalised stereotypes[8] regarding that way of life and toward an understanding more akin to that of a 'setting' or 'feel' for the wartime experience.

One example of this duality at work is the importance of standardised uniforms, both as a tool of discipline within the army and as a semiotic tool that transforms the soldier from individual to abstract sign. As described in a 1927 article tracing the day-to-day life of Union soldiers during the US Civil War, a dire shortage of supplies and distribution problems led to difficulties in supplying standard uniform, an issue with far-reaching implications that emphasise the dual nature of the kind of form of life in question:

> Three regiments from the same state had no less than five distinct colors of uniforms: blue, gray, black and white striped, dark blue with green trimmings, and light blue . . . Still other regiments affected the brilliant red, baggy breeches, and the turbans and fezzes of the Algerian Zouaves.[9]

As the article writer continues, the 'worst effect of this variegated display was that, when Union troops met Confederates likewise bedizened, it was difficult to distinguish between friend and foe, and fatal blunders resulted'.[10] These mistakes, reminiscent perhaps of the infamous 'someone had blundered' in Alfred, Lord Tennyson's celebrated war poem 'Charge of the Light Brigade', result in real and fatal results: real in that a miscommunication within the rigid, austere military mode of symbolic communication leads not to a 'slip of the tongue' or to 'confusion' but to violence and death.

The above anecdote serves as the first step into the contradictions and difficulties of military life in more ways than one. On the one hand, it showcases, as stated, the glaring discrepancy between Western military ideology (order, regularity) and the realities of war (disorder, uncertainty), especially in the context of current wars that are identified by low-intensity combat with often ununiformed enemy combatants.[11] However, it also foregrounds another possible aspect of the intricacies of the life of soldiers, at least the soldiers in the armies under discussion in this book, which is that, at least to some degree, the measure of confusion, surprise and uncertainty associated with the entrance of American or British soldiers into battle can be said to be directly linked to the preceding expectation of order and regularity. Put otherwise, the catastrophic consequences of the multicoloured uniforms used among

Union soldiers in the Civil War, and perhaps even their very perception as catastrophic, are perhaps linked to their earlier training, one which taught these soldiers to use uniform as a stable, immutable symbol of friend or foe. This is but one example, of course, but it does illuminate not only the uniqueness of military life, but also the connection that life has with the symbolic breakdown or injury that later affects some soldiers. As seen in Cicero's recounting of the story of Midas's capture of the Dionysian Silenus, the experience of chaos and the shock of violence and death could be said to be intimately tied to the desire for order, clear-cut categories and a perfectly stable means of communication born out of a positivist notion of life – that life is something describable and the language used to construct that description is reliable, or at least can be made to be reliable. When one incessantly, perhaps obsessively, seeks a unified, absolute truth, one is destined to face a black and horribly meaningless abyss of chaos:

> There is also told a story of Silenus, who, when taken prisoner by Midas, is said to have made him this present for his ransom – namely, that he informed him that never to have been born was by far the greatest blessing that could happen to man; and that the next best thing was to die very soon.[12]

Here are despair and pain as, perhaps, related to the expectation of, or desire to achieve, certainty in war.

War as Mechanical and Chaotic

One way in which regularity is instilled in those about to go to war, and perhaps one of the most distinct features of war for modern and contemporary Western soldiers, as contrasted with other encounters with sudden violence, is war's supposed or perceived lack of suddenness. If anything, the process of entry into military life and war – also known as 'militarisation'[13] – is a painstakingly gradual one, at least in the three major conflicts discussed here: the Falklands War, the Iraq War and the War in Afghanistan. And the process of acculturation into war usually takes the form of this somewhat simplistic narrative: a civilian volunteers to enlist in the army, for any one of several reasons (aiding the motherland, seeking adventure, seeking a college education and so on[14]); a novice soldier is placed in uniform and receives basic training meant to provide him with fighting skills; a trained soldier is sent to a war zone situated far from his home (South America, the Middle East, Central Asia); the soldier engages in warfare; the soldier's tour of duty culminates/the conflict ends; the soldier travels back home from that remote location; the soldier continues to serve and is eventually relieved of duty, returning to civilian life.

Even in this somewhat schematic outline of the soldier's insertion into war and return from war, two immediate points emerge: firstly, the surprise, or lack thereof, in the encounter with violence; and secondly, the artificiality of the experience itself. In the first place, and in radical opposition to other forms of violent encounters or experiences, soldiers in the conflicts mentioned above volunteer to join the military, train and gain various skills, all in order to use those skills eventually in potentially life-threatening situations. Obviously, the element of surprise is not completely absent, since, by enlisting into the army, one cannot tell exactly when and where that violence will occur, but the complete surprise experienced by victims of natural disaster or sexual assault is replaced by what could be called a gradual anticipation or anxiety and, in some cases, also excitement. That anticipation has also changed through the years, and even in the last century. Soldiers fighting in the trenches of World War I not only knew when they had arrived at war but often when they had arrived at the 'front' or the 'trench', as described beautifully in David Jones's post-World War I masterpiece, *In Parenthesis*. As Jones's soldiers slowly approach the trenches of the front, they pass through more and more signs of war and thus transition from the pastoral French countryside to the scars of artillery explosions, and all the way to the entrance to war itself – a 'little gate':

> Someone seemed to be stirring in front; they bunch their heads in the next file: Pass the message back – who – where's the sergeant – to move on.
>
> Stand fast you.
>
> Stand fast 2, 3 and 4.
>
> Move on No. 1 – get 'em into file corporal – move on by section – put those cigarettes out – no lights past the barrier.
>
> Past the little gate.
>
> Mr. Jenkins watched them file through, himself following, like western-hill shepherd.
>
> Past the little gate, into the field of upturned defences,
>
> into the burial-yard –
>
> the grinning and the gnashing and the sore dreading – nor saw he any light in that place.[15]

Naturally, for contemporary soldiers who fought in Iraq or Afghanistan there was no 'little gate' into a trench in rural France and yet that basic structure, of a slow, measured advance toward the site of danger and violence, 'the burial yard' and 'the field of upturned defenses', has very much remained. In some ways, moreover, the form of the post-modern battlefield is such that the transition is even harsher. While the encounter with violence itself was still and always a surprise, it was an even more structured one than the experience of soldiers fighting in Iraq and Afghanistan, for example, who manœuvre in densely populated or mountainous areas where violence can come as unexpectedly as an improvised bomb in a crowded market or a roadside ambush, and who face mostly ununiformed military forces.

The very segmentation of the experience itself plays another significant part in creating a soldier's mechanical experience of war, and one that may set it apart from the way in which civilians experience wartime violence. Those encountering violence as unassuming victims, such as civilians during war, rape victims, and victims of rail and car accidents, have to take on and deal with a sudden encounter with violence embedded in their normal, everyday life. They do not pass through the 'little gate', in other words, or by a slow process approach the 'scene of war', but experience a confusion of war and everyday life. As H. D. writes in 1944's 'The Walls Do Not Fall' of the experience of walking amongst the ruins of London during the Blitz:

> Trembling at a known street-corner,
> we know not nor are known;
> the Pythian pronounces – we pass on
>
> to another cellar, to another sliced wall
> where poor utensils show
> like rare objects in a museum.[16]

Civilians during war encounter the defamiliarisation of their everyday surroundings, as the surprise of aerial bombardment turns one's own partially demolished home into something resembling an ancient ruin or objects in a museum. One 2003 post by the Iraqi blogger known as Riverbend illustrates this point, describing how the fear of war and violence had undone and warped everyday life while also emphasising the gap between war as it is mediated by the news and its grim, uncertain nature:

> Seeing [the war] on the various networks covering the war is nothing like living in its midst. Watching the 7 o'clock news and hearing about 'a car bomb in Baghdad' is nothing like standing in the street, wary of the moving

vehicles, wondering if one of them is going to burst into a flying ball of flames and shrapnel. Seeing the checkpoints on Al-Jazeera, CNN or BBC is nothing like driving solemnly up to them, easing the car to a stop and praying that the soldier on the other side doesn't think you look decidedly suspicious . . . or that his gun doesn't accidentally go off.[17]

Everyday war, in other words, whether in 1944 London or 2003 Baghdad, is a confusing mix of the domestic and the traumatic, an experience, then, set apart from the articulated, orderly manner in which civilians turn into soldiers, train for war and transit to war zones. For Michel Foucault, through his discussion of what he calls the birth of 'discipline', of which the military is but one type in *Discipline and Punish*, this process is tied to the Western thrust of *discipline*, in which societies turn toward fashioning the kinds of system that would result in obedient, productive and, to an extent, predictable individuals. Prominent among those disciplines is the military one, in which, as the above process shows, a man is turned into a soldier:

> By the late eighteenth century, the soldier has become something that can be made; out of formless clay, an inapt body, the machine required can be constructed; posture is gradually corrected; a calculated constraint runs slowly through each part of the body, mastering it, making it pliable, ready at all times, turning silently into the automatism of habit; in short, one has 'got rid of the peasant, and given him the air of the soldier'.[18]

Foucault's conjuring of the image of the machine both touches on the machine I suggest is constructed following wartime experiences, the prosthesis – the soldier as military prosthetic to the symbolic social whole – and links this mechanisation with a larger cultural thrust. In other words, not only is the military the symbolic stand-in of nations, but the manner with which soldiers are fashioned out of 'formless clay' represents a materialising of cultural ideals having to do with stability, durability, pliability, universality and predictability. Thus, to take apart and build anew, that which soldiers later perform in their poetry, begins also as a mode of transitioning into military life, of becoming a soldier, tool and symbolic or social prosthesis:

> The human body was entering a machinery of power that explores it, breaks it down and rearranges it, a 'political anatomy,' which was also a 'mechanics of power,' was being born; it defined how one may have a hold over others' bodies, not only so that they may do what one wishes, but so that they may operate as one wishes, with the technique, the speed and the efficiency that one determines.[19]

Another aspect of the mechanisation of the body is the body's relation to other objects, which is one of discipline, such as in the use of weapons (guns, planes, drones) and equipment, as well as that special relation to objects we call improvisation. In discipline, as Foucault continues: 'Over the whole surface of contact between the body and the object it handles, power is introduced, fastening them to one another. It constitutes a body-weapon, body-tool, body-machine complex.'[20] A soldier, identified by uniform, is to train so as to make his relationship with arms and equipment automatic to the point of considering them as extensions of his own body. This parallel between weapon and body can be glimpsed in the Marine Corps chant, made famous in Stanley Kubrick's Vietnam War film *Full Metal Jacket*, in which trainees gesture toward their weapon and crotch, respectively, while singing: 'This is my rifle, this is my gun, this is for fighting, this is for fun.'[21]

One poetic manifestation of the constant breaking of the bounds of integrity and sincerity, to use Donna Haraway's formulation,[22] of the body through its proximity to the tools of war is Gerardo Mena's poem 'Rocket Man', published as part of his 2014 collection *The Shape of Our Faces No Longer Matters*. True to post-war writing's commitment to the indexical and memory of the past, 'Rocket Man' begins with a brief prose note, describing the event to be depicted in the poem:

> For Corporal Benavidez, affectionately called 'Rocket Man' by the platoon after the explosion on December 9, 2006, launched him from his gun turret on the vehicle, through the air, and safely onto the sand fifty meters away.[23]

This detailed introduction – citing the specific date, time and place of the protagonist's brush with death – speaks to a function that is central to many of Mena's poems: the act of remembering, precisely, what has happened in war, and those to which it has happened, which will be the focus of Chapter 5. 'Rocket Man' is one of several poems in *The Shape of Our Faces No Longer Matters* that is prefaced by such a localising headnote, and the book's dedication honours ten of Mena's friends, each one listed with the precise date he was killed in action. In 'Rocket Man', Mena gives us the corporal's exact location prior to his 'launch' (the gun turret), as well as the exact distance that he travelled before landing safely. In doing so, I would argue, Mena performs an ethical act, asking us to remember the situation with him, and giving us the data we require to do so. The identification of rank – 'corporal' – and a date in the middle of Operation Iraqi Freedom tells us that the poem is about a specific war and reminds us, if we recall anything about that

IED-infested arena (IED meaning improvised explosive device), that the outcome of most such incidents was anything but comic. As the speaker remembers and cites these facts, he asks that readers mark and remember them as well. But then, in the stanzas of the poem proper, we get a less localised picture:

I dreamed that I opened my mouth and slowly
swallowed an entire rocket.
When I awoke,
I was a rocket.

I had rocket guts and rocket blood.

My rocket feet were plastic fins.
My rocket arms surmounted into a steeple.
My rocket hands held a blast wave
and smoke.

I screamed into the earth,
became wind.[24]

The meaning of 'rocket' here is clearly different from that in the Elton John song to which the platoon members allude. In the song, a space traveller rides safely *inside* a rocket-propelled vessel: he is captain of a ship that he controls. In Mena's poem, Benavidez is transformed into a projectile – an object whose function is not transport but destruction. In the dark humour of the poem we see an articulation of the soldier–weapon complex, or at least an articulation of the tension between the human and tool aspects, where the soldier has become an object that he cannot control. Through the first-person narration, we encounter the confusion and violence that comes from being not the operator *of* a rocket but literally a man-*as*-rocket. This part of the poem should not be read as necessarily an interpretation of Benavidez's own experience. While the title refers to the nickname given to him following the incident, his experience is not a private one. In fact, it violently exposes the objectified nature of the soldier–weapon complex in a more general manner, as soldiers like Benavidez are being hurled through the air, as helpless as objects. Mena's use of the metric measurement here indicates what type of object is being hurled, as well as highlighting the military setting. In that context, the human body, fashioned to work in unison with an object, turns out to have more in common with that object than may have been expected. Only partly human now, it has assumed a hybrid identity, possessing not just mechanical limbs but even 'rocket guts' and 'rocket blood'.

The poem's last lines serve to tie the different aspects of the poem together – the commemoration of others and the first-hand interrogation of the soldier–weapon experience – into the complete poetic object. The 'Rocket Man' of the speaker ultimately fails as both rocket and man, a sense of futility found elsewhere in Mena's poetry: as a man by the very fact of becoming a rocket, a tool or object, and perhaps also by becoming an instrument of violence, and as a rocket as a result of what could be thought of as an ineffective launch. In other words, the rocket fails to strike a target and instead strikes the ground, turns to air: 'I screamed into the earth / became wind.' Despite the dual failure of the rocket to perform either function, the transformation into a speaking object ultimately results in a kind of success: the scream of anguish of the soldier–weapon mode of existence and, at the same time, the bewailing of the loss of lives among soldiers less fortunate than Benavidez. All the while, however, a scream and wind do nothing more or less than imitate the blast effect of any detonating explosive. This is a scream and a wail, in other words, that still sound like just another rocket exploding.

One last mechanising aspect of the military experience, echoes of which can be also seen in the post-war prosthesis that is Mena's poem, is military language itself, with its slang, units of measurement and official designations. It is a form of speech influenced by the two functions of military life discussed above – mechanisation and improvisation – and thus characterised by two similar aspects: functionality and improvisation, exemplified by unofficial military lingo, or slang. On the one hand, military language is made up of orders and responses and is geared at transmitting the most data using the least amount of words. As Wittgenstein writes in his discussion of language games in *Philosophical Investigations*:

> It is easy to imagine a language consisting only of orders and reports in battle. – Or a language consisting only of questions and expressions for answering yes and no. And innumerable others. – And to imagine a language means to imagine a form of life.[25]

Thus, the form of life whose borders we are attempting to trace here is such that it stresses these functional aspects of communication – so much so that any impractical or inefficient modes of speech would not survive and persist in it. As Frederick Elkin writes:

It is assumed throughout this discussion that the language adopted by a soldier is functional. Had the new expressions not in some way satisfied a need or a disposition of the soldier, they would not have been adopted, and the soldier would have spoken as he did in civilian life.[26]

The same goes with brevity, as Elbridge Colby writes in his study of soldier speech published in 1936:

Brevity as well as taciturnity is a common army habit, brevity even to a fluency in the use of abbreviations. So the use of the initials is a common characteristic among these men of few words who are forced to pay more deference to the persistent verboseness of army regulations and orders.[27]

Moreover, in its functional, disciplinary aspect, military language is not and cannot, at least not within the confines of specific units, develop dialects that defy its universal aspect. Put otherwise, soldiers, from the same unit and speaking the same mother tongue, such as English, must be able, to use Roman Jakobson's terms, to decode the message addressed in their orders, commands, reports and updates, whether they are 'organic' members of said unit or not. This universality is, as with the universality of training, uniform and hierarchy, again geared at brevity, efficiency and precision, but also harbours part of what could be called the improvisational aspect, for such universality creates the necessary condition to replace one soldier with another without the system missing a beat, as if soldiers had been identical spare parts for the same giant machine. This aspect of military life bears tremendous ramifications, it should be added, for the attempt to 'demilitarise' after war, the deep sense that one had functioned as part of a larger mechanism and is now discarded. As Ken MacLeish writes of one veteran struggling to integrate into civilian life following an unexpected discharge: 'His physical and mental integrity were directly interwoven with military prerogatives of mobilization and demobilization – that is, the ability to put people and resources in motion for war-making purposes and then to release or abandon them as needed.'[28] To return from war is, again, not a simple homecoming but a cultural shock, one hidden in the seeming sameness of signifiers. And yet, despite and perhaps because of this extreme focus on functionality, the military way of life is still a fertile ground for creating a language that would best fit its disjointed, uniform reality. One such well-documented and socially influential reaction is the creation of an unofficial language of war, or, in other words, military slang and jargon.

Military slang is a significant part of inter-soldier communication, both as a means of personal communication and also, to an extent, solidified as part of official speech (orders, radio etiquette and so on). This includes the military tendency for abbreviations, which could be said to be both official and slang, such as IED (improvised explosive device), MIA (missing in action), DOA (dead on arrival) and so on.[29] But slang also means the construction of new concepts and words meant, as with all slang, to mediate between official speech and personal experience. As Elkin writes, this mode of speaking solidifies, with newer members of the community learning it much as one would a new language or dialect:

> [I]n most cases the learning is completely unconscious. A soldier hears an expression, unconsciously learns its meaning in context, and soon employs it himself. Even for the more deliberate recruit, the expressions soon become his unconscious normal way of speaking.[30]

As Elkin continues, this mode of speech is directly related to a reaction to a new way of life, 'since in the soldier's expressions we find implied attitudes and values, we can derive therefrom a spontaneous reflection of his reactions to Army life'.[31] Driving in this notion of a developing language, Colby describes it as 'the military vernacular', the

> slang that is direct, brief, vivid, figurative, and, in successive generations of soldiers, lasting. It is a living language, often reckless of regulations and their formal phraseology, as we have seen in 'khaki.' It passes from mouth to ear among men and women who read little in the books and pamphlets of formal orders and instructions. It describes the dishonorable discharge as a *kick* and the discharge without honor as a *blue ticket*, from the color of the paper on which it is printed. In this language, a soldier does *bunk fatigue*, wears *dog tags*, eats *dog biscuit*, sports *hash marks*, and sleeps in *pup tents*.[32]

A glimpse into one way in which new terms are coined or, as this example shows, modes of speech are created, is given in one of Elkin's remarks, showing a unit introducing an ironic term as a result of an officer's slip of the tongue: 'Mimicking an officer who once told his men to "chop down those wooden trees," the men placed "wooden" before the name of any wooden object they had occasion to mention.'[33] Here too, in what has to be my favourite military anecdote, the conflict that brought on the creation of the new word, or inserted meaning into an old one, is the disharmony, one made ridiculous by the soldiers, between the mechanical, systematic officer and the chaotic environment in which he is placed.

One could even go as far as saying that it represents a conflict between the mechanical and the organic, as such, the mechanical attempt failing precisely because it is asked to address the organic reality of trees using the unnecessarily symbolic 'wooden'.

Soldiers' speech and slang, in fact, was fully formed enough to require its own dialect guide or dictionary, used not by the soldiers themselves, who were taught how to speak by observation and experience, but by civilians and academics wishing to understand more about army life. Thus, a 'Glossary of Army Slang' appeared in a 1941 edition of *American Speech*,[34] detailing hundreds of entries, ranging from the obvious ('A.A. – Anti-Aircraft') to the figurative ('Rats – Balls of lint that suddenly appear on the floor during an inspection of quarters; see *mice*'). Similar glossaries and treatments have also been published regarding specific units following the Second World War, such as the US Marine Corps,[35] the US Navy[36] and the US Air Force.[37] It would have been tempting to tie in one specific example provided in the glossary – 'typewriter', used to mean 'machine gun' – to ideas of violence and writing, a nickname perhaps linked to what it is soldiers see as 'writing' during war, or, at the very least, to what could be perceived as the relationship between mechanical language and mechanical violence. However, as with everything in the military form of life, it is more likely that sound brought on the creation of this new sign in language, one that takes a symbol and reverts it into an icon. This is because the sign *typewriter* is a habitual one, given to explain or describe the function and action of its references – it, quite simply, writes by typing. However, the army sign *typewriter* is an icon, a sign referring to its referent by ways of similarity – you say *typewriter*, in other words, and hear a machine gun, and, of course, the other way around.

War as Symbolic

As with all human endeavours, war is entrenched in communication and symbolism, mainly, and perhaps most straightforwardly, because it is above and beyond in itself a symbolic act in which signs do battle to determine the fate of designated referents. Soldiers and armies are not, after all, countries themselves; nor do they, in the modern and Western iterations of war, represent each community within their countries, in what Elaine Scarry describes as a kind of symbolic game.[38] Armies and soldiers are, both as individuals and as the army as a whole, stand-ins, metonyms of their homeland sent in the name of their community to do battle with the representatives of another community (which also gives a clue as to the complexities of civil war, in which all sides of the conflict represent the same community, indeed the same families). As such, war not only is the scene of professional, mechanical violence – violence being an essential part of war – but also serves as an exemplar of the workings of a sign–referent concept of language, of the sort that has dominated the Western tradition. In short, the function of signs of communication, violent communication included, is dependent, at least to an extent, on the reconstituted separation between a sign (the American army) and its referent (the United States). This subsection will break down the various symbolisms at play in war: from the representation of a nation at a battlefield by unit or soldier to the insignia and uniform that create symbolic subcategories within each side or unit.

The meaning of these symbols, however, within the military or war-semiotic context, at least in the British and American armies in question, is unchanging, concrete and final, resulting in a kind of transformation. Symbols, then, that represent through social agreement, such as flags, uniform, insignia, turn into indices, signs with an existential link to their referents. So, a uniform that signifies the US army as a result of international agreement *must* and *will always* signify one's ties to a specific military and a specific nation.[39] In fact, the necessity of uniform signifying a concrete, real and constant meaning is so entrenched in the form of life that is war that the very act of wearing the uniform of one nation while fighting for another is considered a violation of the Laws of War. Thus, not only must the uniform remain a stable sign, but it also, in the ethical rules of engagement, *ought to*:

> When, therefore, the soldiers of one army wear, not their own uniforms but those of the enemy for purposes of deceiving the latter, we have again a breach of a tacit understanding arising out of the use of symbols of recognized meaning. In this, as much as in the cases involving the use of the other symbols, there would seem to be a breach of faith amounting to forbidden perfidy, and that quite as much whether the use of the enemy's uniforms took place before or during actual combat.[40]

This line is also drawn in bearing the symbols of another unit or rank within one's own army, where rank and unit are seen as indexical signs assigning a concrete, existentially linked referent. As Zygmunt Bauman writes: 'Nobody can become an army officer just by buying an adequate uniform. Because of this restriction, however, we can assume with confidence that any individual bearing the proper designations is indeed an army officer.'[41]

However, this basic, literal level of symbolism is also tied to the larger representational role the various sides in battle take on during war, and which creates the symbolic relationship that is war itself. The military of any nation, and, by direct extension, the soldiers that make up those armies, not only are those parts of a country's population in charge of that nation's defence or the fulfilment of its political aspirations by way of force, but they do so as metonymic stand-ins for that country. One nation's army defeating another's does not defeat that nation literally, or at least not only literally, since victory in terms of twentieth-century warfare does not mean the decimation of the rival nation or, to give just one example, place a soldier in every square inch of that country. Instead, victory or success is garnered through the very act of defeat of one portion of the victorious army to the parallel portion of the defeated country. Thus, again, a kind of transformation takes place: the army, serving as an iconic metonym for its nation, takes on an indexical or existential role – its defeat does not represent the defeat of a nation but, instead, *is* the defeat of that nation. Thus, Second World War battles waged between Germany and the United States, for example, and involving thousands of soldiers, served as a metonymy or metaphor for a battle between Germany and the United States as countries. Victory in war, in other words, does not require the personal surrender and subjugation of each and every citizen of the defeated country – as the origin of the word subjugation, Latin for 'bringing under the yoke',[42] would suggest – or the conquest of every square mile of the defeated country. Once one army surrenders, the country that that army represents effectively admits defeat.

Moreover, this definition of war, at least in its traditional form, as a symbolic battle, teases out another difference between the army at war and other uniformed forces that are also understood to represent the country: that police and fire-fighting forces are seen as symbols or representatives of the authorities, of the regime, while the army stands for the country and its people. This symbolic move, in which, effectively, signs are sent to defeat other signs, ultimately results not only in a semiotic relationship between the warring sides but also in a semiotic relationship between the 'nation' or 'the people' and the military as a whole and soldiers as individuals. In many cases, as Carl D. Buck writes, the 'words for "army" mean also, or are cognate with words meaning "people, host, band, multitude," etc. The "army" was "the people" (in arms), or "the (armed) host".'[43] Thus, as symbols, soldiers are sent into an arena in which they represent a nation, and in the public eye back 'home' they continue to serve as symbols. Not only are they symbols of the nation and that nation's political aspirations, which is their function during war, but they are also a symbol of national values, whether positive (courage, ingenuity, camaraderie) or, as seen in the wake of such incidents as the abuse of prisoners at the US military prison at Abu Ghraib, negative (cruelty, imperialism, political chauvinism). As Richard Kohn writes regarding the American version of this symbolic manœuvre, the

> American soldier has been a symbol, a political and cultural artifact for a nation diverse in culture, uncertain in unity, and concerned through much of its history with proving its superiority to the rest of the world. Of necessity has been anonymity, which has further muddied the truth and contributed to the making of myths.[44]

However, as Kohn later states, that symbol never existed, both because the makeup of the fighting force itself never consisted of a homogenous mass of soldiers (socio-economically, racially, ethnically, sexually and politically), and because the stereotype of a 'soldier', in this case the American soldier, was always just that, a stereotype: 'The truth of the matter is that the "American soldier" never existed; the most pernicious myth of all is that there has ever been a prototypical American in uniform.'[45]

While the above symbolism has been the mark of every modern instance of warfare involving American and British troops in the twentieth century, the structure of relation between those symbolised and those symbolising has undergone a marked change, at least concerning the conflicts in question here: conflicts in the Falklands, Iraq and Afghanistan, such that the distance, both physical and conceptual, between community and war is growing, as soldiers on the ground are watched from afar by the home front. As Robin Norris writes of the gap between war epics and those facing the realities of war today:

> Because the geography of the North American continent insulates it from direct attack, while modern technology allows troops to travel great distances to do battle, only the warrior class in contemporary America is directly affected by armed conflict, while the rest of us become its audience.[46]

Moreover, the distance of spectators and participants is also, perhaps logically, one not only of concept but also of effect:

> Whereas the deaths of Beowulf and Hector resulted in extinction for their people, in twenty-first-century North America and across most of Western Europe, the death of a leader is unlikely to result in slavery, exile, or dispossession for the average citizen.[47]

War as it is perceived by the American and British publics is, then, a place apart, one understood by those who had experienced it, what Eric J. Leed refers to as a 'disjunctive' rather than 'integrative' experience, adding: 'What men learned in the war set them irrevocably apart from those others who stood outside of it.'[48] And that gap, as a letter from a soldier fighting in the First World War to his sweetheart shows, is one of culture:

> I agree with Robert when he says there will be two classes of men in America after the war -- the ones who went, and the ones who did not. And I believe as he does the ones who went are going to be the ones who will have charge of affairs when they get back for, if a man stands this war and still comes out smiling, he is a man.[49]

'The men who went', as the letter puts it, and in terms of understanding war as a symbolic space, are those who could be said to have been involved in this mixing of the symbolic and the immanent, violent and personal.

Tying in this notion of being severed from both society and, as a result, life, due to the encounter she dubs Force, Weil writes: 'The man possessed by this twofold need for death belongs, so long as he has not become something still different, to a different race from the race of the living.'[50] Those 'who did not', however, endure that experience and, for the most part, retain a confidence in what could be called the distance between symbol and referent – one describes the other, the object and its label. That gap is perhaps the gap seen in Currall's 'Burying the Dead': those who understand words as having the one meaning that communal use and custom have determined and those for whom words are able to carry simultaneous, multiple, painful and personal meanings as well. One way in which this tie between symbolism and violence, or the experience of violence – 'coming up against' – could be said to exist is that war, at least the mechanical, communicational, symbolic and terse style of war associated with Western militaries such as those discussed in this book, is violent, or violent in its own unique way, precisely because of its deep connection to the aspiration for a clear, transparent, universal and distinct communication. Put a little more briefly, the form, order, regularity and mechanical nature of Western armies, which serves ostensibly to ensure that fighting between various forces is as moral or distinct as possible, is a major driving force behind both its violence and the reaction of its soldiers to that violence. For those affected by that violence, a new relation between the symbol and its community, or referent, is created in the ruins of the old, which leads us to the issue of the communal aspect of war.

War as Communal

The communal aspect of war, set apart in this subsection for method-ological purposes, is an inherent part of the military or war experience, and as such has been present, whether explicitly or implicitly, in all of the previous categories. It is mechanical–chaotic, as the first category argues, but never mechanical or chaotic outside of a communal context. Soldiers are made to be soldiers – enlisted, trained, inserted into battle – as part of the soldier or military community. For the most part, they do not enlist alone, train alone or experience violence alone. Moreover, in all their actions they are a community that represents, symbolises or stands in for another community, the often larger community waiting at home, and on whom the success or failure of the soldier on the battlefield has a direct influence. This goes, as Scarry writes, both for the absolute control the community has over soldiers' bodies, and thus the meaning of their participation in war, but also for the wounds and scars those soldiers endure in the name of that meaning. The wounds, in other words, meaningless in and of themselves, are charged with whatever meaning the community provides. As Scarry writes,

> the incontestable reality of the body – the body in pain, the body maimed, the body dead and hard to dispose of – is separated from its source and conferred on an ideology or issue or instance of political authority impatient of, or deserted by, benign sources of substantiation.[51]

In addition, as we have seen for the symbolic aspect, it is a community that shares certain anthropological traits and mores: from the wearing of uniform and the following of orders, to the development of unique dialects and language, also referred to as soldier slang. In other words, and perhaps stating the obvious when it comes to war and through Foucault's understanding of the military as just one way in which the cultures of discipline have developed in recent centuries, soldiers are part of a unique, even exemplary community. It is a community sharing a common goal, a common language, and in which the individual is but a tool for what could be called 'the greater good'. Individuality, in this form of life, means nearly nothing:

> The Army's image of him does not correspond to his own image of himself. He sees himself as a person with preferences, dislikes, pride, and sensitivities; not so the Army. The soldier vaguely understands that some theory of efficiency underlies this.[52]

In this coming together of an extreme personal index, in the form of an individual encounter with violence, and a strong communal aspect, war serves as an exemplar of the effects of violence on language as a result of a basic tension between the individual's need to communicate his own form of life and that form of life's inherent rejection of the ability to communicate as those components are made to stand out distinctly from one another. This tension is also, as mentioned earlier, behind the very need to create a more personal dialect or slang. As Elkin writes:

> To the sociologist the most significant feature of such expression is that, once diffused, like all other soldier expressions, they give the soldier a unique universe of discourse which helps distinguish him, and thus they become a binding in-group force. This tends to give him a greater feeling of freedom among other soldiers, for he can speak the expression which more easily comes to his mind, many of which would not be understood or must consciously be avoided when he is among civilians.[53]

Again, this is true regarding the militaries in question – both Western, both sharing similar military forms and ideals, and both involving a profound and coterminous stress on symbolism and communality. It is these characteristics that provide the backdrop and context of the injury I have discussed in the previous chapter, one similar to that experienced by victims of other encounters with violence and death, but also quite different. One example of how such a coming together of the indexical and communal is expressed is 'Burying the Dead':

> Burying the dead is a metaphor.
> They don't literally mean bury the dead
> Try not to think too much about it
> They mean put things to rest
> Pull your socks up
> Stop harping on
> Get on with it
> Let things lie
> Get a grip
> Forget.
>
> They've never buried the dead.
> Literally.[54]

The gap between the soldier and his community, as it is expressed in 'Burying the Dead', is not simply one of experience, but is similar to contact between different nations or civilisations which practice different customs while speaking a similar language. In this case, though, these civilisations use the same words, often live under the same roof and appear, at least externally, to share the same cultural values. The same can be said of Croft's poem, quoted earlier, in which a veteran cannot seem to tell fireworks from gunfire – the very fact that the two are intertwined in his experience of 'explosion' sets him apart from those around him, who seem to be able to make that exact separation. It is not the kind of cultural gap that would necessitate a dictionary, moreover, since the words are, so to speak, there, but it would require an understanding of a different way of life, one with irony at its core.

War as Ironic

A soldier is an individual but also a member of a community that downplays, if not completely annihilates, the place of the individual: a member of a larger community that he represents and, to many returning soldiers, a foreigner in his own community as a result of his wartime experiences. But above all, soldiers are individuals who, under the pressure of community and symbolism, either encounter violence and death or expect to encounter violence and death in a way that leads some to injury that destabilises the line that connects them to their communities. As I have already mentioned in the previous chapter, the experience is such that something *did* happen, and yet it cannot be described or even placed; the individual experiences an event but cannot relay that event – in many ways, the event of shifting to another form of community, or of belonging to a community accustomed to death and violence – to the community that is 'home'. That split, as Schlegel puts it, a subject I shall expand upon in the following chapter, between 'necessity' and 'impossibility' lies at the heart of wartime irony.

Additionally, if we are to go back to Whorf's analysis of the factory mishap based on a linguistic error, it is an irony of events and words not seeming to fit together. Soldiers, not unlike the man who suddenly understands that the word 'empty' does not necessarily mean 'safe', not only are repeatedly bombarded with situations and events that are difficult to process as a result of a linguistic fixation rooted in a certain common-sense attitude, but undergo this experience for a relatively protracted period of time. A pertinent example of the kind of wartime events that become the norm in the war form of life can be seen in a case described by Jonathan Shay:

> Battle is full of bizarre ironies that seem to have been scripted for black comedy, such as the man in the bunker who throws himself on a grenade to save his comrades. The grenade is a dud, but because he is on the ground he alone survives when the enemy bursts into the bunker and guns down all the others. What happens when the sacrifice, or the sincere willingness to sacrifice, does not 'work'?[55]

What is illuminating here is not just the bizarreness of the event described above, the irony that it could be said to represent, but an imagining of the kind of form of life in which events such as these take place, and the kind of linguistic attitude that this form of life could be said to foster. In other words, it is a story that, much like the poems themselves, exposes a way of human life through the way in which linguistic categories are repeatedly and *physically* challenged. If we are to return to Bruce Weigl's statement, 'The war took away my life and gave me poetry in return,'[56] we see that the taking away of life is both literal and figurative, an event that exists in the space between the individual and the community. An undoing of the link between personal experience and one's 'home', so to speak, is this act of death or taking away of life. The poetry that comes, as a prosthesis, in its stead is but a replacement, an artificially constructed and ironic tool which shows a new relation to life and death, as opposed to being stranded from life altogether. It should be stressed that Weigl's comments, as well as this book, do not suggest that everyone emerging out of modern warfare turns to poetic irony, or to poetry in general, as most soldiers do not become poets, but instead that the poetry that is created in various ways addresses a kind of linguistic cave-in. Poetry, or at least the conscious attempt to create poems, is, if I may turn for a moment to Judith Butler's terminology, one kind of reaction to 'coming up against'[57] a lack of defined safety, one that attempts to capture irony in a verbal object. Before moving on to look at how, historically speaking, this inherent irony has manifested itself in the poetry produced after war, I would like to stress one last point pertaining to the idea of an ironic community, which returns to the last point made in the introduction to this chapter – individual experience 'in its own terms'.

While, as this book claims, poems written after war function as prosthesis as a way of dealing with linguistic injury, thus making a generalisation concerning war's after-effects on soldiers, the way in which each writing soldier goes about it is his own. Much as the statement 'injured soldiers use prosthetic limbs' describes a general phenomenon without predicting the shape and form of each limb produced, my own argument does not make claims about the way each poet and each poem serves individual needs. Where community enters the issue, I would argue, and perhaps as opposed to other forms of encounter with violence as well as other uses of irony, lies in the fact that soldiers experience these encounters within the confines of community, and thus are aware, at least to a certain extent, of the particularity of their own reaction or needs. By experiencing war as part of a community, soldiers are aware that not everyone shares their reactions to war, similarly to other collective experiences. Poetry created in the wake of twentieth- and twenty-first-century warfare could thus seldom be said to emerge from a feeling that everyone coming out of war is a poet, or that the artistic response to war is the *only* way to deal with the linguistic aftermath of war. Instead, poetry or art in general is seen as just one personal way of dealing with the effect war could be said to have on language, making the different categories of dealing with war poetically into different ways of human coping. It could even mean that not everyone is affected, or that some are affected in a way they interpret as positive or life-affirming (moving up the ranks, the thrill of combat, camaraderie and so on). There is a way, moreover, in which the irony inherent to the form of life that is war, and which shapes its day-to-day experiences and figures of speech, has been linked to the production of literature after war. Most famously this was one of the topics advanced by perhaps the seminal work on modern war writing and irony, Paul Fussell's *The Great War and Modern Memory*, published in 1975. And it is because of the centrality of irony in our contemporary understanding of both war and war writing, in great measure following Fussell's analysis, that I would like to articulate the manner in which irony could be said to fulfil a role in my understanding of the prosthetic in the following chapter.

Society at War

Despite the many aspects that make war a different kind of living, much of which has been discussed, albeit partially, above, it should be stated that war, or the fact of being at war, also serves as an extension of the society from which these troops were dispatched. While it is true that soldiers going out to and returning from war function as social symbols, they are also participants in the society they represent and thus export, so to speak, some of the social issues that plague that society. And while these issues are perhaps felt less by those soldiers who approximate a kind of social ideal in those contexts – the 'Marlboro man' image of the wind-swept, white, male soldier, for instance – they are indeed a significant part of the wartime experience for those who do not fit that mould and any discussion of the form of life that is war would be remiss not to include these issues as well.

With growing diversity in terms of gender, sexuality and ethnicity in the UK and US militaries, especially in combat and commanding roles, the theatre of war has changed. That growing diversity brings with it an increasing variety of military experience, especially since the onset of the influential waves of feminist, racial and post-colonial critique of the latter part of the twentieth century, such as the gradual inclusion of female soldiers into combat roles. What that means is that while, for instance, African American soldiers had taken part in every major American military engagement since 1776,[58] the increased role and impact of soldiers of colour, especially following the civil rights movement, means that those experiences are given more and more expression[59] and that more attention is given to the particularity of, say, the African American or Hispanic experience of war and post-traumatic reaction to battle.[60] The same goes for the relatively recent and growing integration of women into combat roles, which means we are able to receive personal documentation regarding women in battle now more than ever, following a long history of female writers describing war in diaries and civilian writing, with prominent examples including Civil War-era letter writing, Great War nurses' diaries and so on.

The significance of these shifts in terms of the form of life of war is that for both women and soldiers of colour war involves not only the experience of, for instance, sudden violence and mechanical training, but also the continuing influence of some of the social behaviours and discriminatory experiences that have marked their civilian life. For women this could include the persistence of sexual assault, trauma and discrimination during their training and combat experiences, with a significant portion of women serving in forward combat roles reporting sexual harassment, unwanted advances and sexual trauma,[61] a trend that seems to be on the rise in the US military[62] as well as in its British counterpart.[63] Moreover, positioned in a dominantly masculine, heterosexual system, female and lesbian, gay, bisexual and transgender (LGBT)[64] soldiers may sense the ongoing effects of institutional oppression, as some women report their allegations of sexual assault and rape were dismissed by commanding officers and military legal officials both during and after their military service. One such story, that of the rape of former Airman 1st Class Jessica Hinves, involved what Hinves described as the compounded effect of military sexual trauma (MST) and her estrangement from other members of the unit. As PBS reported in 2013: 'After the assault, Hinves could not return to her old life. And instead of finding support in her fellow service members, she found resentment. She said her unit was angry at her for getting her attacker in trouble.'[65] Writing in an anthology of veterans' poetry organised by the Oxford Brookes Poetry Centre, Jamie Lorente writes of the ubiquity of sexual harassment and MST among women serving in the military: '[E]very woman has a story and that falls on a spectrum somewhere probably, but every woman I've talked to has a story of MST, experiencing MST in the military at some level.'[66]

In her poem 'My Body Is' Lorente writes of her experience of being raped while stationed on a military base in Germany in a manner that brings together the military form of life – hierarchy, commands, insignia – and her vulnerability as a woman within that cultural setting. There is no clear-cut notion of, say, a battlefront to which one travels – Lorente is, in fact, stationed at the 'rear' of a military base on German soil – and yet the gap between the casualness of her assault and its destructive aftermath is startling. In this specific poetic prosthesis, one very much informed by gender difference and power relations, the work of measuring distance does not home in on the all-encompassing trauma of wartime violence but on the implosion of the military social mechanism itself and the manner in which it targets its female members. The 'plot' begins with the unlikely character of a military cook who, despite not being Lorente's commander, acts as a messenger of a different kind of order: *I've a message for you: meet me out back after dinner.*'[67] Lorente obeys, despite acknowledging that this man 'is not my chain of command', only to receive a second message later: '*Meet the officer at midnight.*' As the poem's speaker digests the chain of events, the cook adds: 'He drove past you, he liked your smile.' Lorente's speaker is embroiled further and further in a power structure that is defined by her military context – she is to meet an officer at his request – and at the same time has to do with another, presumably different, power structure, one linked to her being a women being 'ordered', both figuratively and literally, by a man. As the recollection continues, the officer is 'disarmed', turning into 'a friend' and yet becoming a kind of clichéd image of the brave war veteran, one that conceals the power he wields over female soldiers. He becomes, as Lorente writes, 'a refracted image on a television screen / talking to Oprah about leadership. / He seems kind still, this war-torn veteran.'

Despite the apparent removal of danger, her 'close call' and the anticipation of being 'ordered' to meet the officer, the rape itself, as with the more conventional form of military violence, arrives unexpectedly. The moment of assault, like everything that has taken place up until this point in the narrative, is an aberration, a violent moment seemingly coming out of nowhere, as well as being completely in line with what could be called a chain of gendered command described up until that point – as 'kind' as that process had been. Driving that insight further is the syntactical placement of the incident as a run-on sentence, overloaded with ironic understatement:

> His friend the lieutenant though,
> he raped me in Hanau while I was sleeping.
> This was unexpected.
> A scattered group of us sleeping it off
> after a party in an officer's apartment.
> He too seemed kind and he had a fiancée back home.
> That's what I was thinking: *but I thought he had a fiancée back home.*
> There is a man, one arm against the wall,
> peeing onto a suitcase beneath the window.[68]

The image of the 'kind', 'war-torn veteran' speaking of leadership, that of his 'kind' friend, is juxtaposed with the suddenness and violence of rape, bringing both the officer and Lorente's speaker to the common state of 'war-torn', each for their own different reason. And similarly to other poems I have thus far discussed, 'My Body Is' includes the kind of detail meant to anchor the traumatic memory into a concrete setting, mooring the image of violence into the wall of the real, personal moment – 'he raped me in Hanau while I was sleeping', 'This was unexpected' – and of course the poem's title is anchored down by the prominent index: 'My Body Is.' However, the aftermath of the attack represented in 'My Body Is' is not marred by the smoke and sounds of war but, again, by the casual, mundane, almost matter-of-fact reality of rape: 'There is a man, one arm against the wall / peeing onto a suitcase beneath the window.'

Ultimately, as harrowing as the recollection of that incident is, we have a clear view as to how the poem itself functions as Lorente's prosthesis, as her speaker shifts from an indexical, traumatic, disoriented view of her own body to a position of a kind of reclaiming and ownership:

> I wrap my hand around my wrist
> to remember when I was a child:
> my body is
> my body is.
>
> My body is mine.[69]

The mantra 'my body is', which also serves as the poem's title, is the indexical linchpin of the poem's sense of traumatic unfeeling and alienation. Events take place, orders are given, and the almost numb beat of the poem and its violent action proceeds uninterrupted, not even by the drama and horror of rape: 'His friend the lieutenant though, / he raped me in Hanau while I was sleeping. / This was unexpected.' Thus the indexical act of touching the body – 'I wrap my hand around my wrist' – at first reminds both reader and speaker that there is a body here, her body, and that this is not one flowing, all-consuming narrative but one interrupted by the reality of the attack and the reality of her own body. What is more, in terms of the internal workings of the poem, the phrase 'the body is' works both as a kind of reaffirmation of that existence – 'the body exists, the body is here' – and as a broken-down, incomplete, indexical sentence – 'the body is' – in a manner that resembles Emily Dickinson's use of the index, such as in 'Without this – there is nought –.'[70] It is, in other words, an amputated sentence, one indicating not the certainty of meaning but the search for a meaning that had been severed in the wake of a traumatic experience of violence. All these converge – the existential, the personal, the corporeal – into a making real, a prosthetic kind of real, of the rape and a regaining, perhaps reclaiming, of her own body: 'My body is mine.' The poetic restructuring of memory is, then, as with any prosthetic text, a painful revisiting of the past from which one may emerge with a new poetic limb.

Before moving on to one other important variety of military experience, I think it is worthwhile revisiting Chantelle Bateman's poem 'Lists and Scales', which I discussed in the Introduction and which serves as a complementary piece to Lorente's. If we argue that the military experience is radically different for women, then we must briefly address the manner in which that difference also creates an altered mode of return, one that may be more complex and nuanced. And Bateman's poem, with its stark interrogation of the gendered experience of combat PTSD and the attempt to limp back to life, is a stirring addition to the complexity of the female veteran experience. It sheds light on the double task facing female veterans, of working hard to adapt to life after war while straining under the pressure of gender difference, as seen in the way in which the poem depicts her interview at the VA as a form of sexual assault:

Down the list
'Were you ever raped or sexually assaulted?'
Rape is sexual assault douche bag
And your question is reminiscent of the act
Penetrating and touching me without my consent.[71]

Bateman's speaker here is supposedly 'doing the work' of post-war life and attempting to stumble back into the civilian world, yet encounters a gendered hostility that is, on the face of it, seemingly separate from war and entirely part and parcel of the wartime experience for female soldiers and civilians. How does one, then, return from war if the war, whether political or gendered, does not end? When is the trauma of war intermingled with MST, only to be confronted with continued institutionalised obtuseness and retraumatisation? And what is more, in what way do other social categories, such as race, further complicate the work of the prosthesis? One way they do so, which I will discuss shortly, is through ethnic and political identity, or the experience of soldiers of colour who participate in the act of going to war, which, at least for most of the cases cited in this book, involves going to war far from home to the Middle East and Central Asia, where they find themselves shocked by the similarities they share with the 'enemy'.

The theme of sensing a common fate across battle lines has, of course, a rich history, one of identifying the humanity of opposing forces or as sharing a common burden of war. The mind goes to classic examples such as Priam's appeal to Achilles' shared humanity in an attempt to gain possession of Hector's body in the *Iliad* and, more recently, as a feature of World War I poetry such as Wilfred Owen's 'A Strange Meeting',[72] as well as the dedication that opens David Jones's epic post-war poem *In Parenthesis*, which ends thus:

> to the enemy
> Front-fighters who shared our
> Pains against whom we found
> Ourselves by misadventure.[73]

Another powerful example is Isaac Rosenberg's classic Great War poem 'Break of Day in the Trenches', in which a pest known to both trench lines – the 'cosmopolitan' rat – links English and German soldiers as they endure the same fate:

> Now you have touched this English hand
> You will do the same to a German
> Soon, no doubt, if it be your pleasure
> To cross the sleeping green between.[74]

Most notably, the identification of opposing forces as human or more friend than foe is also common in situations where that identification is more immediate, such as in the writing following the various civil wars.

However, the context in which American and British soldiers of colour encounter this notion of sameness or relation to the enemy is marked by colonial and post-colonial historical strata, wherein these soldiers, coming from personal and historical experiences of discrimination or oppression, find themselves on the side of the oppressor while identifying with the oppressed. These post-colonial and colonial overtones are, of course, present in some of the work already mentioned: namely, Jones's position as a Welsh British subject, as well as Rosenberg's position as a Jewish man. That influence is magnified, I would argue, by the addition of an ethnic element to the contemporary military conflicts that involve British and American armies operating in Central Asia and the Middle East, as seen in a few of the poems by veterans that touch on this topic.

One striking example of this added layer of struggle between identity and an all-subsuming collective, and which involves both race and gender, can be found in Nicole Goodwin's 'Unsaid (Confession)', part of her *Warcries* collection, in which the poet distances herself from the mistreatment of Iraqi prisoners by white female US soldiers and identifies a kinship with the prisoners themselves. In that way, Goodwin's speaker finds herself relating to the 'enemy' more than to her fellow American soldiers, identifying a familiar and shared source of oppression:

> I and the other black girls.
> Never did that.
> Never lost cool.
> Not on my watch.
> Not once.
>
> Maybe 'cause we knew.
> We saw.
> How they looked.
>
> They resembled us.
> Family distanced by time.
> This war separated us by nation.
> But shade united us.[75]

The identity- and power-based issue raised by Goodwin here elicits a different type of prosthetic response. Whereas in many of the other poems discussed in this book there had been a focus on the tension between an 'I' and the expression of the experience of war though public language, in

'Unsaid (Confession)' that tension shifts from an experience of the 'I' to that of a collective 'us'. Goodwin is linked, in other words, to a group – 'I and the other black girls' – and thus her poetic prosthesis is associated with that group and the new collective she forms with the Iraqi prisoners: 'They resembled us. / Family distanced by time. / This war separated us by nation. / But shade united us.'

One other instance of the intermingling of war, violence and identity is the work of Maurice Decaul. Decaul, who, like Lynn Hill, had also participated in the *Holding it Down* project initiated by musicians Mike Ladd and Vijay Iyer, writes in his 'Space Behind My Eyes' of a dream-like encounter with an Iraqi person who he identifies as 'cousin', adding:'

> The canon makes little reference to either of us
> Cousin
> but we find ourselves together
> after six thousand generations
> & this notion of nations
> we shake hands.[76]

As with Goodwin, the encounter with the presumed 'other' of the war turns into a kind of family reunion, two relatives meeting after 'six thousand generations' and sharing two distinct common traits – a love for poetry and exclusion from the Western canon of literature: 'The canon makes little reference to either of us.' And as Decaul writes later on in the poem, the wartime encounter shifts in light of this common link to an educational one, in which the two individuals can sit and teach each other about, for instance, the famed medieval Muslim dream interpreter 'Ibn Sareen the washer of dreams', who lived and worked in Basra, modern-day Iraq. For Decaul, then, the dream state and the tradition to which that dream state is linked are essential aspects of his poetic prosthetic, whereas in other cases the emphasis was placed more on the factuality or 'reality' of wartime experiences. A dream of war and perhaps of war's effects has emerged, in other words: one not unlike the more general category of 'dream' that I have discussed in this book in terms of Peirce's work, as well as my own conceptualisation of the poetic prosthesis. What the speaker in Decaul's poems yearns for is the interpretation of that dream or the ability to reconnect with the kind of cultural tradition that would aid in that interpretation: one that, ironically, is indeed part of a cultural canon, just not the canon of the American culture from which he is sent to war but that of the culture against which he finds himself fighting. Thus, and perhaps as opposed to Goodwin's experience of sudden kinship, Decaul's is less ethnic in the political sense but is based on a shared sense of culture, tradition and exclusion. The indexical 'us', then, does not denote, as in Goodwin, those of a similar 'shade' but instead those with a similar understanding and practice of culture, set apart from the bloody and 'uncultured' context of war.

War at Home

Much of what has already been stated in this chapter already clarifies, I think, the inherent strangeness and violence of the form of life of war, an otherness that only serves to deepen the gap between returning veterans and their immediate communities. At times, as in the cases just discussed, the wartime environment may serve to emphasise further an existing sense of alienation and, at times, social oppression. What I hope at least some of this discussion achieves is a better understanding that the difficulty of translating military experiences into a civilian setting does not amount to a simple misunderstanding of terms – 'What does "burying the dead" mean?' – but is also a literal clash of cultures and worldviews. The encounter is made that much more difficult and complicated with the added issue that the person whose culture is effectively decimated and made confusing by war is, on a surface level, the same person who had left for war some weeks, months or years prior. In other words, just as the word 'hose' remains the same despite new and horrible meanings attached to it, as seen in my earlier reading of Jarrell's 'The Death of the Ball-Turret Gunner', the signifier that is the person himself – physically whole, communicating, 'seeming the same' – is misleading in its sameness. Just as the pre-war soldier had to adjust, and violently so, from a world of expectations and cultural beliefs regarding war to the actual 'reality', and similarly must adapt to the unchanged home to which he returns, there is a great deal of work and hardship facing that same home – to adapt to a forever altered child, sibling, partner or parent.

I will be the first to admit that this book, with its focus on returning veterans, has placed a premium on first-hand experience: not a premium on the 'reality' those veterans face, but on the manner in which their experiences seem to have shaped their way of thinking, how they speak and, ultimately, the new mode of living they are forced to construct for themselves via the poetic prosthetic. However, returning soldiers do not just represent in themselves the injury of war; in many ways, they are part of a wider injurious process or event, setting off emotionally complex situations for themselves and their immediate support community, the latter burdened with much of the veterans' initial 'impact' upon their return. To say this more simply, soldiers returning from the 'culture of war' have a significant, complicated effect on their families and support networks. When the influx of veterans is sudden and extensive, such as following the two world wars or, to some extent, the war in Vietnam, the swell of familial and marital tensions can produce dramatic responses, such as the re-evaluation of the importance of marriage counselling in the UK, which Henry Dicks writes about in the wake of the Second World War.[77] In the case of the constant trickle of returning veterans from conflicts such as those taking place in Iraq and Afghanistan, change is slower and perhaps less perceptible. The severe and at times violent impact of this invisible form of repatriation, however, bears results that are no less devastating for military families and their support networks,[78] who may also require a new way of writing and speaking after their loved ones' return from war.

In this section I would like to discuss not the ways of life of war but poetry written by those who have had to come to terms with the lengths to which their loved ones had changed in war, and the manner in which that change alters their post-war home life. Since, as I have argued throughout, war is not an event which ends upon the return home, that lingering effect and increasing tension between veterans and their loved ones affect more than just the veterans themselves, as the bounds of the form of life of war are found to be much more porous than might have been expected by both soldiers and their families. As Kenneth T. MacLeish writes, the 'precariousness' of post-war life 'also afflicts the soldier who has returned home, and the spouses, lovers, parents, and friends who remain bound to soldiers while they are away'.[79] Much of Kate Gaskin's work focuses on the equally important aspect of life without a partner away from war, as well as providing a fascinating insight into those aspects that define these most contemporary conflicts where, for example, the husband away at war can conduct a video call with his wife in her US home, the topic of Gaskin's poem 'Poem in Which You Leave':

He is rolling over
front to back, back to front

as you crouch
in the desert and cradle

your phone. A miracle
to see it at all

from so many miles, the planes
that drone, the wind

that scabs the brush, your face,
the crust of salt and dust

you wear like skin.
Again, you say. Again.[80]

Through the modern technology of the smartphone, Gaskin sheds light on a bizarre other world, one in which the war culture so minutely detailed in this chapter effectively infiltrates the home. Gone is that false sense of safety around what Alexandra Hyde calls the 'false binaries' of military power, those of gender, of space, of the split between home and front,[81] and Mary Favret calls experiencing war 'at a distance', wherein all families could do was find some certainty in a violent world where such certainty was all but absent. For those at home for the first two centuries of 'global war', beginning with the Napoleonic Wars, the task was, as Favret writes, 'to find sentient ground for what often appeared a free-floating, impersonal military operation, removed from their immediate sensory perception'.[82] As she continues, later global wars, such as those waged in Vietnam and the First Gulf War, are 'mediated'[83] to those at home. And yet Gaskin writes neither of a mediated war nor of a war removed from 'immediate sensory perception', but one that is parallel to her everyday life. That confusing here/now nature of the home–war hybrid is beautifully exemplified as Gaskin weaves her husband's ability to see his baby begin to roll over with her own ability to witness her husband roll over in real time. Moreover, the lines break in a manner that renders the 'miracle' being witnessed ambiguous – is it the miracle of a baby slowly growing into an infant, that of seeing the starry desert skies at night, or of being able to experience it all with a parent thousands of miles away? Are the planes droning and the stars part of the night-time in the desert or a depiction of baby toys and accessories?

However, as pertinent as Gaskin's depiction is of the modern simultaneity of war, I would argue that the manner in which she paints the uneasy return from war is as instrumental, if not more so, to our understanding of the impact that veterans' return has on family life. It is important not only because it repeats the age-old trope of the changed soldier but also because it reinforces that trope within the seemingly flowing cohabitation of modern warfare and modern communication mentioned by Hyde and Favret in the essays cited above. That 'being with them' via email, video chat and social media, may not prevent the more general injury to veterans' identities and to their family life. One poem that illuminates the persistent unease of return is Gaskin's 'The Foxes', which describes family life after war, the buying of a new home, an attempt, as it were, to 'move on', all the while sensing a lingering malady. A disease, moreover, the cure for which is not and cannot be 'moving on', in both a literal and a figurative sense:

They came like emissaries
from a fairy tale. In twilight, framed

by wisteria vines that burdened
the backyard's powerlines, they dozed

like cats all summer. Awake,
they tussled up and down the honeysuckle,

still kits, all muzzle, light feet.
This was years after your friend

froze to death on the concrete staircase
outside his Florida apartment.

Years after you loaded your last
bomb. Years of desert deployments.

And now this house, its kind porch
and open rooms, the foxes we inherited.

Though eventually they too left,
and the sickness that follows us took root.

Wherever we go, these black blossoms.[84]

A chance encounter with the wild, natural world is at first couched in the language of wonder – 'fairy tales' is how we are introduced to the coming of the foxes. Young, harmless and delicate, they are 'framed by wisteria vines'. And yet, like a canary in the mine, 'they too left', causing one to wonder about the nature of the ominous 'sickness', the source of 'black blossoms', that seems to be haunting the home. A clue to that question can perhaps be found in the two incidents that mark the poem's past, ones that it seems she and her veteran partner were desperately trying to escape: a friend who had frozen to death outside his home and the partner's military service. The disease is, then, a war-related one that had plagued the returning veteran and his anticipating family – as seen in the above discussion of Gaskin's 'Poem in Which You Leave' – possibly as well as others who had returned too, such as the friend who had, for some untold reason, managed to freeze to death outside his own home. Was his friend locked out of his home by his own partner? By himself? Was there a fight? What was the source of their disagreement? Or had the friend perhaps lived alone and got locked out, or maybe was inebriated, lost consciousness and died on the steps to his apartment? Whatever the definitive answer to some of these questions, the disease the poem refers to is nonetheless linked to war and its lingering sickness, the sense that whatever it is that changed upon the husband's return from war – the degree to which he had changed, the degree to which she had changed, perhaps – had settled into a permanent condition. The sickness is the 'black blossoms', a life lived again, a garden blooming and yet touched by an unsettling undertow.

One other source of some of the most stirring contemporary accounts of partners' encounter with the reality of post-war change is the work of American poet Elyse Fenton. In one poem, 'Conversation', Fenton also addresses the lingering unease of post-war family life as she too, interestingly, uses the family's garden as a site of both promise of spring and renewal, and that promise's ultimate implosion:

> We're desperate as men counting
> miles across an ocean renamed home
> you and I and the heart's joists that keep
> the roof from warping under
>
> pipes and wind. *No one marries during war,*
> I'm told and yet I'm married to the thought
> of you returning home to marry me
> to my former self. The war is everywhere
>
> at once. Each eggplant that I pick
> is ripe and sun-dark in its own inviolable
> skin. Except there is no inviolable anything
> and you've been home now for a year.[85]

Fenton's poem, written in the wake of her husband's service, highlights a sense of a severed self that I have hitherto discussed in terms of the soldiers' experience but which is shared by those who live in abeyance, awaiting their return. And here too there are hints of the need for mechanical supports to prevent the 'warping' of the psyche, described as the 'heart's joists', in line with the sense of a severed identity – 'you returning home to marry me / to my former self'. The sense of a falling apart, moreover, is not aided in any way by the return of the military partner, which, I think, is the source of the true tragedy 'Conversation' presents: that at times the long-hoped-for return can aggravate the wartime split.

However, another aspect of Fenton's poem also relates to how the poetry of those who wait can be said to differ from those who leave and return, and that is the opposition of the painful split between the mechanical state inherent to the war form of life and the state of nature. As with Gaskin's 'The Foxes', the natural world acts as a foil to the anguish of a life undone. All those things considered to be natural or complete – the wholeness of one's identity, one's relation to family or loved ones, the division between war and the home – are revealed as frayed, diseased and, in Fenton's poem, violable. As Favret writes concerning Stanley Cavell's notion of the violence of the everyday, Fenton and Gaskin's writing seems to make manifest the 'pained effort to bind what is present and familiar with another reality, absent and destructive'.[86] Where Gaskin's foxes were an uncanny apparition related to the ghosts of the couple's wartime past, as well as a symptom of the 'sickness' that those ghosts represent, Fenton's poetic speaker is confronted with the natural wholeness of the 'inviolable' eggplant, that which cannot be corrupted. But, as she pricks the eggplant, she discovers, as with herself, with her partner, with their relationship, that even as far away as Eugene, Oregon, one may still be hit by a stray bullet from Iraq.

There are many ways, I think, in which a depiction of the form of life of war would have been sufficient in exploring, even if rudimentarily, the culture of war and its effect on both language and the language gap created between soldiers and their communities at home. It is a mechanical, pragmatic, overtly symbolic and violent habitus from which one does not simply 'return' or 'demilitarise'. However, what I hoped to show in this last section is that while this form indeed warps, if I may borrow a word from Fenton's poem, there is quite a bit of damage being done on the home front even before repatriation and certainly following the return home. To say this somewhat more plainly: to ignore the impact veterans have upon their return is perhaps to enable the flawed narrative of the isolated, autonomous hero sent to the isolated scene of danger and expected to return 'whole'. Those individuals were never isolated to begin with, and to reintegrate them into a field of memory and coping that includes how they are affected by and affect others is a painful and necessary step on the limping way back to life.

Notes

1. Max Weinreich, 'YIVO and the Problems of Our Time', *Yivo-bleter* 25, no. 1 (January–February 1945): 13.
2. Susan White, 'Professor Helps Mental Health Care Providers Understand Military Culture', *Contact* (Spring 2009): 8.
3. Brison, *Aftermath*, 104.
4. John Keegan, *The Face of Battle: A Study of Agincourt, Waterloo, and the Somme* (London: Penguin Books, 1983), 303.
5. Rachel Woodward, 'Warrior Heroes and Little Green Men: Soldiers, Military Training, and the Construction of Rural Masculinities', *Rural Sociology* 65, no. 4 (2000): 646.
6. Ibid.
7. Scarry, *The Body in Pain*, 112.
8. For a comprehensive summary of the kind of generalised notions of soldiers' experience of war, specifically American soldiers, see Richard H. Kohn, 'The Social History of the American Soldiers', *The American Historical Review* 86, no. 3 (June 1981): 553–67.
9. Fred A. Shannon, 'The Life of the Common Soldier in the Union Army, 1861–1865', *The Mississippi Valley Historical Review* 13, no. 4 (March 1927): 472.
10. Ibid.
11. Hautzinger and Scandlyn, *Beyond Post-Traumatic Stress*, 23.
12. Marcus Tullius Cicero, *Tusculan Disputations*, translated by Andrew P. Peabody (Boston: Little, Brown, and Company, 1886), 48.
13. See Michael Geyer, 'The Militarization of Europe, 1914-1945', in *The Militarization of the Western World*, edited by John Gill (New Brunswick, NJ: Rutgers University Press, 1989), 65–102; and Catherine Lutz, 'Making War at Home in the United States: Militarization and the Current Crisis', *American Anthropologist* 104, no. 3 (September 2002): 723–35.
14. Kohn, 'The Social History of the American Soldiers', 558-9; Kohn largely debunks the clear-cut distinction between exclusively 'patriotic' American soldiers in the late nineteenth and early twentieth centuries as against a more 'practical' enlistment in the late twentieth century.
15. David Jones, *In Parenthesis* (London: Faber and Faber, 2014), 31.
16. H. D., 'The Walls Do Not Fall', *Trilogy* (New York: New Directions, 1998), 4.
17. Riverbend, 'Jewelry and Raids . . .', *Baghdad Burning*, 9 October 2003. Available at: <https://riverbendblog.blogspot.com/2003/10/> (last accessed 23 February 2022).

18. Michel Foucault, *Discipline and Punish*, translated by Alan Sheridan (London: Penguin Press, 1978), 135.
19. Ibid., 138.
20. Ibid., 158.
21. Carol Burke, 'Marching to Vietnam', *The Journal of American Folklore* 102, no. 406 *Vietnam* (October–December 1989): 427; Fred Turner, 'This is for Fighting, This is for Fun: Camerawork and Gunplay in Reality-Based Crime Shows', in *Bang Bang, Shoot Shoot: Essays on Guns and Popular Culture*, edited by Murray Pomerance (New York: Simon and Schuster, 1999), 175.
22. Donna Haraway, 'A Manifesto for Cyborgs: Science, Technology, and Socialist Feminism in the 1980s', *Socialist Review* 15 (1985): 81–2.
23. Mena, *The Shape of Our Faces No Longer Matters*, 30.
24. Ibid.
25. Ludwig Wittgenstein, *Philosophical Investigations*, translated by G. E. M. Anscombe (Oxford: Blackwell, 1968), 19.
26. Frederick Elkin, 'The Soldier's Language', *The American Journal of Sociology* 51, no. 5 *Human Behavior in Military Society* (March 1946): 414–15.
27. Elbridge Colby, 'Soldier Speech', *American Speech* 11, no. 1 (February 1936): 50.
28. Ken MacLeish, 'Churn: Mobilization–Demobilization and the Fungibility of American Military Life', *Security Dialogue* 51, no. 2–3 (2020): 195.
29. 'Department of Defense Dictionary of Military and Associated Terms', *Joint Chiefs of Staff* website. Available at: <http://www.jcs.mil/Portals/36/Documents/Doctrine/pubs/dictionary.pdf> (last accessed 1 August 2018).
30. Elkin, 'The Soldier's Language', 416.
31. Ibid.
32. Colby, 'Soldier Speech', 60.
33. Elkin, 'The Soldier's Language', 417.
34. 'Glossary of Army Slang', *American Speech* 16, no. 3 (October 1941): 163–9.
35. Donald Howard, 'United States Marine Corps Slang', *American Speech* 31, no. 3 (October 1956): 188–94.
36. C. Douglas Chrétien, 'Comments on Naval Slang', *Western Folklore* 6, no. 2 (April 1947): 157–62.
37. Robert Shafer, 'Air Force Slang', *American Speech* 20, no. 3 (October 1945): 226–7.
38. Scarry, *The Body in Pain*, 62.
39. Nathan Joseph and Nicholas Alex, 'The Uniform: A Sociological Perspective', *American Journal of Sociology* 77, no. 4 (1972): 720.
40. Valentine Jobst, 'Is the Wearing of the Enemy's Uniform a Violation of the Laws of War?', *The American Journal of International Law* 35, no. 3 (July 1941): 440.
41. Zygmunt Bauman, 'Semiotics and the Function of Culture', in *Essays in Semiotics*, edited by Julia Kristeva, Josette Rey-Debove and Donna J. Umiker (The Hague: Mouton, 1971), 286.
42. 'Subjugate', *Oxford English Dictionary* Online. Available at: <http://www.oed.com/view/Entry/192724#eid20063788> (last accessed 11 December 2014).

43. Carl D. Buck, 'Words for "Battle," "War," "Army," and "Soldier,"' *Classical Philology* 14, no. 1 (January 1919): 9.
44. Kohn, 'The Social History of the American Soldiers', 556.
45. Ibid., 560.
46. Norris, 'Mourning Rights', 284.
47. Ibid.
48. Leed, *No Man's Land*, 74.
49. 'Letter from Lloyd Maywood Staley to Mary Beatrice Gray, May 29, 1918', *Letters Home from War* website. Available at: <http://www.u.arizona.edu/~rstaley/wwlettr1.htm> (last accessed 23 February 2022).
50. Weil, 'The *Iliad*', 21.
51. Scarry, *The Body in Pain*, 62.
52. Elkin, 'The Soldier's Language', 420.
53. Ibid., 415.
54. Currall, 'Burying the Dead'.
55. Shay, *Achilles in Vietnam*, 74.
56. Weigl, *The Circle of Hahn*, 5–6.
57. Judith Butler, *Frames of War* (London: Verso, 2009), 34.
58. See Christine Knauer, *Let Us Fight as Free Men: Black Soldiers and Civil Rights* (Philadelphia: University of Pennsylvania Press, 2014); Michael Cullen Green, *Black Yanks in the Pacific: Race in the Making of American Military Empire* (Ithaca, NY: Cornell University Press, 2010); Wallace Terry, *Bloods: Black Veterans of the Vietnam War, An Oral History* (New York: Ballantine Books, 1984); and Kimberly L. Philips, *War! What Is It Good for? Black Freedom Struggles & the U.S. Military* (Chapel Hill: University of North Carolina Press, 2012).
59. Emma Moore, 'Women in Combat: Five-Year Status Update', *Center for a New American Security*, 31 March 2002. Available at: <https://www.cnas.org/publications/commentary/women-in-combat-five-year-status-update> (last accessed 23 February 2022).
60. See, for example, Bruce P. Dohrenwend, J. Blake Turner, Nicholas A. Turse, Roberto Lewis-Fernandez and Thomas J. Yager, 'War-Related Post-Traumatic Stress Disorder in Black, Hispanic, and Majority White Vietnam Veterans: The Roles of Exposure and Vulnerability', *Journal of Traumatic Stress* 21, no. 2 (April 2008): 133–41; Michele Spoont, David Nelson, Michelle van Ryn and Margarita Alegria, 'Racial and Ethnic Variation in Perceptions of VA Mental Health Providers Are Associated with Treatment Retention Among Veterans with PTSD', *Medical Care* 55 (September 2017): S33–S42.
61. Lori S. Katz, Lindsey E. Bloor, Geta Cojucar and Taylor Draper, 'Women who Served in Iraq Seeking Mental Health Services: Relationships Between Military Sexual Trauma, Symptoms, and Readjustment', *Psychological Services* 4, no. 4 (2007): 239–49; Sheila Jeffreys, 'Double Jeopardy: Women, the US Military and the War in Iraq', *Women's Studies International Forum* 30, no. 1 (January–February 2007): 16–25; Cynthia A. Leardmann, Amanda Pietrucha, Kathryn M. Magruder, Besa Smith, Maureen Murdoch, Isabel G. Jacobson, Margaret A. K. Ryan, Gary

Gackstetter, Tyler C. Smith and Millennium Cohort Study Team, 'Combat Deployment Is Associated with Sexual Harassment or Sexual Assault in a Large, Female Military Cohort', *Women's Health Issues* 23, no. 4 (July–August 2013): e215–e223.

62. Department of Defense, 'Appendix B: Statistical Data on Sexual Assault', 2019. Availableat:<https://www.sapr.mil/sites/default/files/3_Appendix_B_Statistical_Data_on_Sexual_Assault.pdf> (last accessed 23 February 2022).

63. Ministry of Defence, 'Sexual Offences in the Service Justice System 2018', 2019. Available at: <https://assets.publishing.service.gov.uk/government/uploads/system/uploads/attachment_data/file/790324/20190321-Sexual_Offences_Statistics_2018_report-FINAL.pdf> (last accessed 23 February 2022).

64. Kristin M. Mattocks, Anne Sadler, Elizabeth M. Yano, Erin E. Krebs, Laurie Zephyrin, Cynthia Brandt, Rachel Kimerling, Theo Sandfort, Melissa E. Dichter, Jeffrey J. Weiss, Jeroan Allison and Sally Haskell, 'Sexual Victimization, Health Status, and VA Healthcare Utilization Among Lesbian and Bisexual OEF/OIF Veterans', *Journal of General Internal Medicine* 28 (2013): 604–8.

65. 'Former Air Force Servicewoman Feels Betrayed by Military After Sexual Assault', *PBS News Hour*, 23 May 2013. Available at: <https://www.pbs.org/newshour/nation/former-air-force-servicewoman-feels-disposed-of-betrayed> (last accessed 23 February 2022).

66. Jaime Lorente, 'Jamie Broady', in *My Teeth Don't Chew on Shrapnel: An Anthology of Poetry by Military Veterans*, edited by Niall Munro (Oxford: Oxford Brookes Poetry Centre, 2020), 47.

67. Ibid.

68. Ibid., 49.

69. Ibid., 50.

70. Emily Dickinson, *The Complete Poems of Emily Dickinson*, edited by Thomas H. Johnson (Boston: Little Brown and Co., 1960), 655.

71. Bateman, 'Lists and Scales'.

72. For more on this theme in 'A Strange Meeting' see, for instance, Santanu Das, *Touch and Intimacy in First World War Literature* (Cambridge: Cambridge University Press, 2005), 169–71.

73. Jones, *In Parenthesis*, xvi.

74. Isaac Rosenberg, 'Break of Day in the Trenches', in *Poetry of the First World War: An Anthology*, edited by Tim Kendall (Oxford: Oxford University Press, 2013), 136.

75. Nicole Goodwin, *Warcries* (Scotts Valley, CA: CreateSpace Independent Publishing, 2016), 60.

76. Maurice Decaul, 'Space Behind My Eyes', *Warrior Writers*. Available at: <www.warriorwriters.org/artists/maurice.html> (last accessed 23 February 2022).

77. Henry V. Dicks, *Marital Tensions: Clinical Studies Toward a Psychological Theory of Interaction* (Hove: Routledge, 2015), 1–4.

78. See, for example, Michelle D. Sherman, Fred Sautter, M. Hope Jackson, Judy A. Lyons and Xiaotong Han, 'Domestic Violence in Veterans with Posttraumatic Stress Disorder Who Seek Couples Therapy', *Journal of Marital and Family Therapy*

32, no. 4 (2006): 479–90; Andra Teten Tharp, Michelle D. Sherman, Ursula Bowling and Bradford J. Townsend, 'Intimate Partner Violence Between Male Iraq and Afghanistan Veterans and Their Female Partners Who Seek Couples Therapy,' *Journal of Interpersonal Violence* 31, no. 6 (2016): 1095–115; and Briana S. Nelson and David W. Wright, 'Understanding and Treating Post-Traumatic Stress Disorder Symptoms in Female Partners of Veterans with PTSD', *Journal of Marital and Family Therapy* 22, no. 4 (1996): 455-67.

79. MacLeish, *Making War at Fort Hood*, 93.

80. Kate Gaskin, 'Poem in Which You Leave', *War, Literature, and the Arts: Folios* 2 (2019): 2. Available at: <https://www.wlajournal.com/wlaarchive/folio2019/Gaskin.pdf> (last accessed 23 February 2022).

81. Alexandra Hyde, 'The Present Tense of Afghanistan: Accounting for Space, Time and Gender in Processes of Militarisation', *Gender, Place & Culture* 23, no. 6 (2016): 864.

82. Mary Favret, *War at a Distance: Romanticism and the Making of Modern Wartime* (Princeton: Princeton University Press, 2010), 9.

83. Ibid., 12–13.

84. Kate Gaskin, 'The Foxes', *Poetry Northwest* (Winter and Spring, 2019): 23.

85. Elyse Fenton, 'Conversation', *Clamour* (Cleveland, OH: Cleveland State University Poetry Center, 2010), 64.

86. Favret, *War at a Distance*, 159.

CHAPTER 4

Prosthetic Irony – The Ghost in the Machine

Irony is not just a figure of speech or a way of saying things in a round-about way, although it is those things as well. It is also an insistence on ambiguity, one entrenched in the form of belief that one cannot say certain things directly, that the game of meaning is just that, a game, and one that must be played carefully. It is that brand of irony, of that meaning of the word, that plays a central role in the form of life that is war, whether through ironic or absurd events taking place, or through the seemingly ironic use of language and slang. However, irony is not only a characteristic of these military experiences, but also what could be called its underlying philosophy. Irony, the 'ghost' shifting between alive and dead that travels between index and symbol, represents a new way of thinking during and after trauma and war, one tethered both to one form of life coming to an end as well as to the enacting of that life through poetry – a life lived in irony. Similarly to the man injured in the factory warehouse explosion, new information or information of a dif-ferent kind is taken in; it does not provide a better grasp of one's safety or sense of life but challenges those distinctions and, consequently, desta-bilises communication and one's self-identity as human. In the case of veterans, this means a lesson not only in what violence can do or in the fragility of one's own body, but also in the nature of communication, humanity and time – that one can be at a loss for words, that one can feel like an object, and that one can be at war and at home simultaneously.

It seems counterintuitive to ascribe 'irony' to that lesson, to a sense of dissipating borders, since what we have in mind when we think of irony, again, is aligned more with an evasive discourse, a way of saying things in a circumventory manner rather than 'getting to the point'. I think I have made it clear thus far that 'getting to the point' is not something soldiers can or even wish to do, seeing that the point in question is painful, paralysing and to an extent inaccessible. In the wake of my own military experiences, one of the facts that troubled me the most was this double sense that I felt as if I 'had' to describe what I had seen and felt, and yet finding that I cannot 'get it right'. It was only when I gave up – out of pure frustration, to be sure – and described not the scene but the feeling created by that scene, in what would become my novella *Nartik Yahalom* (Diamond Purse), that I found out that I had discovered what I was looking for somewhere else. To speak more generally, there is a sense in which evasiveness, going artistically AWOL – what I have called elsewhere a resistance to reality, plays a decidedly productive role in the ironic element of the poetic prosthesis. In order to illustrate what I mean by irony better, a detour is required into the differences between this irony and the more commonly used variants of the concept. Our first stop, however, will be a familiar one – the previously cited comment by Vietnam war veteran and poet Bruce Weigl:

> The war took away my life and gave me poetry in return. The war taught me irony: that I instead of others would survive is ironic. All of my heroes are dead. The fate the world has given me is to struggle to write powerfully enough to draw others into the horror.[1]

War teaches in a way that seems different from the gradual, time-consuming and community- or authority-based instruction that is so characteristic of military training, as seen in the previous chapter. As Eric J. Leed writes in *No Man's Land*, whatever it is that war is presumed to 'teach' 'is qualitatively distinct from any [learning] gained indirectly through traditional "schools"', later adding: 'In war men are shown, not just told, and they are shown not by an orderly presentation of reality but through radical juxtapositions of violence and stillness, utter fear and utter boredom.'[2] You are not told that war ends your life; in other words, as Weigl notes, it is something you learn once your life has ended. And while the concept itself is obviously not without its theoretical controversy,[3] irony as Weigl uses it here refers, I think, to the attempt to use language while somehow still adhering to an ethical stance, according to which practically any and all language used in the wake of war is impossible and immoral. It is immoral since to speak or communicate about war can be perceived by war veterans as somehow dishonourable toward the experience of war, as well as, sometimes, toward fallen comrades. Providing a way out of this fidelity to the past, as Dominick LaCapra puts it, while somehow 'respecting' it, is, as I shall argue throughout, the function of irony and the poetic prosthesis exemplified in Weigel's very statement.

As a way to home in further on the relevant definition of irony I would like to rule out the idea of irony, at least in these cases, as being *simply* a rhetorical or figurative device: the very indication of a direct link between wartime experiences and a 'teaching' is ironic. I would argue that this teaching, intimately tied to a sense that language has failed in the presence of violence, is already present in Weigl's short statement. One aspect is that war did not take Weigl's life in any literal sense, or through an ordinary use of the word 'life', since its usual meaning would have us believe that Weigl died or was killed in war, a fact which the use of the index 'my' and the very existence of the statement seem to disprove. In other words, the combination of the symbolic 'taking away life' and the indexical 'my' creates an ironic tension, since the use of the first-person possessive seems to contradict logically the taking of the speaker's life. This is a very roundabout way of saying: 'Dead people don't write books.' It is the same kind of ironic interplay of index and symbol on display in the title of Maurice Blanchot's 'The Instance of My Death', in the ending to Randall Jarrell's 'The Death of a Ball Torrent Gunner' – 'When I died, they washed me out of the torrent with a hose,' as well as in the line that ends Madeleine Doiret's testimony as given in Charlotte Delbo's *Auschwitz and After*: 'I died in Auschwitz but no one knows.'[4] One other instance of index–symbol irony can also be seen in the contemporary war poems discussed here, such as, albeit in a different manner, the title of Gerardo Mena's 'So I Was a Coffin'. So, given all that, 'Bruce Weigl isn't dead' seems to be the logical answer to that curious conundrum.

However, while it is likely that Weigl was not dead when he wrote that his life was taken away, it is just as likely, and equally important, to rule out the possibility that the above comment is the result of a special use of the word 'life'. Another version of this argument would be that, while Weigl understands what 'life' means or how the word is used in a sentence, he deploys it in a 'figurative' manner, meaning that he writes 'life' but actually means something else: say, the ability to feel secure, the ability to communicate, and so on. This account of Weigl's comments, or of any ironic tension of the kind I have alluded to above, assumes, of course, a correct or at least normative use of words and signs, separating it from the kind of use that is, somehow, intentionally breaking these rules, by way of a joke, figurative speech or rhetorical play. So, the argument would go that while Weigl says he is dead, he does not *mean* he is dead. As Kierkegaard writes, this reading amounts to accusing Weigl's comment of not being 'serious about its seriousness'.[5] And while this kind of reading excludes what I argue is a non-rhetorical irony presupposed to produce such a statement, it does raise the very relevant issue of seriousness. I would argue that Weigl is serious, *dead* serious. But how can that be? How can a walking, animated person – who seems to be alive – refer to his own death, seriously?

Writing in *The Concept of Irony with Constant Reference to Socrates*, Kierkegaard refers to the kind of seriousness that is involved in his conception of irony, one intimately tied to being 'serious' about nothingness. In terms of the quotation from Weigl, or really any other instance in which soldiers write or talk about being dead, whether in their poetry or in therapy sessions, this amounts to the fact that Weigl is very serious, not necessarily about any one aspect of his comment but about its cumulative effect: that being dead or the feeling of being dead is not, to paraphrase Currall's poem, a metaphor. Or, said otherwise, that the feeling of being dead is anchored to a moment of death, that indexical mooring that is the element of post-war poetry that anchors it – a feat of the imagination – to a very real and painful past. As Kierkegaard writes:

> In the last analysis the ironist must always posit something, but what he posits in this way is nothingness. Now it is impossible to take nothingness seriously without either arriving at something (this happens when one takes it speculatively seriously), or without despairing (this happens when one takes it personally seriously). But the ironist does neither of these, and to this extent one may say he is not really serious about it. Irony is the infinitely delicate play with nothingness, a playing which is not terrified by it but still pokes its head into the air. But if one takes nothingness neither speculatively nor personally seriously, then one obviously takes it frivolously and to this extent not seriously.[6]

Within my own terms, this attitude could be said to be the seriousness of every aspect of the wartime experience: the seriousness of war's intentions and one's participation in it; the seriousness with which one senses fear of death and/or the experience of death; the seriousness of the communicational breakdown during and after war; and finally, the seriousness required to create an artistic or verbal object that is 'posited', to use Kierkegaard's word, so that the experience is communicated to others. All these factors have an immediate, personal stake in the lives of those emerging out of war, or at least serve, as I argue, as some of the most serious after-effects of war. As Wills writes, 'there is a real urgency' in the need to write the prosthesis, 'for it is always death that one finds lurking behind a case of prosthesis'.[7] In the construction of the post-war prosthesis, in fabricating with words a way of using language that is ironic, first and foremost, toward the very attempt to communicate at all, a relation toward nothingness and death is displayed that could be read, as in Weigl's comments, as 'unserious'. Here, I would argue, lie exposed two very different kinds of seriousness.

On one hand, there is the seriousness that is born out of a serious/ unserious distinction as the very act of both recognising and adhering to that divide, which is another way of linking seriousness with a kind of social conformity or 'responsibility'. So, when a group of soldiers in World War I, described in Fussell's *The Great War and Modern Memory*, opts to kick a soccer ball toward enemy lines as a show of bravado, they are performing, under this type of seriousness, a very unserious and irresponsible act. One soldier, reporting seeing a similar soccer game during a battle between British and Turkish armies near Beersheba (not far from where these very lines are written), wrote: 'One of the men had a football. How it came there goodness knows. Anyway we kicked off and rushed the first [Turkish] guns, dribbling the ball with us.'[8] This is similar to the trench art I previously discussed, where the soldiers 'playing' with ammunition and wasting valuable and recyclable cartridges are not what some army generals would call 'being serious'. A 'serious' way to treat ammunition, at least as far as the military regulations are concerned, is to shoot the enemy (marked by uniform and insignia) with the live rounds, and to collect the spent shells for recycling and reuse. Here, again, is an element of safety, of unnecessarily handling live rounds or spent ammunition, of not 'fooling around'. Thus, under this definition of 'seriousness', to be serious is to demonstrate one's adherence to the community-based rules and regulations, such as demonstrating the ability to keep oneself away from dangerous situations (speaking to the dead, in some cultures at least, could be construed as a very unserious undertaking, while in others it is very serious indeed). As one last point regarding this kind of seriousness, it would be fairly easy to see how it aligns itself quite nicely with two aspects already discussed: the use of symbols in language as a way of demonstrating seriousness – 'For God and country' – as well as the very serious attempt to use community-regulated words in order to describe one's experience of war, along with the many hurdles that attempt faces.

However, there is another kind of 'serious' more relevant to the type of 'play' demonstrated in the construction of the poetic prosthesis, and this is intimately linked to Weigl's statement. Thinking, for instance, of Mena's 'So I Was a Coffin', there is a way of reading an ironic bent or at least what seems like a less than serious tone in sentences such as 'They said no, you are a bad spear,' in which the soldier's failure to perform 'seriously' is represented in a tone resembling that of a chastising parent. It is, in a way, then, the very voice of seriousness itself, berating the soldier for their apparent inability to be serious enough – to be a good soldier, to be a good symbol (flag) and so on. And yet that irony, again, is indeed serious in that it is based on the assumption, firstly, that there is no definitive way to be serious successfully, or no definitive way to secure one's safety, like the man smoking next to empty petrol barrels; and secondly, that, oddly, certain situations, objects, experiences seem to indicate that some things can be safe and unsafe, serious and unserious at the very same time. I would argue that this type of seriousness, of a kind that takes 'everything' seriously, requires one to take Weigl, again, at his word as he uses language: 'The war took away my life and gave me poetry in return,' or Jonathan Shay's veteran patients as they proclaim 'I died in Vietnam'. The space created between the signs in that sentence, of not being able to grasp fully the meaning of a life being taken without it actually being taken, is what, in other words, these poems present with the utmost seriousness: not the meaning of these words necessarily, or the times, places and people the indices seem to pin down or frame, but the kind of space they create. That space, void of direct meaning and the product of an always moving, always ironic mode of meaning-making, is what the poetic prosthesis generates, the energy it produces, which imitates the movement of life. When I had trouble describing my war experiences 'precisely', I was left only with the bitter aftertaste of failing to get it 'right'. But when, in a kind of creative desperation, I wrote a narrative in which my soldierly past was made to interact, for instance, with settings outside its own time – a meeting with my mother's grandfather who died in Auschwitz, for instance – a space opened where I was able to pin something down precisely by 'fooling around'. It is a space that appears to be blank, 'unserious' or producing 'nonsense', and yet is packed with a different mode of meaning. This reminds me of what Kierkegaard writes of the space of irony in discussing 'an engraving that portrays the grave of Napoleon':

> There is nothing else to be seen in the picture, and the immediate spectator will see no more. Between these two trees, however, is an empty space, and as the eye traces out its contour Napoleon himself suddenly appears out of the nothingness, and now it is impossible to make him disappear. The eye that has once seen him now always sees him with anxious necessity . . . it is this empty space, this nothingness, that conceals what is most important.[9]

The empty space, the shape of which is determined by its borders – what indices are used, what symbols, and how they are made to interact with each other – is the irony of post-war poetry, one which communicates facts and uses words in a way that reconstructs not a landscape of war but a diagram of its aftermath. Finally, perhaps rudimentarily, it is language through which this tension between necessity and impossibility is recreated. This is an ironic 'fate', which Weigl seems to assume is essential to a reading of soldier poems, in that they serve to replace a lost connection to language and community – or 'life' – with an attempt to play ironically with the building blocks of that language to fashion a prosthesis that allows the renewal of communication, with a difference – 'poetry'.

One manner of addressing that distance, the empty space which post-war poems create, while struggling with the bonds of post-war seriousness, is addressed in the poem 'What Being in the Army Did', written by Iraq and Afghanistan veteran Graham Barnhart. The subject of the poem is ostensibly what its title suggests – things Barnhart had been taught in the army. Much of the discussion revolves around examples having to do with the measuring of distance or relation – the relation between the scientifically precise kilogram or metre, for instance, and his own body weight and estimate of length. In other words, the poem displays the serious ways of measuring distance – utilitarian, pragmatic, lethal – that one had been taught in the army. One such moment involves the military technique of using torsos to measure distance through the scope of a gun:

The army taught me torsos
and tailgates

are useful for gauging distance.
That swaying grass

or flags or scarves
can estimate windspeed,

and traveling from an artifact
to a fundamental constant

requires loss.
It takes me sixty steps

to walk one hundred meters.[10]

And yet, as the poem concludes, it appears the distance Barhart is measuring, the relation on which he has his sights, so to speak, are not those relations that the army had taught but those that the army, as the title suggests, *did*. Those relations are in language: the immeasurable distance, for instance, between those experiences and the home, signified by the presence, as in this next section, of the speaker's girlfriend, or, more essentially, the gap between the language available to the war veteran and the war experiences themselves. Unlike the perfect kilogram mentioned in the poem, 'Le Grand K', there is no ultimate standard in language that enables us to pinpoint precisely what it is that being in the army 'did':

When I say things like that
my girlfriend asks if I'm proud

of being dangerous.
I can safely say

I used to be and now at least
I know the dull machine chunk

of a rifle's sear reset between rounds,
a sound my father asked about once.

He asked if I knew any words
that sound like a prison door locking.

Abduction? Deconstruction?
He shook his head.

So I said maybe there is no word.
Maybe if there are bars,

describe the feeling
of the air between them.

If there are keys, the distance
between the sound of them

touching and the sound
of them touching the door.

The weight of your days
approaching that closure—

No, he said,
there is definitely a word.[11]

The poem ends with a dispute between Barnhart and his father regarding the ability to pin experience down with just one word, that one 'perfect' utterance that will, for instance, describe the reality of the war experience. Effectively, this is a dispute between the two kinds of 'serious' just mentioned – his father seeks to pin down a moment with one word, echoing the military style of spare pragmatism, while Barnhart's speaker is looking for something else, for a gap, a space that would elicit the desired communicational effect. That space is, of course, the space of the poem itself, a poem like 'What Being in the Army Did', for instance, that opens up what I have been calling an ironic space between that elusive, traumatic experience and the seemingly inadequate vocabulary.

* * *

It should be said that, aside from creating some distance between my own sense of post-war irony and the ways in which the term is generally used, there is also a need to create one other distinction that Weigl's comments regarding irony and war may elicit in the context of war and the writing of war. Perhaps most relevant in this regard is Fussell's treatment of the concept in his seminal work on World War I poetry, in which irony is, to a great extent, the essence of modern war. Fussell provides several ways in which irony and war are related, such as his comment: 'Every war is ironic because every war is worse than expected. Every war constitutes an irony of situation because its means are so melodramatically disproportionate to its presumed ends.'[12] Fussell seems to claim here that war is essentially ironic, hinting at a basic structural or situational absurdity that marks its irony. It is, however, the effect this irony has on the way soldiers speak and write which I shall focus on here. Elsewhere in his work, Fussell refers to one type of ironic effect in which British soldiers, dealing with harrowing, dehumanising violence, received speedily arriving letters and packages from home. Fussell indicates that this duality was part of what 'makes experience in the Great War unique and gives it a special freight of irony [. . .] the ridiculous proximity of the trenches to home'.[13] Fussell mentions yet another case of ironic duality via 'a curious prophylaxis of language', related both to an idea of a blurred 'security' and to how a loss of said security could result in linguistic confusion: 'One could use with security words which a few years later, after the war, would constitute obvious *double entendres*.'[14] Fussell's comment juxtaposes two elements having to do with language use after war that seem to echo Weigl's earlier remark: while the Vietnam veteran and poet spoke of irony replacing life, Fussell points at an irony created where 'security' once was. Again, as with Weigl, irony comes to prominence when concepts such as 'life' or 'security' are destabilised. Once the certainty, control and order of the world are pulled away from a life, the poet, with as with J. Hillis Miller's example of Wallace Stevens, has to 'walk barefoot into the world'.[15] Irony, I would argue, is born out of this void, not as an attempt to reinstate a new and ordered system in place of the old (such as a turn toward nihilism, pantheism or relativism, to name but a few) but as a means of both mourning and living, of expressing impossibility and necessity at one and the same time – of opening a fictive space of possibility.

The irony I am reaching for here, however, in the context of the form of life of war, and, as I shall extrapolate in the following section, in the inner workings of those poetic prostheses created after war, is discussed only as far as it can be seen and analysed in the poetry written after war. To put this another way, the discussion, while leaning on an idea of irony as inherent to war, does not include those soldiers who do not write poetry after war, and who most obviously make up the majority of the veteran population. Some return home to a very normal life, some pursue a military career, all the while never feeling the need to address their experiences through verbal art. How, one could ask, does this fact sit with Weigl's comment about war teaching him irony? Are those soldiers turning to poetry the only ones affected by the difficult conflation in terms which I claim war creates and which I claim results in a kind of poetic response? The answer to that question seems to be two-sided. For one, the attempts to write poetry after war are the very source from which this notion of irony and an ironic prosthesis emanates. In other words, I am reading and thinking here through those who have addressed an issue with communication through their poetry. Thus, for the purposes of this argument, all that I need to show is that the poems that have been written function as poetic prostheses, constructed and assembled as an attempt to reconnect with language and community. But, on the other side, it would seem to me that hermetically limiting any hypothesis as to the more general effects of war on language dealt with here, as well as irony's place in this process, seems to miss the mark as well. It surely does not lie within the scope of this book to attempt to determine whether or not irony and ironic prostheses can be used in wider psychological or sociological terms. On the other hand, to claim that issues of communication affect only those who attempt to deal with them through poetry or the arts would be tantamount to claiming that Primo Levi was the member of a select group of Holocaust survivors who suffered a significant enough blow to language and representation, or that, as a writer, he was among the few affected by the horror of Nazi concentration camps. Within the very limited scope of this book, therefore, I would only go as far as saying that those soldier writers are not the only ones experiencing the profound linguistic difficulty which follows such events or happenings, since I see this place of scepticism as, whether unconsciously or consciously, essential to what we would call the experience of trauma.

On the other hand, we cannot dismiss the fact that claims regarding the linguistic effects of war or trauma are made and expound a general theory of, say, linguistic confusion, by a select few who were driven to write and sometimes publish a poetic response to this confusion. What those creating art are doing in the wake of war is not, thus, just reacting; rather, they are engaged in the act of living. Those living their lives, whether through agony or relief in the wake of war, and who do not produce artistic responses to that experience are those who can. A necessary addition to that statement, moreover, is the experience of those who cannot live life after war at all, also through the range of severe psychological conditions which may follow war and which are treated with therapy, medication and sometimes confinement. Those suffering from PTSD do not lead a normal post-war life, in a way that is painful to a degree most cannot imagine. And, of course, there are those who literally cannot live after war, with veterans, sometimes especially those on the younger side,[16] committing suicide.[17] So, perhaps going backwards, those who use language in order to indicate something about the limits of language, both in war and in everyday life, are those who cannot live without it.

Index–Symbol Irony

The form of life that is war, then, along with its embedded sense of symbolism and its unique mode of communication, is the backdrop against which soldiers experience what I have called the 'injury' to their ability to communicate. The connection between this injury and the choice of poetry as a means of addressing the post-war injury I have called indexical poetics is related to irony in two parallel ways. Firstly, the split between self and community is linked to certain concepts of split irony, such as those proposed by Schlegel and Kierkegaard, and, in return, to philosophy or art via *poesis*; and secondly, this so-called tension is somehow inherent to war and the wartime way or form of life. The term irony as it is used here is, as I have already stated, one of constant tension in relation to language – of a sense of its inherent unreliability, as a result of wartime experience, along with an urgent, existential need to communicate both that unreliability and the experiences that brought it about.

As such, however, irony, an infamously difficult concept to grapple with, cannot refer to the 'situational' and 'verbal' division offered up by D. C. Mueke in his book *The Compass of Irony*.[18] Perhaps mainly, this is because the very division Mueke applies is one between experience and the tool used to describe experience (situation versus language), and irony, as soldiers following war experience it, is precisely an unsettling of the ability to use one to describe the other. This unsettling, as previously argued, is based on a blurring of certain basic divisions or distinctions, some of which are essential to the experience of reliable, constant communication. The mode of witnessing created in the attempt to link oneself to such experiences while keeping one's distance, so to speak, is not unlike what Shoshana Felman describes as 'second-degree' witnessing in her chapter about Paul de Man's theoretical writings:

> Such second-degree testimony is complex and can no longer be direct. Because it seeks above all to preserve the distance necessary for the witnessing (the inner distance of the radical departure), it requires not the involved proximity of memory (that of the submersion of the witness) but the *distancing* of this submersion through the reflectiveness of *theory* . . . [N]ot (as some would have it) as a cover-up or a dissimulation of the past, but as an ongoing, active *transformation of the very act of bearing witness*.[19]

I would add that to be 'direct' about testimony is to be serious, to try to testify of a change in language while retaining the parameters and divisions that had been undone in war. And while these war poets do not distance themselves, as de Man did, through theory, in the same manner, they perform this preservation of distance through what I argue is the application of irony.

One instance of such ironic distancing is Ed Poynter's long poem 'Memories of War', written, as he states in his introduction, 'here and now (April 2012) as I stare at the screen of my desktop PC and find my thoughts drifting back to the summer of 2007 in Basra, Southern Iraq'.[20] A cataloguing of experiences, smells, names and places, 'Memories of War' presents irony not as purely situational or verbal, but as a condition of being in which experiences that disturb the ability to communicate leave one with what appears to be nothing more than a list of plain facts:

And the tastes and smells . . .
the acrid, searing smells.
Cordite.
Salt from sweat and dust.
Human waste and rotting vegetables.
Diesel.
Cigarette smoke.
Iron.
Burning plastic.
Watermelon.[21]

As with other poems discussed earlier, such as Chris from Kandahar's 'A Soldier's Winter' or Lynn Hill's 'Capacity', the listing of facts achieves a double purpose. The catalogue displays the ability to recognise, categorise and name, the performance of a now empty, passively observing sense of humanity, as well as the effort to resist an annihilating layer of reality aiming to end all differentiation and individuality, or, in Hill's case, her own undoing ('There's a limit to madness'). And it is this tundra of erasure that Poynter grapples with in the poem's final lines:

A catalogue of frozen tableaux and sensory collages.
But where did the laughter go?
Where are the fond remembrances?
Are these the feats to tell with advantages?
Where are the friends I lived and fought with?
We laughed through these experiences.
We cried through these experiences.
We drank tea and played chess.
We loved.
I lived!

Why does only this remain?[22]

Similarly to the previously discussed loss of 'life', or 'the sanctity of life', the speaker in Poynter's poem mourns the loss of 'laughter', 'friends' and eventually 'love' and 'life'. The separation of the indexical from the symbolic, in Peircean terms, the 'I' from the 'life', the 'we' from 'love', and the displaying of this severed or split self, to borrow another of Lacan's terms,[23] in material form or in writing is what could be called irony. The act of communication that is created in the wake of the understanding that 'only this remains' – the 'frozen tableau', comprised of fragmented images and sensations that tell nothing of the experience in a 'precise' manner – is, as I argue, inherently ironic and essentially disruptive to the situational and verbal designation of irony.

Irony, in this way – the spirit of the continuous degradation and resuscitation of meaning through a constant oscillation of meaning that stands at the heart of the poetic prosthesis – can be paralleled to Richard Rorty's use of the terms 'irony' and 'ironists'. In his *Contingency, Irony, and Solidarity* Rorty defines ironists as those who reserve a constant and basic doubt regarding what he calls the 'final vocabulary' – 'the words with which we tell, sometimes prospectively sometimes retrospectively, the story of our lives'.[24] As per my discussion of Wilfred Owen's preface in Chapter 2, this rejection is parallel to Owen's undermining of 'Poetry' as a means of describing war, a vocabulary that includes words such as 'true' and 'good', as well as 'England', 'kindness' and so on. Those who take up a sceptical position as to the ability to hold any set of final vocabularies reliably or definitely are ironists since they are 'never quite able to take themselves seriously because [they are] always aware that the terms in which they describe themselves are subject to change, always aware of the contingency and fragility of their final vocabularies, and thus of themselves'.[25] Obviously Rorty's position here is a philosophical one, perhaps even an ethical one – irony as a position of constant critique and instability, in that sense sharing the essence of what I refer to as the work of the poetic prosthesis – never sure, always limping, almost moving. And yet as opposed to the anxiety-filled version of that lack of assurance – hyper-vigilance, flashbacks, phantom pain – it is the kind of instability or oscillation that enables something new to sprout from its constant motion: language.

The concept of irony I suggest here could be described, if I may indulge in some explicit Peirceanisms, as the effect of the indexical ('real', situated, specific) and symbolic (general, communal) elements of language being made, artificially, to inhabit the same space and, sub-sequently, undermine their respective functions. Put simply, words that are usually meant as a kind of placeholder which no one really ques-tions or thinks about, words that refer to the place, time and speaker, for instance, suddenly become receptacles of unsaid meaning regarding the war experience. At the same time, words that are taken to mean things in the most general sense and are thus used frequently for community-based communication are suddenly exposed as arbitrary or at the very least unstable – 'The war took my life' or 'I died in Auschwitz'. As both processes take place simultaneously, something new rises out of that motion, which is that object we may call the poetic, the 'dream' or the prosthetic. The ironic effect, then, is a destabilisation of the manner with which these signs operate, so as to maintain, to a point, their so-called main function, much as soldiers maintain the ability to name and report, all the while subverting that same ability, bringing about an indeterminate vibration or oscillation of meaning. This subversion, again, does not completely topple the respective meaning; nor does it entirely shift the function of indices and symbols, if for the very fact that this form of poetic communicative irony is meant, despite its own scepticism regarding communication, to communicate precisely that inability through a placing of objects in a new set of relations. A distance, or tension, is kept between the speaker and his means of communication, in a way, however, that includes both in the same structure – specifically, in the same place, at the same time. This is to maintain, as Felman writes, the ironic or poetic distance of Ishmael floating to life on a coffin, as opposed to the very real, ontological and fatal finality or lack of movement that is Ahab's final and fatal attachment to the white whale.[26]

An arresting example of this force at action, of the push-and-pull of meaning within the ironic space of the poetry, is yet another poem by Graham Barnhart. In 'Everything in Sunlight I Can't Stop Seeing' Barnhart beautifully sketches the outlines of index–symbol irony by using the indexical 'in me' as a way to locate war following the return home. Returning soldiers, to reiterate, are alienated from their home environments and from themselves, feeling dead while surrounded by life, real while surrounded by fake and so on. In the following example, then, Barnhart indexically locates the war experience in the only space it exists at home: him. Dedicating the poem to Bruce Weigl, to whom I have devote the majority of this current chapter, Barnhart writes:

I fry an egg over easy, and eat it
between two slices of wheat toast.
Through the kitchen window I watch a workman
prying up the old street.
Brittle sparks
jump from the brick top when he strikes it.
Or it's the shovel tip scoured to chrome
bouncing off the clay.
I leave my sister's house,
and the intersection transformer is still
humming somehow. I'm used to the electricity
quieting in the wire when the sun
scrapes its knee bloody up the porch step.

> I walk beneath the orange
> fluorescent street lamps
> and the white fluorescent street lamps turning
> the air around themselves resinous
> with bluing rings like flooded drainage ditch
> ripples around dropped earrings.
> Tree branches, black
> in the dawn sky, resume their grays and browns
> by lunch, but the black wrought fences continue
> leaning into their rust, rigid and failing.
> —there is no war in this but me.[27]

The poem is mostly taken up by seemingly mundane depictions of every-day life as they appear through the speaker's view, or through a kitchen window in his 'sister's house', an everydayness disrupted only somewhat through the tense, violent tone of some of its detail, most notably the sun's 'bloody' knee. Again a relation is set up, one in which the speaker viewing life from the window serves as one pole and the outside world as the other, the latter characterised by a steady, dumb continuity – the branches that 'resume their grays and browns' and the fences that 'con-tinue leaning into their rust'. This is a world of constants, of continu-ity, of cyclic change. All these images, however, are then drained, to use Barnhart's word, into the indexical 'this' in the poem's final line. 'This', in other words, meaning 'everything just described as continuing', is then immediately countered with 'me' – war cannot be seen or read in any of these features and aspects, and one would not be blamed for miss-ing war in that landscape, for it simply is not there. Where it is present, however, is in 'me'.

Indices, as just seen in Barnhart's poem, become impregnated with seemingly unsayable meaning, and are often used in the poems under discussion as markers for the wartime or post-war upheaval as a whole or as the generators of tension between wartime experiences and post-war reality. In other words, the case of soldiers' post-war poetry, whereof one cannot speak, to paraphrase Wittgenstein, is often pointed toward with an index. That is the case in Poynter's poems discussed above ('Why does only *this* remain?'); in Currall's 'Burying the Dead' ('Get on with *it*'); Croft's 'When the Men Came Back' ('*It's* still *here*, 20 years on'); Chris in Kandahar's 'A Soldier's Winter' ('*This* isn't real *this* is only a dream') and so on. 'This', 'that', 'it', 'now', 'then' are all signs meant to attach, as per Peirce, abstract meaning to a specific subject, time and place, and yet as they are used in these poems, affected by this ironic tension, they seem to point at the very heart of that which the speaker cannot put into words. This effect of a nearly collapsing index, which, at the same time, both performs its function as existential anchor and takes on an almost mystical breadth, recalls Agamben's discussion of Hegel's analysis of the possible meaning of the indexical *This* in the *Phenomenology of Spirit*. While writing, obviously, without direct reference to Peirce's work, which would appear later in the nineteenth century, Hegel writes of the possibility that *This* serves to indicate not a specific meaning but a kind of concrete nothingness:

> The This is, therefore established as *not* This, or as something superseded (*aufgehoben*); and hence not as Nothing, but as a determinate Nothing, the Nothing of the content, viz. of the This . . . *Suppression* [*das Aufheben*] exhibits its true twofold meaning which we have seen in the negative: it is at once a *negating* and a *preserving*. Our nothing, as the Nothing of the This, preserves its immediacy and is itself sensuous, but it is a universal immediacy.[28]

The 'determinate Nothing' Hegel writes of seems at least partially appropriate to the mode the index takes on in post-war soldier irony, in which indices indicate both the specificity (the 'here and now' of personal experience) and the vagueness or void ('get on with *it*'; 'only *this* remains'; and 'there is no war in *this*') that lies between indescribable personal experience and reportable community speak.

However, the impregnated index is only part of the ironic movement, providing a kind of framework of distance in which the prosthetic drama takes place. One other aspect, as indicated previously, is the draining or destabilising of symbolic meaning, the effective toppling of authority over language and meaning. This process can be seen in how irony twists the way in which we understand symbols, words whose meaning is generated by communal agreement. Meant to function, at least according to Peirce's analysis, as the more 'meaningful' or 'abstract' and conceptual parts of communication, these agreed-upon symbols are drained or bled of their meaning. Common victims of this subversion are the kinds of words or concepts most noticeably targeted by war poems in the last century or so. For Owen it was 'heroes', 'deeds', 'honour'; for Wittgenstein it was the words of metaphysics such as 'ethics', 'the feeling of being absolutely safe'; and, similarly, for the online writers discussed here it is 'healer', 'time', 'life', 'love' and others. A striking example of the way with which this destabilising oscillation takes place is, again, Mena's compelling poem 'So I Was a Coffin'. By attaching the symbolic and human ('life', 'meaning') to the indexical and non-human (indices, 'it', 'that'), Mena could be said to generate the kind of irony I have been referring to:

> I found a man. They said he died bravely, or he will. I encompassed him
> In my finished wood, and I shut my lid around us. As they lowered us
> Into the ground he made no sound because he had no eyes
> And could not cry. As I buried us in dirt we held our breaths together
> And they said, yes. You are a good coffin.[29]

Not only does the poet subvert or complicate the speaker's own human-ity by identifying it, like Melville's Ishmael, with an object of death – a coffin – but the poem also influences other symbolic and indexical aspects such as time. A possible reading of 'They said he died bravely, or he will' seems to attack the concept of bravery by suggesting that one does not die bravely at the time of one's death but, somehow, only later. In other words, that 'bravery' is an artificial add-on, a label placed by the community-based or communication-prone elements of society, not necessarily attached to the act of dying itself.

Destructive Irony, Constructive Irony

The oscillation that serves as the life force of the poetic prosthesis is, then, irony. It is at the core of the 'was and not was' paradox that hovers over the act of writing after war: I have to say it, it cannot be said; it happened, it couldn't have happened. The result is, again, a prosthetic aimed at regenerating movement, at re-enabling possibility and thus fracturing the painful and wordless solipsism of post-war life. And yet the idea of irony or movement or oscillation being a counter to that paralysis may not be the most immediate to those who are aware of the issues that plague war veterans, who seem to yearn, if anything, for a sense of stability amid post-traumatic unrest. To 'heal' from post-war pain, reason may have it, is tantamount to make 'it all' stop moving – to arrest the sense of a porous, parallel time in which flashbacks and hyper-vigilance make every moment charged with the possibility of Vonnegutian time travel, to stop the assault nightmares and obsessive thinking, and, generally, put an end to all the 'noise', to rid oneself of the constant hum of collapsing past and present, of a past violence and present paralysis. Brian Turner, in his aptly titled 'Phantom Noise', beautifully describes this idea of post-war mental 'noise':

> There is this ringing hum this
> bullet-borne language ringing

shell-fall and static this late-night
ringing of threadwork and carpet ringing
hiss and steam this wing-beat
of rotors and tanks broken
bodies ringing in steel humming these
voices of dust.[30]

I do recognise that this book offers very little by way of 'peace' or stability as understood by those who wish, understandably, for literal peace and quiet, for a space in which this 'noise' ceases completely. The constant movement of irony is work, which may seem a task too far for the already exhausted. And yet the poetic prosthetic offers, at least that is what it did for me and perhaps for others mentioned in this work, stability of a different kind, one in which the resumption of life and the ability to communicate with those around us involves action and movement. To consider the idea of the poetic prosthesis, then, is to reject the notion that the always-moving, always-shifting emotional experience is diametrically opposed to the goal of returning to life after war. There are, no doubt, ways of moving that are not of the oscillating, poetic kind I have discussed thus far and that are, for all intents and purposes, a moving away, a distancing of oneself that, I think, would not result in the same sense of regained agency, of the limp of walking back into life. And yet the transition, if I may, into the poetic is not such a shift, though it perhaps might seem that way – 'Why can't you just get over it and tell me what it was like?' To be ironic, in this regard, is to harness the movement of irony in order to talk about what war has done to you – not to run away, but to step closer.

The way irony is sometimes understood, as evasive, as a 'way out' of speaking directly, can be seen in one classic example of verbal irony given by Dan Sperber and Deirdre Wilson in their seminal 'Irony and the Use-Mention Distinction'.[31] In Sperber and Wilson's text one person, standing in the middle of the pouring rain, says to his friend: 'What lovely weather,' ostensibly as a way to point out that the weather is not 'lovely', thus communicating 'the weather is not lovely' in a roundabout way. To be ironic in this sense is to circumvent unnecessarily, or perhaps to be creative where one may have just been direct and said: 'Horrible weather.' However, as addressed above, the kind of ironic stance toward language found in post-war poetry is not of the sort in which one word is used to mean another. The issue, in other words, is not one of paraphrasing or euphemising but rather of exposing the distance between experience and communication, and doing so using *the only means of communication available*. This is not a vaguer, less direct way of saying things but one that sustains 'the inner distance of the radical departure', to reiterate Felman's phrase, from one's 'final vocabulary', as per Rorty's formulation. It is the kind of irony that is so closely associated with the creation of art in general, and the one that, at least in my experience, makes so many artists reluctant to talk about their work, feeling that the work had done 'all the talking'. It is the irony of creating an object that would serve as a particular instance of the state of mind or way of life that irony presents, which would expose a gap in language while using the material of language itself. That conception of irony, I would argue, as creating a space of possibility that is inherent to art is closer to the Romantic idea of irony, of the kind advanced, if not invented,[32] by German philosopher Friedrich Schlegel.

Romantic irony serves as the most relevant definition of an oscillating irony that I am thinking of here because it could be said to address the basic tension the wartime linguistic injury brings about: that an experience, fact or event is impossible to communicate and yet *must* be communicated. As such, it is an irony defined not as a rhetorical device but as an expression of an essentially split or oscillating stance toward or use of communication. As Schlegel writes in one of his most cited philosophical fragments:

> Irony sustains and provokes a feeling of the irresolvable conflict between the conditioned and the unconditioned, between the necessity and the impossibility of a complete communication. Irony is the freest of all forms of license since it allows one to go quite beyond oneself, but is equally the most binding since it is unconditionally necessary.[33]

Importantly, Schlegel's definition stresses not only the sense of a split communication but the fact that the gap that wartime experiences bring about is irreconcilable, much in the same way that Rorty describes the ironist's constant suspicion concerning their own final vocabulary. The discomfort of communication, one that I will later link to the discomfort of the prosthesis, remains a constant, unyielding characteristic. Irony, thus, at least as it is defined by Schlegel, is the rhetorical or poetic counterpart of the post-war experience of language: split, irresolvable, necessary and, as I will argue, ethical. Such a stance could be seen, for instance, in the attitude expressed in many of the post-war poems already discussed but notably in those composed by veterans of the Falkland War, who unfortunately have had more experience dealing with the persistence of the past, even thirty and forty years on. That attitude can be traced in Croft's previously discussed poem:

It's still here, 20 years on,
and every firework
that you casually let off
proves that time
is not a healer.[34]

It also is evident in another poem by Falklands War veteran, Tony McNally, titled 'PTSD', which ends thus:

I was 19 in June
Under a bright crystal moon
I died that day
But I'm still here to say
For the brave and the free.
My award – PTSD.[35]

Whatever it is that happened in war, designated, as it often is in these poems, by the index *it*, is, using a temporal–spatial index, 'still here'. The gap between experience and its communication, or the community, signified by 'you', persists, despite what the community considers to be true regarding wounds in general – that time 'heals' them. 'Heals', I would suggest, is in itself a suggestive word in this context, used to represent the communal expectation of 'healing'– that a healed body returns to a pre-injury state. That, however, according to the poem's speaker, and according to veterans' own reports over the years,[36] is not an option, since the gap still persists, even '20 years on'. The ethical aspect, to reiterate, is brought out by the stark difference between the manner in which the war veteran experiences fireworks – not necessarily believing they are bombs, but being unable to differentiate their detonation from the explosions of war – and the 'casual' manner attributed to the community and characteristic of those for whom the sense of language as a reliable communicator is intact. This is the gap not just between those with or without experience of violence, then, but between two types of speaking communities, using the same signs in a radically different manner.

This insistence on the ongoing, manageable and yet unhealable nature of the impossible/necessary gap in this understanding of irony marks what one might call the ethical aspect of what is a linguistic and aesthetic discussion. If irony is a gap that cannot be resolved in communication that is the essence of a mode of thinking or making art,[37] and one only communicable itself through a kind of ever-moving shift in meaning, then irony and the problem it presents mirror the unresolvable issue of the post-war wound. Thus, an attempt to close or resolve that gap would result not only in 'bad' art, from a Schlegelian point of view, but also in art that perpetuates the post-war mental split and that is, ultimately, unethical. Examples of non-ironic works such as these could include works of art with an explicit message to communicate, such as political art, propaganda; or, on the other hand, a kind of solipsistic artistic enterprise that avoids the issue of communication altogether (because it is either impossible or unimportant), and, from a reading point of view, the professed use of ideology as a decoding or interpreting mechanism. As Felman describes it in her discussion of Paul de Man, this means the kind of Ahab-like mode of 'direct', 'stable' and 'consistent' communication that latches on to the reality of the traumatic event to the point of absolute silence and, at times, death. This hardwired attachment to trauma and pain, one that seemingly forgoes the attempt to communicate and instead chooses somehow to represent trauma or safeguard trauma, I think, is something like war re-enactments or cosplay, in which participants literally repeat the past. And yet while this fidelity to pain indeed provides the stability that is in demand after war, it is seldom in itself a banishment of pain and at times serves as its escalation.

It seems worthwhile noting that the conception of art as provoking and sustaining tension is also related to more modern theories of art than Romantic poetry: namely, Russian formalists such as Viktor Shklovsky's notion of defamiliarisation[38] or Jan Mukařovský's 'foregrounding'.[39] In defamiliarisation, works of art create these gaps through the attempt to make words and concepts that have become 'habituated' in our use strange or unfamiliar. In the terms presented by Schlegel, the work of art, in accordance with Shklovsky's seminal 'Art as Technique', takes the communal, holistic, reliable or 'healthy' version of the object-word connection and makes it other-than-healthy. It does this not, again, by imagining an entirely different universe or by coining new terms as a way of bypassing an essential problem with communication, but by taking the same words, phrases, situations and events that have become habitualised and allowing them to emerge anew. Examples of this kind of move would be Currall's 'Burying the Dead', in which a specific idiomatic phrase, the poem's namesake, is broken down or defamiliarised, and Croft's challenging of the word 'heal' or defamiliarising of the habitualised experience of fireworks. Another pertinent example is Bernie Bruen's 'On Issue War Stock':

Slashed Survival-suits
Survived as slashed suits, not as
Suits/(slash)/Survival;

But a slashed Suit (survival)
As a Survival-suit (slashed)
Survives suitably
To splash below parachutes.[40]

One can imagine a form of life, one perhaps prior to Bruen's wartime experience, in which one could confidently, habitually or 'casually' utter the words 'survival suits'. However, as the poem seems to show, war experiences undermine that 'security', as survival suits neither survive nor ensure the survival of those wearing them. This may seem like a trivial discovery, since to be surprised that survival suits do not completely protect their wearer from harm seems extremely naïve – the survival suits, after all, do not *vouchsafe* survival. And to a degree, that statement seems to be true: no one wearing such a suit, one would think, believes it renders them immortal. What does take place is the slow degradation of the meaning of the word 'survival', one that may have wider linguistic consequences or, at the very least, point to the tenuous, unstable link between whatever it means to 'survive' or 'not survive' during and after war. What is more, these exercises, I would argue, do not demonstrate the absurd and complete negativity of irony as, say, a nihilistic practice geared at rendering all communication absurd or impossible but rather, firstly, enable a prosthetic, albeit uncomfortable and artificial contact with language, communication and society, as opposed to no communication at all (a solitary island); and secondly, create a work of art, a singular, material manifestation of an otherwise philosophical, solipsistic conundrum.

The ethical aspect of this insistence on such words as 'irresolvable' and 'sustained' is embedded in what I have discussed as 'being serious', or the 'stakes' involved in the creation of ironic prosthetic, perhaps related to Kant's evocation of the serious play in his analytics of the sublime:

> On the other hand, the feeling of the sublime is a pleasure that only arises indirectly, being brought about by a feeling of a momentary check to the vital forces followed at once by a discharge all the more powerful, and so it is *an emotion that seems to be no play, but a serious matter in the exercise of the imagination.*[41]

In poetry written by soldiers after war, as discussed in the previous chapters, the ethical aspect could be articulated like this: the gap between necessity and impossibility *ought* to be understood as a real one and one that has a real-life effect on the human being who created the object that is being understood as being ironic. In this form of the ethical, to reduce the ironic to any one pole, to close the gap that the poem seems to trace – Weigl is not serious about being dead, or Weigl is using the word 'dead' in a figurative way, or Currall is not serious when he discusses the phrase 'burying the dead' – is an unethical act. Taking a soldier's poem as pacifist in nature, via a political interpretation, or, inversely, stating that the same poem glorifies war and shows its necessary nature, is just as unethical. This notion of a gap as serious, at least in part, is linked with the fact that, at least for these soldier poets, it is experienced as a real, everyday problem and not an abstract exploration of the meaning of words and the ability to communicate. As Manfred Frank writes concerning Schlegel's concept of irony, seen thus, 'irony already gives evidence in this world for the truth of that which should be, which must, in the meantime, appear as nothingness'.[42]

Irony, in this sense, does not represent an attempt to disallow or hinder communication but rather an effort to communicate while evoking a relation of tension between what has to be said and what can be said, a tension that creates an empty space of fluctuating meaning. In other words, it is a relating not of words and their connection to things, a connection that is almost a habitual one by definition, but the enactment or the attempt to communicate relation. As Schlegel writes: 'Irony [is] merely the surrogate of that which should go into the infinite.'[43] This foundation is then taken up by Kierkegaard, who identifies Schlegel's irony as an offspring of the Socratic idea of irony, as taking nothingness 'seriously' by positing, or, more accurately, creating 'some-thing'. In other words, the very construction of a new object, with an understanding of nothingness as infinite possibility, is, in and of itself, an ironic gesture. To return to Kierkegaard's statement discussed earlier: 'Irony is the infinitely delicate play with nothingness, a playing which is not terrified by it but still pokes its head into the air.'[44] Irony, according to Kierkegaard's reading of Schlegel, is always a very 'serious' form of 'play', in which something new is posited, put forth as a physical object while in some way hovering between the impossibility of its very positing and the absolute necessity of the act of positing, as such. Referring to Hegel's famous criticism[45] of Schlegel's irony as destructive, Kierkegaard rejects the former's intimation that irony is the destructively frivolous play with meaning. What Schlegel, instead, is promoting, according to Kierkegaard, is that irony born out of taking both nothingness – or the inability to communicate – and something – the necessity to communicate – as seriously as possible, at one and the same time:

> It may therefore be said of irony that it is the seriousness with nothingness insofar as it is not the seriousness with something. It conceives nothingness continually in opposition to something, and in order to emancipate itself seriously [for seriousness] with something, seizes upon nothingness.[46]

It is for these reasons that I see Schlegel's comment on irony as, at the very least, interacting with the ethical, since his stance implies an ethical point regarding the inherent impossibility of the complete, unequivocal communication that is essential for the creation of art and, perhaps, as a human point of departure. That irony, again, *should/ought to* 'sustain' a gap between communication and experience. The significance of this conception of irony is threefold in terms of the veteran poetry that sits at the heart of my discussion. A direct implication of this proposed tie, furthermore, would be that the tension expressed in these poems is an ironic one, and that the irony manifest in the poems is one inherently tied to Schlegel's gap between the necessity of wartime events and experiences – they did, as far as the soldier is concerned, happen – and the seeming difficulty, perhaps impossibility, of conveying the *effect* these events had, or the significance they hold for the soldiers in question. Before moving on to discuss the function this sense of irony has not only for literary output after war but also for the wartime experience itself, I would like to address one last parallel between the Schlegelian and Kiekergaardian concept of irony to the poems analysed here: this is the notion of communication as conversation as opposed to transmission.

I would argue that a habitual, 'natural', reliable or casual use of language, the kind undone or shaken by war, is not predicated on conversation, *per se*, but on authority and, experienced within a military form of life, on transmission or reporting: words mean what they do, in other words, because you are told so. Successful communication under this linguistic model, one seemingly distilled to its purest form in the pragmatic terseness of military speech, would consist of using the precise labels to describe the objects and events associated with them, in an attempt to provide an accurate description of a certain state of affairs under the gaze of authority. This is the kind of thinking of communication, in other words, exemplified by the father's voice in Graham Barnhart's 'What Being in the Army Did': 'No, he said / there is definitely a word.' Language is used as a one-way tool, connected to things and events in the world only in that it names or describes them. However, the advent of injury or the experience of death in war shifts that understanding of words and what they do, if only for the basic reason that words fail in fulfilling their descriptive role regarding personal experience. Thus, aside from a changed, ironic take on language and its ability to transmit facts concerning personal experience, there is also the possibility that the attitude toward language seen in poems written after war also exhibits a move away from language as a tool for precise use ('there is definitely a word') and toward language as a tool of conversation or play.

Stressing the notion of irony and conversation, Schlegel frames irony as the natural ingredient of conversation, of a collective philosophical and artistic endeavour that strives toward the space of relation, as opposed to monolithic, solitary knowledge. Moreover, it is a conversation enacted through endless communal work,[47] 'a universal, infinitely progressive, living work which never achieves completion'.[48] In that way, irony, while sometimes interpreted as disrupting communication – for example, by claiming that poems are less communicative than everyday conversation – is a mode of conversation that aims to resist the expectation for an all-encompassing, accurate, holistic communication. As Maike Oergel writes, the ironic 'dynamic dialectical process is not so much the path to an eventual solution, but the main event itself'.[49] Interestingly, this concept of irony as essentially conversational is related to Peirce's definition of language as essentially conversational as well. Notably, this notion of communication and the infinite work of conversation, as opposed to the final work of scientific discourse, is, as Anne Freadman writes, also a hallmark of Peirce's endeavour to break down the kinds of signs we use in communication as such:

> Rather than being the form of the manifestation of the world to the mind, the 'sign' thereafter is Peirce's attempt to formalize the pertinent event unit of conversation. Signs matter in practice because signs are the matter of practice. Semiosis is the name of the process whereby, in practice, signs displace one another and are transformed. They do so through the interpretant, the point of mediation that orients toward their consequences, entailing their upshot with their uptake. In principle, this process is infinite.[50]

Perpetual movement is the seed of communication as well as its byproduct. So, when soldiers create ironic prosthesis, or poems, they are, taking both Peirce and Schlegel into account, initiating what they see as an 'honest' or 'real' conversation with their communities, one which reinstates the conversational seed – irony – as the governing factor. In other words, the only kind of knowledge that can and should be engaged in and transmitted – as much as possible – is the kind involved in constant conversation. Thus, it is the kind of conversation in which Kierkegaard's empty space serves as an enabling source, not subject, in which one points to certain kinds of facts – as do indices – without attempting to break them down hermetically or reductively.

Going back, then, to Peirce's analysis, ironic statements are attempts to communicate which express difficulty or challenge in dealing with an index–symbol tension. And this is precisely where this tension is at its most personal, since symbols represent meaning given by social contract and accepted by society ('apple', 'knife', 'hat', words that we understand to mean what they do because we are told so), while indices are those signs which point directly, sometimes physically, at a meaning that seems beyond social consent, at once personal, interpersonal and immediate. Thus, an irresolvable gap between symbol and index, in terms of real social communication or interaction between a personal subject and its society, means not only a language gap between that person and its society, and a real one as well, but also one that, somehow, changes the way one sees language as operating. It is a change, basically, between thinking events are communicated and thinking events and communication stand on both sides of an irresolvable tension – are, in fact, changes in the way one sees oneself as related to communication and society at large. But, more than just giving a theoretical concept to this gap, this ever-moving conception of irony, together with Peirce's analysis, enables a demarcation of the poems discussed in this book by eliminating those works or attitudes which quite conceivably could arise in the wake of war and in response to the communication issues war raises but that would not be considered ironic. This is because, I argue, the 'irrevocability' Schlegel speaks of can come into view only when an attempt to communicate it is undertaken. Put differently, soldiers who chose to remain silent cannot be said to be partaking of an ironic mode of communication, simply because there is no communication to speak of.

However, on the other side, perhaps more vaguely, lie those soldiers who do write poetry concerning their wartime experiences only in an entirely 'indexical' manner, using words that stress only private and incommunicable experiences. I do not mean 'private' in the sense of displaying one's personal use of a commonly employed word or phrase, but the kind of attempt at a description of a private experience which, to an extent, disregards the existence of an addressee. In this case, thus, no communication is attempted, and thus the 'impossibility' of communication is avoided. In other words, poems written in the wake of war are, by the very attempt to write down experiences which seem to evade comprehensive communication, ironic in and of themselves.

It is when that irony is seen as the driving force of these poems, and not just its major obstacle, that they serve the function of prosthesis.

* * *

Despite the centrality of the conversational element of both irony and Peirce's notion of language, note must be taken of what can be called the limits of irony: namely, the danger of irony stagnating as dogma, and the role such terms as 'prosthesis', 'artificiality' and 'discomfort' have in maintaining irony's inherent tension – in other words, the possibility of attributing a conceptual stability to what is in reality a constant flux and tension. This would be the place to discuss briefly Hegel's famous warning against irony for irony's sake, the danger that the notion of an irresolvable tension itself could be read or understood as a solution to that tension. Perhaps paradoxically, the very attempt to provoke and sustain a gap between the impossible and necessary could, in and of itself, close that gap, perhaps in situations where the ironist herself detaches from Schlegel's perpetual conversation and sinks into ironic solipsism. This is an issue directly taken up by Hegel in the *Aesthetics*:

> In that case, he who has reached this standpoint of divine genius looks down from his high rank on all other men, for they are pronounced dull and limited, inasmuch as law, morals, etc., still count for them as fixed, essential, and obligatory. So then the individual, who lives in this way as an artist, does give himself relations to others: he lives with friends, mistresses, etc.; but, by his being a genius, this relation to his own specific reality, his particular actions, as well as to what is absolute and universal, is at the same time null; his attitude to it all is ironical.[51]

In what I consider to be another warning against a dogmatic reliance on 'distrust' as replacing the dogmatism of 'trust', Maurice Blanchot writes:

> Trust–distrust in language is already fetishism; it amounts to choosing a particular word in order to play on it with the delight and the malaise of the perversion that always assumes a straight, if hidden, usage. But writing: the detour that would disqualify the right to any language at all (even to a twisted, anagrammatized one) – the detour of inscription (which is always description) . . . Writing, friendship for the ill-come unknown, for the 'reality' that cannot be made evident and that escapes every possible utterance.[52]

Hegel's criticism and Blanchot's caveat highlight the importance of Schlegel's emphasis on both the provocation of irony, which seems to be the point Hegel is aiming for, and its sustaining: a sustaining which brings together seemingly disparate parts – rationality, mythology – in order to create a limping, ironic whole.

However, since irony, as it has been explored here, is manifest in a split mode of communication, one doubtful as to the ability to communicate, then that element preventing it from slipping into dogma is what could be called its artificiality or element of discomfort. Writing of Schlegel's irony, David Kaufer states that it is 'not simply an artificial device invented by a speaker or writer, but an outlook of detachment'.[53] I would insist, nonetheless, on precisely this artificiality: not, perhaps, artificiality as it is used here, one similar to Hegel's notion of an unfettered, destructive and counterfactual element, but artificiality in the way that life with the prosthesis is always a life experienced as sustained by means other than life. It is only when one uses and reads irony as not only an expression of detachment but also an expression of discomfort with the tool invented to deal with that detachment that free, undogmatic irony takes form. Dogma is the subsuming of the artificial element into an organic self without this experience of discomfort or tension, the creation, as I shall explore in the section on prosthesis, that post-humanists such as Bernard Stiegler, discussed in Chapter 1, have dubbed a cyborg. As I have already argued, this dogmatic subsuming of the prosthetic ignores the discomfort of existing as a cyborg. That stump, however, persists, as these poems have shown, along with its discomfort, phantom pains and, finally, the prostheses it necessitates.

Notes

1. Weigl, *The Circle of Hahn*, 5–6.
2. Leed, *No Man's Land*, 28.
3. Don Fowler, 'Postmodernism, Romantic Irony, and Classical Closure', in *Modern Critical Theory and Classic Literature*, edited by Irene J. F. De Jong and J. P. Sullivan (Amsterdam: Brill, 1994), 233.
4. Charlotte Delbo, *Auschwitz and After*, translated by Rosette C. Lamont (New Haven, CT: Yale University Press, 1995), 267.
5. Kierkegaard, *The Concept of Irony*, 265.
6. Ibid., 286–7.
7. Wills, *Prosthesis*, 143.
8. Fussell, *The Great War and Modern Memory*, 27.
9. Kierkegaard, *The Concept of Irony*, 56–7.
10. Graham Barnhart, 'What Being in the Army Did', *Beloit Poetry Journal* 69, no.1 (Spring 2019): 22.

11. Ibid., 23–4.
12. Fussell, *The Great War and Modern Memory*, 7.
13. Ibid., 64.
14. Ibid., 23; emphasis in the original.
15. J. Hillis Miller, *Poets of Reality: Six Twentieth-Century Writers* (Cambridge, MA: Harvard University Press, 1966), 7–8.
16. Kara Zivin, H. Myra Kim, John F. McCarthy, Karen L. Austin, Katherine J. Hoggatt, Heather Walters and Marcia Valenstein, 'Suicide Mortality Among Individuals Receiving Treatment for Depression in the Veterans Affairs Health System', *American Journal of Public Health* 97, no. 12 (December 2007): 2193–8.
17. Herbert Hendin and Ann Pollinger Haas, 'Suicide and Guilt as Manifestations of PTSD in Vietnam Combat Veterans', *American Journal of Psychiatry* 148, no. 5 (May 1991): 586–91.
18. Douglas Colin Muecke, *The Compass of Irony* (London: Methuen, 1969), 42.
19. Felman and Laub, *Testimony*, 140; emphasis in the original.
20. Ed Poynter, 'Memories of War', *War Poetry Website*. The version of the poem that includes the author's comments is no longer available due to changes to the *War Poetry Website* (last accessed 2013). The poem itself can be found on the *LiveJournal* website. Available at: <https://war-poetry.livejournal.com/693813.html> (last accessed 24 February 2022).
21. Ibid.
22. Ibid.
23. Jacques Lacan, 'The Subversion of the Subject and the Dialectic of Desire in the Freudian Unconscious', in *Écrits*, translated by Bruce Fink (New York: W. W. Norton, 2001), 678, 691.
24. Richard Rorty, *Contingency, Irony, and Solidarity* (Cambridge: Cambridge University Press, 1999), 73.
25. Ibid., 73–4.
26. Felman and Laub, *Testimony*, 137.
27. Graham Barnhart, 'Everything in Sunlight I Can't Stop Seeing', *The Iowa Review* 47, no. 1 (Spring 2017).
28. G. W. F. Hegel, *Hegel's Phenomenology of Spirit*, translated by A. V. Miller (Oxford: Clarendon: 1977), 68. Cited in Agamben, *History and Infancy*, 14–15.
29. Mena, *The Shape of Our Faces No Longer Matters*, 55.
30. Brian Turner, 'Phantom Noise', from *Phantom Noise* (Farmington, ME: Alice James Books), 35.
31. Dan Sperber and Deirdre Wilson, 'Irony and the Use-Mention Distinction', *Radical Pragmatics*, edited by P. Cole (New York: Academic Press, 1981), 295–318.
32. Maike Oergel, *Culture and Identity: Historicity in German Literature and Thought 1770–1815* (Berlin: Walter de Gruyter, 2006), 82.
33. Friedrich Schlegel, *Philosophical Fragments*, translated by Peter Firchow (Minneapolis: University of Minnesota Press, 1991), 13. Cited in Bubner, *The Innovations of Idealism*, 209.
34. Croft, 'When the Men Came Back'.

35. Tony McNally, 'PTSD', *War Poetry Website*. Available at: <https://www.warpoetry. uk/falklands-war-1982> (last accessed 24 February 2022).

36. See, for example, Tracy Karner, 'If Only Time Healed all Wounds: Post Traumatic Stress Disorder in Older Men', *Generations: Journal of the American Society on Aging* (Spring 2008): 82–7; and Charles R. Figley and Seymour Leventman, *Strangers at Home: Vietnam Veterans Since the War* (New York: Routledge, 1980).

37. Lowry Nelson, Jr, 'Romantic Irony and Cervantes', in *Romantic Irony*, edited by Fredrick Garber (Budapest: Akadémiai Kiadó, 1988), 17.

38. Victor Shklovsky, 'Art as Technique', in *Russian Formalist Criticism: Four Essays*, translated and edited by Lee T. Lemon and Marion J. Reiss (Lincoln: University of Nebraska Press, 1965), 3–24.

39. Mukařovský, 'Standard Language and Poetic Language', 226.

40. Nigel 'Bernie' Bruen, 'On Issue War Stock'.

41. Immanuel Kant, *The Critique of Judgment*, translated by James Creed Meredith (New York: Oxford University Press, 2007), 75–6.

42. Manfred Frank, *The Philosophical Foundations of Early German Romanticism*, translated by Elizabeth Millan-Zaibert (Albany: State University of New York Press, 2004), 218.

43. Friedrich Schlegel, *Kritische Friedrich-Schlegel-Ausgabe*, vol. 18, edited by Ernst Behler (Munich: F. Schöningh, 1963), 112, no. 995. Cited in Manfred Frank, *The Philosophical Foundations of Early German Romanticism*, 218.

44. Kierkegaard, *The Concept of Irony*, 286–7.

45. Jeffrey Reid, *The Anti-Romantic: Hegel Against Ironic Romanticism* (London: Bloomsbury, 2014), 9–10.

46. Kierkegaard, *The Concept of Irony*, 287.

47. Daniel Dahlstorm, 'Play and Irony: Schiller and Schlegel on the Liberating Prospects of Aesthetics', *The History of Continental Philosophy, Volume I*, edited by Alan Schrift (Chicago: University of Chicago Press, 2011), 108.

48. Reid, *The Anti-Romantic*, 122.

49. Oergel, *Culture and Identity: Historicity in German Literature and Thought 1770–1815*, 82.

50. Freadman, *The Machinery of Talk*, xxv–xxvi.

51. G. W. F. Hegel, *Aesthetics: Lectures on Fine Art*, translated by T. M. Knox (Oxford: Oxford University Press, 2010), 65–6.

52. Maurice Blanchot, *Writing of Disaster*, translated by Ann Smock (Lincoln: University of Nebraska Press, 1995), 38.

53. David Kaufer, 'Irony and Rhetorical Strategy', *Philosophy and Rhetoric* 10, no. 2 (Spring 1977): 91.

CHAPTER 5

The Prosthesis and Burial,
Or Caring for the Dead

Those whom they caught in the daytime were slain in the night, and then their bodies were carried out and thrown away, that there might be room for other prisoners and the terror that was upon the people was so great, that no one had courage enough either to weep openly for the dead man that was related to him, or to bury him; but those that were shut up in their own houses could only shed tears in secret, and durst not even groan without great caution, lest any of their enemies should hear them for if they did, those that mourned for others soon underwent the same death with those whom they mourned for. Only in the nighttime they would take up a little dust, and throw it upon their bodies; and even some that were the most ready to expose themselves to danger would do it in the daytime and there were twelve thousand of the better sort who perished in this manner.

— Josephus Flavius[1]

In his discussion of the centrality of memory or memorising in the art of rhetoric in *De Oratore*, Cicero details the myth of the invention of the art of memory, or mnemonics. In the tale, the Greek poet Simonides, from the island of Keos, is performing at the home of local nobleman Scopas. Following his performance, Simonides is suddenly beckoned outside; once he is out of the house, the entire structure collapses, killing everyone inside, including Scopas, his family and all of his guests. The ensuing aftermath brought a quite unique problem, to which Simonides' art of memory provided the solution:

When their friends wanted to bury them but were altogether unable to know them apart as they had been completely crushed, the story goes that Simonides was enabled by his recollection of the place in which each of them had been reclining at table to identify them for separate interment.[2]

The myth of Simonides, which, I must admit, has fascinated me and continues to fascinate me, and of which I have written in the past in a somewhat different context,[3] posits a few characteristics of the work of memory and how it intercedes in the work of the poet or artist. One of those characteristics is the poet's relationship to history. While history, and specifically disaster, aim to eradicate human life and human difference – history and war as impersonal mass graves of memory – the writer aims to reassert identity and individuality in the wake of disaster. In Simonides' tale, what I call history is the collapsing roof that shockingly and suddenly erupts in the middle of everyday life and crushes men and women to a consistent, homogenous and undifferentiated human pulp. The role of the poet is, then, to turn that homogenous mass into an account of personal, identifiable lives, one that also enables the act of memorialisation and burial.

One way to counter this erasing of memory is, again, poetry, and perhaps more fundamentally, writing as induced by and shaped by the call of memory – one can even think of the poetic form itself as inherently related to memory, with rhythm and rhyme traditionally used as ways in which long texts could be committed to memory. As writing is that force which etches difference into the blankness of a white page, writing is also the revival of difference from the homogenous ashes of history, to successfully, effectively and, dare I say, beautifully revive those lost to history back to their differentiated, human state, if only for the sake of a proper burial and commemoration. In the case of the myth of Simonides, this is the demarcation of human difference from the collapsed roof of disaster. And within that ancient tradition in which poetry serves to remember and, in a way, bury the dead, or at the very least enable individual mourning, one has only to return to the text that stands at the heart of Weil's investment in Force, the *Iliad*, to notice the striking abundance of personal information, whether names, birthplaces or family ties, that is provided regarding the war dead. Among the countless dead named and either symbolically or literally buried are such major figures as Patroclus, whose death sent his friend Achilles into the fever of battle in search of vengeance, and Hector, to name but a few. But one standout example of the lesser-known men memorialized in Homer's text is the Trojan warrior Ilioneus, briefly discussed earlier. True to the spirit of the role the poetic has in burial, Ilioneus's death is given a time and place, along with a graphic depiction of its manner, as well as information regarding his family. As Peneleos hurls his spear at Acamas the Trojan, Ilioneus is killed in the confusion of battle:

This man's father was Phorbas, whom Hermes loved
More than any other Trojan and who had the flocks

> And wealth to prove it, but only one child,
> Ilioneus. Peneleos' spear
> Went through his eye socket, gauging out the eyeball,
> And going clear through the nape of the neck.[4]

While the *Iliad* is often noted for the sheer immensity of its scope, being the narrative of a decade-long military conflict involving thousands of combatants, this excerpt highlights Homer's investment in the role of burier and commemorator. I mean this not just in the sense of placing the dead body in a marked grave, for there are very few distinguished soldiers to be granted that kind of honour, Hector being the noted exception, but in the kind of poetic commemoration through both indexical and symbolic aspects. It may be called indexical not least because Ilioneus is named but also as Homer describes the indexical force of war: the spear as it violently enters Ilioneus's body. And it is a depiction involving the symbolic or communal as well: the spear-punctured body of the young warrior as belonging to a specific family or community.

Thus, while famously rejecting the Homeric tradition for what was perceived as its rhetorical power over enthusiastic young men edging towards battle and the heroism battle will afford them, it seems that the Trench Poets included in that rebellion another Homeric aspect of post-war poetry – that of specific memorialisation. And it is the spirit of this memorialisation that makes a bold return, I would argue, in the war writing of modern and contemporary writers, a result also, as I have mentioned, of the changing demographics and socio-economic makeup of the American and British militaries. That change, it should be noted, was not sudden but took place over time, and had already shown its effects in post-Second World War and post-Vietnam soldier literature that did, in fact, name the dead much more prominently than post-First World War writings, with noted examples including Kurt Vonnegut's *Slaughterhouse Five* and Tim O'Brien's *The Things They Carried*. The appeal to the memory of the dead, as I will discuss in this chapter, forms a brand of interpersonal, interdependent relations between the returning, grieving soldier and the war dead. This care for the dead may have been sustained throughout the war-writing tradition but has shifted radically in contemporary war writing – from the memory of kings to an almost folk commemoration of individual soldiers.

In *The Disarticulate* James Berger addresses what he sees as the need to engage with both trauma and disability in order to gain a view of the experience of living with disability, whether through a focus on personal pain and a personal past or the social marginalisation and oppression of the disabled. This interweaving of pain and community, trauma and disability, can be described as a kind of codependency or oscillation, not unlike, I believe, the codependency of index and symbol that stands at the heart of what I have been calling prosthetic poetics. The personal experience of pain, the index, evades direct representation as well as participating in the generation of representation through its relationship or interdependence with the symbol. However, this sense of interdependence, in this case theoretical, is part of a larger theme for Berger, which he discusses in terms of care. In other words, the never-ending conversations that post-war poems initiate are part of a community of reading and writing, and thus a form of interpersonal interdependence and mutual care.

Care, as Berger argues, has long been a fraught concept in certain areas of disability studies, relevant to this discussion since, by definition, those soldiers who require a poetic prosthesis are also those marked by disability and pain. And the reason that 'care' has been the source of such controversy is the claim that any care-based relationship is inherently hierarchical and oppressive, in that it involves the person who is cared for being deprived of their rights and autonomy. There is much in this criticism that is intertwined in a wider struggle against social oppression and marginalisation and is the hallmark, as I have already discussed, of a certain strand of disability studies that places the field squarely within other identity-based social critiques. And there is little doubt that some of that criticism seems poignant in the case of war veterans who shy away from any understanding of their situation as that of 'victims' or 'dependents', to the degree that some of those who participated in a study of post-Vietnam PTSD, sensing that they had failed to 'provide' for their families, cut ties with them entirely in an attempt to save face.[5] And yet beyond issues of masculinity or personal agency, some in the field have also been concerned with a power dynamic of a moral or metaphysical nature.[6] To be 'taken care of', in other words, means the relinquishing of agency and acceptance of submission.

Writing of the need to deconstruct the notion of care in terms of feminist critique, for example, Rosemarie Garland-Thomson says: 'This ethic of care contends that caregiving is a moral benefit for its practitioners and for humankind. A feminist disability studies complicates both the feminist ethic of care and liberal feminism in regard to the politics of care and dependency.'[7] In their respective work on a related concept, 'compassion', Marjorie Garber, Candace Vogler and Lauren Berlant discuss the inherent condensation and inequality of compassion, and the sense in which it creates a slanted relationship of control of the 'compassionate' over others conceived as weaker or disabled.[8] For Vogler, moreover, a direct line runs between compassion, conservatism and colonialism,[9] an argument to which I shall return in the conclusion to this book. As Berlant writes: 'In operation, compassion is a term denoting privilege: the sufferer is *over there*. You, the compassionate one, have a resource that would alleviate someone else's suffering.'[10]

However, Berger, through a reading Martha Nussbaum's and Eva Kittay's writings on care, argues that the idea of care as hierarchical and, ultimately, oppressive is rooted in the ideal of the autonomous individual, which, I would argue, is not far removed from the ideal I discussed in the previous chapter of an autonomously operating, perfectly transparent language. According to John Rawls's concept of autonomy,[11] the subject of critique by both Nussbaum[12] and Kittay,[13] the autonomous and completely independent subject is the primary condition for any wilful engagement into contractual relations with others and with society; given that disabilities prevent such autonomy, any contract with persons with disability is, in fact, a legalised form of oppression and divestment of rights. Basing his conceptualisation on Nussbaum's and Kittay's critique of Rawls's notion of autonomy as a pre-condition for entering the social contract, Berger argues instead for a social model based on codependency, one that enables a conception of care that is not strictly hierarchical and that would not deprive the disabled of their rights and autonomy. As Berger writes,

> Autonomy – in effect, invulnerability – cannot, in Nussbaum's and Kittay's views, be the basis for social standing. There must, rather, be a way to articulate social–ethical status that does not derive from the contract and that takes account of the full nature of human interdependence, vulnerability, and finitude.[14]

So, what disability and care highlight, according to Berger's reading of Nussbaum and Kittay, is not the vulnerability of the disabled subject to oppression but the inherent interdependence in any human relation, which seems connected with what I have discussed as the inherently interdependent nature of communicating – language as conversation – in the previous chapter. This is not the grounds to invalidate or marginalise, but a reminder of the power of care: 'Disability of this sort, then, in Nussbaum's view, does not make someone less human, less a valid subject for ethical treatment. But it does place in the foreground the reality of dependence and the need for care.'[15]

I would like, however, to engage with Berger's foregrounding of the centrality of interdependence and care with a social–personal understanding of disability in the realm of memory and the dead. For now, this will not be a discussion about how the community can enter into a relationship of care with war veterans. In a way, that theme dominates, or perhaps underlies, this book as a whole – providing tools to understand what soldiers communicate to their community after war, and preparing the ground for the two to change each other, as well as Peirce's own emphasis on language being, first and foremost, a social tool meant for interpersonal communication. In other words, what binds many of the thrusts presented in this book is, in a sense, a rejection of the kind of autonomy politics Nussbaum, Kittay and Berger critique, and, in its stead, offering an understanding of disability as involved in interdependence: the interdependence of language, being a social tool of communication; the interdependence of the prosthesis, in its marking of an experience of dependence on an object, an interdependence of returning veterans and their home communities; and, as I shall discuss in this chapter, an interdependence of the living and the dead. Put otherwise, the themes explore the way that the burial of the dead and the resulting text mirror the internal mechanism, discussed in previous chapters, of an index that is, so to speak, buried only to transform into language or poetry: 'The war took my life and gave me poetry instead.'

What I would like to focus on in these next few pages, however, is centred around the brand of care that war veterans take of their dead comrades and those otherwise silenced by what Weil calls Force. Specifically, I mean the ways in which the poetic prostheses that are constructed after war, and which enable their creators to limp back into language, also fulfil the function of caring for the bodies of those completely annihilated by war and provide them with a proper burial. In addition, this chapter will also discuss one noted effect of this instance of care: namely, how the impulse to remember and bury the dead results in a kind of burial of a former self, one that results in the transformation of the index of past pain into an icon of art and performance. In other words, I will explore the transformation of the index from anchor to artifice that takes place, as I have argued in previous chapters, on the semiotic level as well as in the content of the poems themselves, as, time and again, veterans gain a new sense of personal and artistic agency as a result of their desire to care for the bodies of the war dead. The performance of burial is understood, then, in two significantly different ways: firstly, the burial and thus commemoration of those killed in war, and who, deprived of a 'proper burial', stand to be forgotten; and secondly, the burial of the 'dead inside' writer or speaker. On the one hand, the retracing of individual names and lives from the ambiguous and annihilatory fog of war is a skill that requires the kind of fidelity to detail and facts we would associate with historical or documentary works. On the other, a creative gesture of letting go of a former self in favour of a fabricated, dramatised and prosthetic self. And it is in this difference in the action involved in each one of those attempts, woven together in the fabric of the post-war literary text itself, that one sees the two rhetorical poles at work: the historical and the poetic.

The burial of others, firstly, is marked by a recurring reference to indices of 'factuality' or 'historiography', such as names, places and units of precise measurement, all geared towards faithfully locating and burying the body of individual soldiers and civilians. In this aspect of post-war writing facts are used to affix, to use Peirce's term, indexically the work of art to a concrete time and place, thus encouraging personal commemoration. In many ways, moreover, the function of Peirce's index in sign systems is precisely the function of 'facts', 'names' and 'numbers' in post-war writing: the pinning down of an almost abstracted, larger-than-life historical event such as war to a particular life and that particular moment in which that life ended. To produce a moment of specificity, as opposed to monolithic death, then, one has to mark the place and time of death: not historically by way of depicting the grand movement of troops in battle, nor commemorating a more general 'those who had lost their lives at war', but via an almost forensic work of history aimed at etching the right name and the right date on a tombstone that is placed above the right body. And it is this axis of the rhetoric of post-war writing that also bears its moral onus, and is most closely associated with the guilt of survival and the ethical obligation to remember those who did not. It is this element that LaCapra describes as 'fidelity to trauma' and which Weigl called his 'fate' following his return from Vietnam. To speak of the dead is therefore a moral mission and an obligation, one tied to the shameful fact of having survived what others have not, as well as to the imperative to speak 'precisely' regarding the fate of others. This preciseness is abundantly apparent in contemporary works of American and British soldier writers. The rhetoric of self-burial, however, is informed not by the language of facts *per se*, but by the power at the disposal of soldier writers to craft their poetic prosthesis to suit their own needs. This, as I shall discuss, manifests itself as a weaponisation, if I may use that word, of metaphor and figurative language or certain structural and formal gestures, such as repetition, line length and more. The effect of the dual process initiated in burying others and oneself is thus equally double: both burial of a former self, and the sense of artistic release and freedom that burial triggers.

In order to understand the significance of burial after war, however, a brief classification is needed of the two seemingly opposing states this chapter discusses. The first is that of the unmarked or mass grave, defined, I would argue, by the threat of the loss of identity and memory after death. That definition includes, as I have mentioned, the lack of a 'proper' burial but also those burial sites that erase the individual identity of those buried or subsumes it in the name of unified, monolithic commemoration – from mass graves to data sheets compiling the numbers of the dead. This image, perhaps nightmare, of forgetting can be represented as a homogenous mass threatening to wipe out the traces of the deceased, both literally and figuratively, whether in the form of the land in which the unidentified body rots, the water into which it disappears, the mass grave – as in the myth of Simonides, as well as the excerpt from Josephus Flavius's *The Jewish War* that opens this chapter – or the monolithic national monument. Together with a long history of the 'restless' unburied dead or the moral issue they raise – in classical Greek literature, the Bible and all the way to the modern horror film – there is also the psychological and philosophical impasse that the unburied dead represent for witnesses. As Ian Finseth explains in relation to writing coming out of the American Civil War, the unburied, unmarked dead come to represent an obstacle to working through wartime experiences, thus necessitating, as I argue, the act of marking through the poetic prosthesis. The 'nameless Civil War dead', as Finseth writes,

> especially when visibly and horribly unburied, represented an extravagant corporeality that made it more difficult to dispose of their complexities symbolically; their corpses embodied an unresolved, liminal, or transitory condition that was intrinsically volatile, both emotionally and ideologically.[16]

The act of burial is, then, first and foremost, that of marking, of writing, as we have already seen in the few poems dealing with burial such as Mena's 'So I Was a Coffin' and Currall's 'Burying the Dead', along with others, such as 'I Remember the Parades', a poem by Afghanistan veteran Colin D. Halloran. Writing of memory in two different ways, Halloran recalls the Independence Day parades of his childhood, as well as a different kind of memory, that of the fallen war dead. The poem ends

with both memories converging, an emphasis on the weight and duty
of memory:

> Those who remember church groups passing
> step in time with high school bands
> to bring joy to those who watch
>
> smiling
> collecting candy
>
> on this a welcome day off
>
> forgetting the weight
> of the wreath that's laid
> for the nameless
> the forgotten
> the ones who died
> in sunshine
> just like this.[17]

To remember, to care for the dead, to provide a proper burial is, then,
the work and the weight of taking the undifferentiated mass of forgetting, along with the convergence of the past and the present, and writing
difference into it, of resisting if not physical decomposition but, at the
very least, the forgetting that that decomposition may bring. In the case
of Halloran's poem, for instance, it is the work of differentiating the ever
confusing mix of past and present, the sunshine in Afghanistan and a
sunshine pinned down by the indexical 'just like this'. And, as in my discussion of irony in the previous chapter, it is a differentiation that also
regenerates movement in the speaker, a digging up of memory and of the
dead that strangely results in increased agency and life. There is, as with
many of the instances discussed thus far, a nagging problem of sameness: that 'burying the dead' is both an idiom and a fact, for instance, and
that the 'sunshine' over the parade is the same sunshine in which men,
women and children have died. To resist the paralysing 'weight' of that
sameness is to etch difference.

Writing of the poetic or literary function of a retrieval of individuality
and, as a result, agency following disaster or trauma, Amir Eshel writes
of the ability to restore agency where agency has seemingly been lost as
'futurity' – the fashioning of a future where no future can be found, only
a bleeding and all-encompassing past.[18] Quoting Israeli author David

Grossman, Eshel seems to point precisely to this work of excavation of lost human forms as inherent to literature. Thus the work of creating character and plot, in Grossman's terms, ceases to be considered a flight of poetic fancy, and takes on the shape of saving those who have been lost, may have been lost, will be lost to a striking image of the immense pressure of forgetting and memory: 'Sometimes I feel as if I am digging people out of ice in which reality has encased them. I write. I feel the many possibilities that exist in every human situation, and I feel my capacity to choose among them.'[19] Evident in Grossman's portrayal of post-disaster life, written less than a year after his son was killed during the Second Lebanon War, are the two functions described here as comprising the poetic prosthesis: the act of self-preservation, seen in Grossman's ability to sense freedom of choice and of opportunity in the world, as well as the saving of others from the wasteland of erasure. In the context of reading and reacting to writing coming out of war and about war, then, we must first consider the writers themselves as having, to some degree, escaped the threat of utter obliteration. They are home, safe and sound, having, as one would say, survived the war. However, and despite this intuition, time and again soldiers return from war, as I have already briefly discussed, describing themselves as somehow dead. And as Shay's line regarding the dead-yet-alive soldiers reminds us, it is a sense of death not unrelated to the actual death of others, whether comrades, enemy combatants or civilians, to the witnessing of the human body as it breaks down and threatens to dissolve into a lack of boundaries. By witnessing the objectification and fragmentation of the human form, by witnessing friends turn into objects under the pressure of Force, being 'washed out of the turret', veterans could be said to witness their own fragility and the utter unlikeliness of having survived war themselves. However, memory and memorialisation have not always been the privilege of all those who had gone to war, both historically and in contemporary writing. It is thus an act of both memory and somehow class fidelity too – to remember those who are forgotten also because they are not 'important' enough to be remembered. And I mention class here since while the act of memory in the wake of disaster is as ancient as the *Iliad*, *who* and *how* those lost to war are remembered seems to be at least partially related to social class.

A wiping out of memory is thus resisted with the etching of literature, whether the writers' own sense of their being on the precipice of the mass-grave abyss, or, at the very least, the danger of friends, comrades, enemy combatants and civilians being crushed beyond recognition by war and by monolithic acts of national and sometimes international commemoration. The notion of being lost to memory in war is, again, as ancient as war itself or at least since the inception of writing about war in the Western tradition in the *Iliad* and the *Aeneid*, and the importance of burial in war is an evident feature of literary depictions of war all the way from works such as Sophocles' *Antigone* and *The Song of Roland* to post-World War II poet Howard Nemerov and his depiction of the 'clean war' in his 'War in the Air'. In contemporary post-war and soldier writing the threat of being forgotten, of being covered by a blanket of undifferentiated matter, of decomposing, is but a continuation of that age-old theme. In 'A Soldier's Winter' the speaker's inability to discern internal from external and to make sense of the perceptions around him are equated to the slow buildup of snow in the Afghani winter that slowly covers the landscape, threatening to cover even the speaker as well. However, while the *Iliad* indeed commemorates the dead, it often does so along lines of social standing, with kings, princes and heroes being remembered while the more common soldiers remain as devoid of a proper burial as their real-life ancient counterparts. As Valerie Hope writes, the remains of combat soldiers, from the Roman Empire all the way to the nineteenth century, were relegated to what I have called the mass-grave model of forgetting. While those stationed in large fortifications were sometimes remembered with individual markers, as a result of their relative proximity to either home or major settlements, 'the fate of the battlefield dead was very different':

> The dignity of an individual grave accompanied by any form of commemoration was not the destiny of those killed in warfare. The bodies would have been stripped, cremated, and then interred in mass graves. Disposal was probably rapid and unceremonious. For practical reasons this had to be the case. Rotting bodies were unhygienic and unsightly, individual identification of bodies would have been difficult, and, if left, exposed corpses could be looted and interfered with by enemies. Bodies were generally cremated, according to Pliny, because this removed the risk of remains being dug up in the future and the graves desecrated. For similar reasons, the graves were probably left unmarked . . . An army on the march needed to look forward rather than backwards; it moved on and left no one to tend or protect graves.[20]

Any commemoration of individual soldiers that did take place, as Hope writes elsewhere in the same text, as opposed to monolithically as part of the dead of a battle or war, was the result of efforts by comrades in arms and class: 'If the soldier failed to save sufficient money his final rites were presumably organized and funded by his comrades. Many tombstones suggest that fellow soldiers, men who had often been designated as heirs in the will, commemorated the dead.'[21] And as she later reiterates:

> The commemoration of dead soldiers, whether they were killed in combat or died at peace, was in general a private matter. The army might oversee the disposal of corpses after a battle, and trophies and triumphs might celebrate the victory, but as individuals the dead men were little remembered, publicly at least. For the vast majority of Roman soldiers killed in action there was no roll of honour or special memorial where their names and individuality were preserved.[22]

This classical tradition to let the common soldier dissolve into the field of battle, leaving no trace behind unless commemorated through a form of folk memorialisation, fits, moreover, the emphasis given in classical war writing on the memory of royal and aristocratic figures. As Paul Meters writes, in the *Iliad*, for instance, while 'the lives and deaths of the great warriors hold our gaze, the masses of soldiers have all the personality of a bee swarm'.[23] Thus, like the works of trench art described in Chapter 1, soldier writing, or at least much of the soldier writing that occupies this book, is a folk art created both for personal use – the prosthesis of language – and for communal use in the remembering of others. It is interesting to note that this notion of a folk commemoration of fellow common soldiers can also be seen much later, such as in the American Civil War, where soldiers would sometimes place temporary 'head-boards' near the remains of the dead in the vicinity of the battlefields so that relatives could later identify the remains of their loved ones for the purposes of enabling a proper burial. One soldier, Tyler Wise, quoted in Jim Murphy's *The Boys' War*, writes in the aftermath of battle: 'I dreamed of my bunkmate last night,' adding that he wonders 'if his remains will be put where they can be found, for I would like, if I ever get the chance, to put a board with his name on it at the head of the grave'.[24] Elsewhere, one Union soldier, writing to the mother of a comrade who had fallen ill and died during the war, notifies the family of the date of their loved one's death – 18 January 1862 – but also attempts to aid the family with the task of burial:

> He used to bring me the letters which he received from you and have me to read them, and by the letters which I have seen and came from you I take you to be a very nice Woman and it appears that you are a poor Woman as well as my own mother and a great many others and therefore I made a motion last night for our Company to put in one dollar a piece and have a head stone put to the head of his grave and whatever there is left to be sent to you and use it as you think proper.[25]

Later, the letter writer, Thomas O. Nickerson, indicates that it would be more practical for the family to come and pick up the remains of their loved one as a result of the improbability of sending the corpse home, adding: 'My Father has turned out quite a number of soldiers out of his family and he has also come himself.' Contemporary war poetry, I think, aligns itself with this notion of a folk memorialisation, a counter to the classical tradition in which the focus was on the conquering, often aristocratic, hero, not the common soldiers, written as a means of enabling the proper burial of those who may be lost to memory. What links, then, the actions of common Romans and their efforts to memorialise their comrades, Civil War soldiers and their 'head boards', and contemporary soldiers' 'burial' of comrades is a return to poetry's ancient function as enabler of burial and mourning. It is a way to properly bury the unnamed, unremembered dead.

That act of burial, moreover, is evident even in a cursory reading of the poems I have already discussed in this book in the theme of the burial of others, exhibiting LaCapra's notion of 'fidelity to the past'. One such example would be Currall's 'Burying the Dead', which not only directly addresses the act of burying in its title and content, but also, I would argue, links the act of burying with that of writing:

> Burying the dead is a metaphor.
> They don't literally mean bury the dead
> Try not to think too much about it
> They mean put things to rest
> Pull your socks up
> Stop harping on
> Get on with it
> Let things lie
> Get a grip
> Forget.
>
> They've never buried the dead.
>
> Literally.[26]

As I have already discussed, Currall's poem clearly separates those who indexically experienced Force and the objectification of the human that it brings about from those who did not experience those things through the ability to recognise the multiple meanings of 'burying the dead'. Said otherwise, it takes a person who had dug a grave to recognise how it is a mistake to tell a soldier to 'bury his dead' so as to convince him, figuratively, to let go of his past. Moreover, to reiterate, that resistance is all the more clear, given the impossibility of letting go of the past, of the index, since the recurrence of the past and its pain is sudden and uncontrollable. What I would like to add at this juncture is the fact that the poem itself looks like an act of digging, the lines narrowing as a dug hole would, just as the speaker is 'digging' through the many possible meanings of the title phrase until 'hitting' the literal meaning that sits underneath. By digging down from communal discourse, or symbols and the symbolic use of 'burying the dead', all the way into the personal, indexical and literal, the poem is also, in a way, re-exposing the corpse of the past, giving it shape and form, even if that form takes the form of a poem. Taking on this notion of the physical shape of the poem as mimicking the act of digging a grave, the 'body' found at the bottom is 'literally' or the literal, actual, specific, concrete and individual dead.

However, while the desire to memorialise runs through the war-writing tradition, the question of who gets remembered differs widely, with some of the contemporary writers I discuss here – such as Gerardo Mena and Maximilian Uriarte (who will be discussed later in this chapter) – not only recalling an abstracted image of a person lost to war but seeming to be dedicated to the memory of specific soldiers. Moreover, the memory relates to the kind of specific soldier that would not have been mentioned in the *Iliad* or even in Tennyson's 'The Charge of the Light Brigade.' In those war poems what is remembered is the event of war, in Tennyson's case, or those glorious kings, princes and gods who led that war. And while the Trench Poets of the Great War marked their work at least partially as a rejection of the heroic, epic tradition of classical war poetry, their writing retains at least that element of the tradition. As Homer focuses mostly on figures such as Achilles and Agamemnon, poets like Wilfred Owen and Siegfried Sassoon home in on the realities of the trenches, a reality viewed by the officer class, in which war remains an event populated by a 'swarm-like' class of soldiers. Thus, the soldiers dying in Owen's poems and those of Sassoon and Rosenberg – the latter an example of a soldier belonging to lower social class than his fellow poets – rarely had names, and often served as a type of war dead, as opposed to existing in moments of memorialisation as private as Mena's dedication to Kyle Powers – 'who died in my arms'. One example is the death of the anonymous soldier that stands at the epicentre of Owen's most celebrated poem, 'Dulce et Decorum est':

Gas! GAS! Quick, boys! – An ecstasy of fumbling
Fitting the clumsy helmets just in time,

But someone still was yelling out and stumbling
And flound'ring like a man in fire or lime. –
Dim through the misty panes and thick green light,
As under a green sea, I saw him drowning.

In all my dreams before my helpless sight,
He plunges at me, guttering, choking, drowning.[27]

Owen's poem is, to be sure, yet another case of marking a specific death out of the unmarked space of the mass grave, represented here in the 'drowning' of the soldier in the flurry of the gas attack. However, and as opposed to at least one dominant tendency seen in contemporary soldier poetry, the soldier that Owen's speaker witnesses remains nameless. This, I would argue, runs at least partially counter to the sweeping argument put forth by historian Jay Winter in *War Beyond Words*. According to Winter, military memorialisation in the West, especially that following World War I, represents a more democratic, 'horizontal' mode of dealing with the war dead.[28] Yes, the graveyards, as Winter writes, are democratic as opposed to the monolithic, martyr-based shape of totalitarian memory. And yet it seems that even that step closer to recognising the importance of the death of a common soldier, which Winter identifies, is not yet the specific, personal commemoration of writers such as Mena and Uriarte.

That many of the great war poets of the twentieth century repeatedly trace the form of the war dead, only to leave them in their anonymity, could be linked, moreover, to the simple fact of changing demographics in the past century or so of warfare in the West, as well as a growing tendency, which David Reynolds identifies as the influence of American democratic values, toward the democratisation of commemoration and naming.[29] In the British military of the early twentieth century, lines of rank often mirrored class lines as well, with officers, who had usually come from middle- and upper-class backgrounds, in command of a largely lower-class contingent. Such was the case with some of the more prominent Trench Poets, such as Owen, Sassoon and Brooke, who themselves manifested the palpable gap between themselves and their soldiers.[30] Added to that is the fact that these divisions also intersected with racial and ethnic lines as well, with the officer class occupied almost completely by white English officers, while the rank-and-file contingent was made up of an array of ethnic backgrounds mirroring the British class system as well as British imperialism and colonialism.[31] However, in the context of the contemporary American and British militaries, in which varied voices of both ethnicity and class play an ever-increasing role,[32] the desire to pay respect to the deceased plays a much more significant role. Whatever the reason, though, names, dates of death and other personal details are a prevalent feature of contemporary war writing, seen in Mena's repeated reference to his fellow soldiers, such as Kyle Powers in 'So I Was a Coffin' and Corporal Benavidez in 'Rocket Man', to give two examples. Thus, the commemorative impulse, what I have been calling the push to remember and bury the war dead individually, seems to have peaked in the wake of contemporary conflicts, as I shall now discuss through somewhat differing examples of the poetry of Brian Turner and the graphic novel *White Donkey: Terminal Lance*.

A Place for Ghosts

The works that stand at the centre of this current discussion are those in which the indexical return of the past, and the manner in which that return is forced on to war veterans, takes on the form of ghosts. And yet, these are not tales of gothic hauntings, for despite the fact that ghosts represent the realm of the dead, that realm, as I have attempted to show in the first part of this chapter, is one with which returning soldiers, who already consider themselves to be partially dead, share a great intimacy and which they sense a duty to commemorate. In its pathological manifestations, however, the appearance of the quite literal ghosts of the past has been recognised as a hallmark of PTSD, whether through hypervigilance against enemy forces, even when home, or hallucinations of the war dead.[33] However, the ghost does bear a very specific brand of burden, one that I have already discussed using LaCapra's 'fidelity to trauma', and that is the moral obligation to bury the dead. Put another way, if the dead body, the living thing undone by Force, is the index of violence that marks past events, the ghost's appearance could be marked as the index of that past in the present, one signalling the lack of proper burial that had left it to wander in pain, divested of a final resting place.[34] Writing of one uniquely ancient manifestation of the post-war or post-traumatic encounter with ghosts, Walid Abdul-Hamid and Jamie Hacker Hughes describe Mesopotamian cuneiform tablets, dated between 600 and 1300 BCE, arguing that this is the earliest known recorded proof of what has come to be known today as PTSD. In one text, ostensibly describing the symptoms of a post-combat mental disorder, the Assyrian expert writes:

If in the evening, he sees either a living person or a dead person or someone known to him or someone not known to him or anybody or anything and becomes afraid; he turns around but, like one who has [been hexed with?] rancid oil, his mouth is seized so that he is unable to cry out to one who sleeps next to him, 'hand' of ghost.[35]

Later, the description adds: 'If his mentation is altered, [. . .] (and) forgetfulness(?) (and) his words hinder each other in his mouth, a roaming ghost afflicts him.'[36] The ghosts of the past, unburied, unmarked, unremembered, haunt veterans in the present, forcing, indexically, their hand to the act of writing. However, as I have discussed, this burial of the unburied dead is only one aspect to that burial the prosthesis enables, along with the dream-like, prosthetic distance from the past that the act of writing affords. One contemporary case, in which burial as commitment to and oppression by the past intervenes with the act of artistic expression that burial allows, is the post-Iraq War poetry of American veteran and writer Brian Turner.

Turner's poetry, perhaps the most celebrated of the current wave of American soldier writers, often treats writing as a form of burial, whether of others or of himself. In his 2005 debut collection, *Here, Bullet*, Turner addresses the anonymity of the unburied war dead in poems such as 'Body Bags' and 'Repatriation Day'. In 'Eulogy', another poem from *Here, Bullet*, Turner carefully memorialises – buries – a fellow soldier who had committed suicide during his service in Iraq, both raising the painful and under-discussed issue of soldier suicide[37] and providing the precise documentary detail that I have associated with the act of burying others:

It happens on a Monday, at 11:20 a.m.,
as tower guards eat sandwiches
and seagulls drift by on the Tigris river.
Prisoners tilt their heads to the west
though burlap sacks and duct tape blind them.
The sound reverberates down concertina coils
the way piano wire thrums when given slack.
And it happens like this, on a blue day of sun,
when Private Miller pulls the trigger
to take brass and fire into his mouth.
The sound lifts the birds up off the water,
a mongoose pauses under the orange trees,
and nothing can stop it now, no matter what
blur of motion surrounds him, no matter what voices
crackle over the radio in static confusion,
because if only for this moment the earth is stilled,

and Private Miller has found what low hush there is
down in the eucalyptus shade, there by the river.

PFC B. Miller
(1980 – March 22, 2004)[38]

The person that 'Eulogy' buries is, of course, first and foremost 'PFC B. Miller', as he is referred to at the end of the poem, with the precise, one would say indexical, time and place of death, as well as a dramatic depiction of the scene of life at the time of his death. The momentary hushing of the world, the shot, are, like the poem, a mark on an otherwise seemingly natural and undifferentiated world. The river does not stop for Private Miller, and yet it is Turner's act of burial that succeeds, for a moment, in achieving the kind of dream in which the water had indeed been held at bay in order to remember the dead soldier. However, in that gesture, in the writer's ability to stop the river in order to remember his fallen friend, we also find traces of the second type of burial, that of a personal past and, perhaps, a past version of the writing self. This power is visible not only through Turner's sudden, divine ability to arrest the flow of nature, reminiscent of the Jewish tradition regarding the silence of nature during the giving of the Torah to Moses on Mount Sinai, but also through the visible role of the index 'it' with which the poem opens. That which is buried is, in other words, not only Private Miller but also 'it', that ominous, catch-all index not only for the death of the soldier but also, to an extent, for the death of the writer. To bury his friend, in other words, is also to bury the index of past pain, and to allow the emergence of a new, limping sense of identity, one that includes a sense of artistic and personal agency. Nowhere is the poet's ability to mark the past as buried, express the past's oppression of the present, and transform that oppression into artistic expression more evident than in another of Turner's poems, 'At Lowe's Home Improvement Center'.

In this poem, published as part of Turner's second volume, *Phantom Noise*, the writer transforms a suburban strip mall hardware store into a fully-fledged wartime evacuation centre, as a returning veteran dropping some nails on the ground experiences a vivid flashback to wartime events. At one and the same time, Turner demonstrates the power of traumatic events, the indices of past pain, to press themselves into an ever-anxious present; takes care of the war dead, in this case Iraqi children; and exhibits his own prowess as a writer. Boundaries of time and space are undone as Lowe's becomes both a hardware store in the United States in the present and a bleeding battle in Iraq in what had been the past. Itself a liminal space between life and death, the evacuation centre is riddled with the war wounded and war dead, with ordinary Lowe's lawn mowers being transformed into helicopters and store aisles into blood-soaked helipads. Moreover, those objects that trigger the onset of wartime experiences are themselves indices of a kind: a box of nails, those instruments used to anchor objects in place, falls to the ground, an undoing that mimics the stream of spent shells from a firing machine gun. Indices come loose, untethering one time or the image of one time and one place from the past, causing it to invade the present. The poem's closing lines, however, depict not only the sudden resurrection of the past, with its unburied dead, through the violence of an uncontrollable flashback, but also, through the prosthetic space enabled by the poem itself, the raising of the unburied dead in the form of ghosts. The unmarked, unremembered Iraqi dead rise from their graves as ghosts that haunt the store, ultimately marking the poem's speaker as wounded:

> Aisle number 7 is a corridor of lights.
> Each dead Iraqi walks amazed
> by Tiffany posts and Bavarian pole lights.
> Motion-activated incandescents switch on
> as they pass by, reverent sentinels of light,
> Fleur De Lis and Luminaire Mural Extérieur
> welcoming them to Lowe's Home Improvement Center,
> aisle number 7, where I stand in mute shock,
> someone's arm cradled in my own.
>   The Iraqi boy beside me
> reaches down to slide his fingertip in Retro Colonial Blue,
> an interior latex, before writing
> T, for *Tourniquet*, on my forehead.[39]

The poetic re-enactment of the wartime scene, the active artistic counterpart to the passive real-life predicament of flashbacks and uncontrollable hyper-vigilance, becomes a space for ghosts, for the memory of the dead to return to haunt the living. They haunt, it should be said, and yet not in the same way that a box of loose nails triggers a war scene, thus representing agency in one's discussion of the past, used to perhaps ward off the complete lack of agency represented by such symptoms as flashbacks, hyper-vigilance and phantom pain. Thus, and importantly in the terms of this chapter, it is a space of writing, of an etching against forgetting a fact made that much more visible in the very act of writing with which the poem ends – not the marking of the poem by the poet, but the marking of the poet by the poem. It is the burying, in other words, of the speaker and poet. The ghosts of the dead are resurrected as a means of remembrance but also as a tool through which the speaker can relate to his own wound. The guilt of others' death, the artistic resurrection, is, then, a way of addressing one's own untimely demise.

It bears mentioning, however, that in the case of 'At Lowe's Home Improvement Center', the commemoration, unlike that in 'Eulogy', is not of a specific, named person, but of what could be called an abstracted Iraqi child or civilian. This is, I believe, an issue hinted at by the poem itself, with its referencing of 'Retro Colonial Blue', the colour the boy's ghost uses to mark the speaker's body, and by the very fact that the victim – the dead child – is marking the perpetrator as wounded. There are, of course, biographical and historical issues to consider here, one being that Turner and his poetic speaker would have known Private Miller personally and thus had been able to name him in the poetic prosthesis commemorating his suicide, while the Iraqi spectres populating 'At Lowe's Home Improvement Center' are not unlike the nameless bee swarm, as Meters calls it, found in war poetry since the *Iliad*. In other words, while there is little doubt the poem serves as the space of writing that enables the marking of Turner's own body as wounded in the war, evident in the ghostly triage that serves as the main scene of 'At Lowe's', there is also a sense that the war in Iraq, regardless of its victims, was something that had happened to Turner's speaker and that was told from his point of view, and that point of view alone. From that vantage point, then, the Iraqi boy can redeem or mark the American soldier but cannot gain a subjectivity all his own, causing what I have referred to as the democratisation of a 'folk' military commemoration to be viewed through a different class-based lens – that of the common American soldier and those who seem to reside in a social stratum lower than even his: Iraqis.

This more general claim, obviously, could also levied at my own analysis, since it focuses on those American and British soldiers going to war in Central Asia and Iraq without reckoning with the other, very significant side to this 'story', which is the local population of those areas; this is because my book focuses on the work necessary for those soldiers to come back to life, not the work that has to be done in the wake of war on a larger, societal scale. Put otherwise, focusing on prosthetic work without dealing with social work is only part of the task at hand, and by focusing on the vantage point of the returning soldier I myself am perpetuating the age-old colonial trope, as Samina Najmi writes concerning Turner's *Here, Bullet,* of the Westerner going off to gain experience in the Orient:

> While Turner's *Here, Bullet* contributes to American war literature specifically and is often compared to the writings of Vietnam war veterans Yusef Komunyakaa, Tim O'Brien, Bruce Weigl, and others, it may also be placed within the broader context of a long history of texts by white authors who venture to distant lands and report back to their home audiences what they have gleaned from their travel.[40]

There is great merit to Najmi's critique here, both of Turner's poetry, at least in some of the cases, and of the war poetry tradition more generally, one that, while focusing on the horrors of war, time and time again restores the glory of the quest to gain experience, all the while avoiding the subject of the victims of that quest. I will address at least that idea, of the victims of the said 'adventure to the orient', in the final chapter, but it is an issue that bears mention at this point as well. The work of working through trauma, of attempting to enable a return back into a new, prosthetic life, does not and cannot serve as a tool to cover over some of the larger social issues brought about or perpetuated by war, be those issues gender, race, class or, in this case, colonialism. One way in which the discourse of trauma, at least in the humanities, has done precisely that is through the image of what writer and veteran Roy Scranton dubs 'the trauma hero' – the image of the broken soldier not as a counter to or critique of past hero-worship, of the kind established by texts such as the *Iliad*, but as a continuation of that trope by different means. Whereas once the bounty of war had been glory won in battle, now the 'bounty' of war could be said to be a knowledge of the 'truth' of war. As Scranton writes: 'The truth of war, the veteran comes to learn, is a truth beyond words, a truth that can only be known by having been there, an unspeakable truth he must bear for society. So goes the myth of the trauma hero.'[41]

The two can, no doubt, coexist at the same time – the need to describe war and to rebuild language in its wake is, indeed, tantamount to restoring mobility as a human being *and* the stories that impetus gives rise to uncontrollably restore or even create the halo of glory around war. That is not to say that there is anything specifically glorious about Turner's poem; replete with signs of paralysis, confusion and emotional horror, 'At Lowe's' no doubt traces a line between the war and the impossibility of life after war, as well as the centrality of writing in maintaining that life. And yet, and this is a topic I will return to in the concluding chapter,

there is a way in which all war writing glorifies war, to an extent, a sentiment echoed by Jane Marcus's pointed statement: 'War stories encourage war. The more literary the history, the more it incites the reader to
approve of belligerence.'[42] And in that way, 'At Lowe's' may be said to
participate in a literary history of war that specifically describes war,
again, as an event that happens *only to the speaker*, not to their subjects
who, in this case, include an abstracted image of Iraqi children and an
emphasis on Turner's experience not as a personal experience of war but
as an equally abstracted self-image as 'the soldier'.[43]

An interesting, even if partial, counter to this abstraction comes from
another context of care: namely, the poetry of former navy medical officer Fredrick Foote. Serving on board the United States Naval Ship *Comfort*
during the Iraq invasion, Foote treated a good deal of Iraqi soldiers and
civilians, a fact that allowed him to gain greater familiarity with names
and personal backgrounds. As with other poems written by servicemen
and women, Foote's work, compiled in his 2014 collection *Medic Against
Bomb*, makes explicit reference to the psychological toll of proximity to
death and injury; as he writes in 'Happy Return', 'Don't think that time
has dulled those / thorns – / they're waiting for you – drawing near.'[44] In
the equally ironically titled 'Safe Home', Foote, who at one time led the
veteran's poetry project at Walter Reed Hospital, describes the boundless, time-confused post-war reality, a horrific mix of survival and the
persistence of death and memory:

> in the wet brain there is no bar
> between
> moonrise and waking days
> and the baby's puke
> is a coil of weeping blood
> the dreams have rhythms like teams
> that make the extra pass
> such fear
> in finding the mind's-soil
> *crackt*
> validation.[45]

Foote indexically locates the struggle of post-war life in the mind and
does so using terminology that both corresponds with his experiences
as a physician – 'in the wet brain' – and symbolically marks the 'wet' or
boundless nature of post-war anxiety. This is a fragmented existence, one
with a constant 'rhythm' and a lack of bounds, one that finds the 'mind's

soil' has, in the words of the poem, 'crackt'. And yet as familiar as this depiction of the pain and fragmentation of post-war life is at this stage of our discussion, the battlegrounds of Foote's writing are quite different: hospital wards, populated by American soldiers as well as by Iraqi fighters and civilians, all of which are exposed to the thunderous violence of the war. In one example, 'Ahmed the Soldier', Foote writes of an Iraqi who had been burnt by a fuel air explosive (FA.E):

> Just like someone had opened up a pop can
> – the skull's lid free –
> still tied into his truck burnt black by
> the FA.E. –
> we saw in awe – but what should least
> have survived that wreck –
> the picture of wife and baby girls – is
> what I'll never forget.[46]

While the poem's subject and title figure, Ahmed, is far from fully realised in the manner that, for instance, Turner's and Foote's speakers are, and while he is viewed in an objectifying way as a burnt body – one whose 'lid' was open – there is undoubtedly more presence to even this lifeless man. He has a name and, as importantly, an imagined life, depicted through what we may presume is an image of his wife and children. It is exactly that background, this fleshing out of his image, moreover, that breaks Foote's speaker down, that marks the man, his name and his life. In other words, a major part of the wartime experience described in the poem, more dramatic than the gruesome physical condition of Ahmed, is the shocking revelation that he had a life, that his subjectivity existed beyond his role in the theatre of war as antagonist and beyond his role in Foote's own poem. The sudden and perhaps unexpected appearance of the human, in other words, is as troubling as the graphic image of a burnt body with its 'lid' open, if not more so.

One further complication of this shock of subjectivity, made more complicated by its discussion of gender roles both in terms of doctor–patient relations and within Iraqi society, is provided in another of Foote's poems. In 'The Iraqi War' Foote further explores his position as observer and care giver to wounded Iraqis, this time through the image of a female civilian, to whom the poem is dedicated – 'For Mounira' – and whose family was killed, seemingly as a result of the war. In one stanza Foote is able to situate her as a woman who had been adhering to the Iraqi social code, avoiding the men's dominos and card games, amid the otherworldly setting of the hospital ward:

> Your children dead
> within the riddled car
> and yet you never cried
> when we made scarves
> you tied one on
> the girl who couldn't move
> you led the prayers
> certified the food
> and never once broke down.[47]

Later on, however, Mounira does indeed break down, a response that the speaker of the poem assumes is tied to the fact that the hospital had begun to disassemble, presumably ahead of moving to a different location. And in doing so, Mounira pierces through the many walls that separate her experience from that of Foote's speaker – gender, class, ethnicity – in a manner that is only vaguely intelligible, as a yelp of pain:

> that was the day you chose
> to fall into the arms
> of Senior Chief Minata
> the one so good with the kids
> a man not your husband
> to sway weeping
> clasped together
> a strange beast
> half uniformed half black
> crying 'Salaam, Salaam!'[48]

The wounds that led to Mounira's collapse were there, visible to the observing doctor who had wondered at her ability to keep them hidden. Unlike the subject of 'Ahmed the Soldier', Mounira bears no physical scars from her ordeal, other than perhaps her black clothing that could be interpreted as mourning garb. And yet those wounds gush open, apparently unannounced, positioning her figure as outwardly disabled as well, a central element of many of the poems hitherto discussed: the externalising or materialising of unseen wounds. And whether or not that externalising can ward off the type of violence-perpetuating readings I have alluded to above is perhaps too big a question to try to grapple with. But it is, I think, certain that this moment of rupture is key in understanding why it bore the significance it visibly did for the speaker. As the poem concludes, Mounira's undoing becomes, as in Foote's 'wet brain', a moment of broken boundaries – the rigidity of formal codes and societal norms undone, and the creation of a stirring Iraqi–American creature of mourning: 'a strange beast / half uniformed half black'. It is, I think, undeniable that Foote's speaker retains a more significant level of agency and personhood, able to observe the minutiae of custom and gender difference in a ward where he is an authority figure and able to record emotions and happenings at a distance, a privilege not awarded to the grieving Mounira, who is embedded at the seeming bottom of the social ranking of the ward. And yet I would argue that, despite these limitations, Foote's poems are able, at the very least, to begin to form that testimonial, that act of care for the dead and their survivors, which serves such a significant part of his writing, that poetically conjures the beast of unarticulated, unbound mourning that is, as he writes, ' half uniformed half black'.

* * *

The notion of a burying of others and a burying of the self has been the central theme of this chapter and perhaps the democratic nature of that commemoration is evident, naturally, in another depiction of the afterlife of the Iraq and Afghanistan wars in contemporary American culture: the TV comedy series *You're the Worst*. While *You're the Worst*'s main focus is not the aftermath of war, but the dysfunctional romance between its two Los Angelino protagonists, the war in Iraq haunts the show through the figure of veteran Edgar Quintero – a housemate of the show's male protagonist. At the series' onset, the figure of Edgar is that of a troubled veteran who fails to hold on to regular employment and stable relationships as he persistently lives under the shadow of a recently traumatic past, continually failing to connect even to the Veterans Affairs office. His initial breakthrough is as a comedy performer and writer, which, along with access to medicinal marijuana, saves him from what I refer to here as being swallowed up by that past, from a complete undoing of his memory and identity. Thus, Edgar finds his way out of pain through the act of writing. And yet in one of the show's more poignant moments he also succeeds in extracting others from invisibility precisely through a similar kind of etching. Upon encountering a group of homeless veterans, Edgar becomes overwhelmed with a sense of guilt at not only surviving but at living a better life than those who had undergone similar experiences. Resolved to help somehow, Edgar teaches the homeless veterans how to write, specifically how to phrase their signs in such a way as to garner more handout money or even just to punctuate their sentences so as to make their messages heard.[49] By writing on their cardboard signs, Edgar is resurrecting the living dead hoards of urban homeless veterans back into life or, at the very least, into the view of the living.

While it would seem unlikely to speak of freedom, agency or even a kind of playful gratification at this juncture, post-war soldier texts and representations of life with disability can be sites of relative freedom. The act of textual self-burial, then, is also a moment of active self-assessment and self-invention through the marking of the no longer undifferentiated mass. This is also, or perhaps even mainly, due to the fact that the writers themselves are in danger of being erased by war, a predicament reflected in the perils they face and the grief they deal with but also with not being able even to remember or note what had happened to them at war. In his study of World War I, Eric J. Leed refers to the odd inability of some veterans to remember their own experiences, using the example of Austrian violinist and World War I veteran Fritz Kreisler as he 'apologizes for the formlessness of his recollections'.[50] Later he quotes Kreisler as saying: 'One gets into a strange psychological, almost hypnotic state while on the firing line which probably prevents the mind from observing and noticing things in a normal way. This accounts, perhaps, for some blank spaces in my memory.'[51] Poetry is that place in language where an apparent 'formlessness' is not only allowed but also, at least in modern times, encouraged – if not in form, then in the form of meaning; it not only 'remembers' but, in a way, enables memory, much in the same way that, as it is directed at the potential loss of others, it enables burial. Thus identity is also resurrected precisely because it contains a fictional element, what I have called in Chapter 1 the resistance to the 'real'. One could think of freedom of this kind in terms of pleasure, a life-affirming activity that is pleasurable, perhaps in the Barthian sense, because it is also dangerous since it is done on the edge of the abyss, and because it is always on the cusp of failing. One contemporary example of such a figure of pleasure in reinvention is the figure of Don Draper from the AMC show *Mad Men*, himself a fictional character draped on the dead figure of army officer Dick Whitman. Like Melville's Ishmael, he is a survivor of violence – in Draper's case the war in Korea[52] – and like Ishmael, invested in a textual recreation of himself.

However, 'So I Was a Coffin', which I have referred to repeatedly at this point, perhaps provides a vividly explicit case in which a sombre act of burial manifests in this brand of freedom, of an internment of a past self that creates new possibility. That 'other' being buried is, as I have already argued, specifically named, and his date of death, as if etched on a tombstone, also meticulously recorded – 'To Corporal Kyle Powers, who died in my arms 04 November 2006').[53] The poem depicts a speaker continuously failing at performing certain soldierly functions: killing (through the image of the spear); national symbolism (through the image of the flag); and saving his comrade's life (through the repeated image of him as a bandage, failing to keep Kyle alive). In the poem's final stanza, however, the speaker finally does succeed in being a coffin, that artificially constructed object that enables and is symbolic of an individual act of burial. For the speaker for be able to bury Kyle, however, he must also bury himself:

They said you are a coffin.

I found a man. They said he died bravely, or he will. I encompassed him
in my finished wood, and I shut my lid around us. As they lowered us
into the ground he made no sound because he had no eyes
and could not cry. As I buried us in dirt we held our breaths together
and they said, *yes. You are a good coffin.*[54]

Using the wrought artifact of the poem–coffin, the poet is then able to bury both the dead and the presumed living, to commemorate a specific name, a specific date and a place of death while also giving voice to the hardly speaking, overwhelmed by the death of others and the guilt that death produces.

One final example of writing as burial in contemporary soldier writing is taken from a field both textual and visual – the graphic novel *Terminal Lance: The White Donkey* by artist and former US Marine Maximilian Uriarte.[55] Beginning its life in 2010 as an online satirical comic strip by the name of *Terminal Lance*, it highlighted the morbid absurdities and quotidian hassles of a 'grunt's' tour of Iraq. However, by the time it finds its way to physical publishing at the beginning of 2016 Uriarte's work turns sharply to the weightier discussion of PTSD and the trials of homecoming after war. Following the fictionalised experiences of its protagonist, Abe, from boot camp to the battlefronts of Iraq along with his close friend Garcia, *The White Donkey* highlights Abe's inability to fit back into his former life, an obstacle symbolised by the recurring image or hallucination of a mysterious white donkey. The donkey first appears following Garcia's death, only to make a reappearance in Abe's post-war nightmares.

Figure 5.1 Maximilian Uriarte, *The White Donkey: Terminal Lance* (New York: Little, Brown, and Company, 2016). Reprinted by permission of Little, Brown, an imprint of Hachette Book Group, Inc.

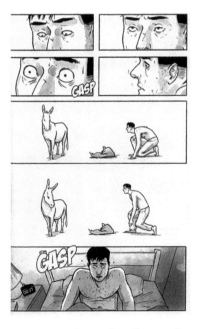

Figure 5.2 Uriarte, *The White Donkey*.

In the novel's final stages, a now completely undone and emotionally paralysed Abe has deteriorated to the point of solitary, solipsistic
alcoholism, obsessively mulling his own death. One striking moment
in the graphic novel is when Uriarte manages, through the visual–
textual medium, to capture the moment of paralysis, of 'drowning' in
post-war reality. As with any example of the genre, the novel is defined
by the kinetic movement of shifting images and pages, making the frozen image of a befuddled and suicidal Abe even more striking. Sitting in
a drunken daze in the same exact position for three double folds, Abe is
made almost inanimate as his girlfriend knocks on the door in a desperate attempt to connect. Abe ultimately goes on a drunken drive with a
loaded handgun, until he is again struck by the image of the silent white
donkey. Frustrated further by the recurrence of the seemingly symbolic
beast, one that had appeared not long after the death of Garcia, Abe follows it all the way to Garcia's grave marker. As with Mena's 'So I Was a
Coffin', here too the marker provides a name and specific time of death,
enabling an etching of yet another individual life out of the homogenous
mass of death. However, at the same time, the drive to bury Garcia, as it
were, to preserve an individual life as a way to prevent it from being lost
in the homogenous pulp, enables the burying of the writer's own index
of the past. And as Mena's power as an artist also revolved around the

Figure 5.3 Uriarte, *The White Donkey*.

transformation of the index from a moment frozen in personal history, the attempt to save Kyle's life, into a moment of artistic prowess, even in the very act repetition, so Uriarte not only buries Garcia but exhibits his own newfound strength. And as with Mena, this power is also revealed in what Derrida called rhythm or tone,[56] in the structural aspect of the work of art, such as the repetition of *The White Donkey* panels in which Abe seemingly does nothing but sit and stare. And, on the level of content, it is revealed in the very rendition of the ghost of a personal painful past and the moral commitment to commemoration through the figurative symbol of the white donkey.

Thus the act of commemoration, that of burying the dead, lies at the ethical epicentre of contemporary works of soldier writing, true to the formula set since Greek and Roman epic poetry. Therein, in other words, lies the guilt. However, the act of self-burial and self-regeneration, that of constructing new ways of saying and showing, a seeming byproduct of the urge to remember others, results in pleasure: that of persisting to the future while still anchored in a knowledge of the past. As Robert Pogue Harrison writes in *The Dominion of the Dead*, his book-length investigation of the link between mourning, burial and writing, the two processes require each other, producing an art forever pulled in both directions:

> The dead depend on the living to preserve their authority, heed their concerns, and keep them going in their afterlives. In return, they help us to know ourselves, give form to our lives, organize our social relations, and restrain our destructive impulses . . . The dead are our guardians. They give us a future so they may give us a past. We help them live on so that they may help us go forward.[57]

Centrally in terms of this chapter, and above any social or cultural concerns that predominate Harrison's study, the idea of the dead 'giving form to our lives' is especially appealing, specifically in a conversation of such forms as poetry and the graphic novel. To attend to the dead, to allow oneself to bury them and be buried among them, is to give form to that liminal, nearly homogenous loss of identity: a coffin that gives shape to shapelessness.

* * *

By way of concluding this chapter I would like to return for a moment to Berger's discussion of interdependence and care. There are ways in which returning soldiers, like Mena, Turner, Uriarte and others, fit the description of Berger's 'dys-/disarticulate'. They are removed from language, removed from humanity, objectified by Force, perceiving themselves as either dead or animals, such that they lie outside of language. In this respect they are figures that require care from others from within the community: family members, support groups, friends and partners. The construction of the prosthesis itself is, as I have argued, an important first step toward receiving care, one in which the veterans create the basic conditions of possibility for care – language and communication, albeit of the limping sort, still punctured by the spear of the past. As Berger writes, then, they are figures stranded in an in-between existence, both human and non-human, active and object:

> The dys-/disarticulate is the figure for the outside of language figured in language. But he is also a representation of a human being living as an individual subject in a social world. And as a person perceived and figured as 'other,' he becomes the focus of ethical considerations. There is in these texts a dynamic of centripetal and centrifugal moral forces, as the dys-/disarticulate figure is thrust away from and drawn back toward the social order.[58]

But, as I have discussed in this chapter, these figures of care, supposedly exposed in their vulnerability to the dominion of care takers, if we are to take Garland-Thomson's critique of care in the context of disability, are also care takers themselves. They are care takers of the individual and personal dead, of the silent, of the terminally inarticulate, terminally objectified and animalised. It is in this way that the rendition of the ghost of the disarticulate past in Uriarte is especially poignant, in transforming the figure of the terminally objectified Garcia into a silent animal – the white donkey. To reiterate Berger's statement that I quoted earlier in this book, post-war writing is a moment of language rising from under water, from a moment without language, from within the homogenous mass I have called the mass grave, and coming into being. By doing so, representation is shown not only to marginalise the disabled, but to give them voice, and create meaning where no meaning had before been: 'Metaphor – or, as I have argued, catharsis – is how language emerges out of not-language, and we should encounter it with the cognitive, aesthetic, and ethical tools at our disposal.'[59]

In a later discussion Berger cites Terrence Deacon's work on cognitive disability and his use of Peirce's division of signs and the category of index. For Deacon, as Berger writes, yelps of pain generated by animals are examples of indexical signs, a communicational outburst that is indexically tied to a physical sense of pain or fear. In the semi-dead, semi-alive existence of the returning veterans, coming from a language-less solipsism into language through the force of the poetic prosthesis, that yelp is retained as a sign of the persistence of the non-linguistic or extra-linguistic in that limping new language, as well as a way of remembering those left in death or silence. To respect the indexical, then, is to bury it, the act of burying itself as central to what the post-war poetic prosthesis accomplishes: burying the index out of a sense of duty and care, and revelling in the resulting agency, artistry and return to society.

If one were to follow, however, the articulated argument this book proposes – from the end of life in war through the reconstruction of life by building a prosthesis, to the faultlines between trauma and disability, and now, the notion of care for the dead and burial – a picture arises that not only emphasises the value of personal regeneration after war but also posits the limits and perhaps even pitfalls of such an attempt. By limits I mean the ways in which the act of prosthesis-making, while being an action drawing both from personal pain and from a communal codependency and care, is one in which there is a danger of encroaching on the rights and bodies of others. And while I have already addressed the gender and race aspects of prosthesis-making, it is perhaps time to acknowledge or demarcate the ways in which the life-affirming task of regeneration can itself, possibly and in certain contexts, become a weapon against others. And it is time to acknowledge that those others, more often than not, are identified as non-male and, moreover, that the sense of care and community I have gestured at is a community of men. I have discussed this issue around the manner in which returning veterans affect their home communities and in my discussion of sexual violence in the experience of female veterans but I shall further address it in this book's concluding chapter.

Notes

1. Josephus Flavius, *The Jewish War*, translated by G. A. Williamson (London: Penguin, 1981), 4.5.3.
2. Cicero, *De Oratore*, translated by E. W. Sutton and H. Rackham (Cambridge, MA: Harvard University Press, 1948), 347–8.
3. See Ron Ben-Tovim, 'The Collapsing Roof of History: James Joyce, Josephus Flavius, and the Duty of Memory', *South Atlantic Review* 83, no. 2 (2018): 47–66; and Ron Ben-Tovim, 'The Feminine Art of Survival in Henryk Grynberg's *The Jewish War*', *Archives of Emigration: Studies – Essays – Documents* (forthcoming).
4. Homer, *Iliad*, lines 502–7.
5. Tracy Karner, 'Fathers, Sons, and Vietnam: Masculinity and Betrayal in the Life Narratives of Vietnam Veterans with Post Traumatic Stress Disorder', *American Studies* 37, no. 1 (Spring 1996), 82.

6. The sense of shame or lack of masculinity associated with war-related psycho-logical struggles is described beautifully in Zoe Wool's *After War*, as well as in Sarah Hautzinger and Jean Scandlyn's *Beyond Post Traumatic Stress*.

7. Rosemarie Garland-Thomson, 'Integrating Disability, Transforming Feminist Theory', *NWSA* 14, no. 3 (2002): 16.

8. Marjorie Garber, 'Compassion', in *Compassion: The Culture and Politics of an Emotion*, edited by Lauren Berlant (New York: Routledge, 2004), 23–25.

9. Candace Vogler, 'Much of Madness, More of Sin', in *Compassion*, 30–31.

10. Lauren Berlant, 'Compassion (and Withholding)', in *Compassion*, 4.

11. John Rawls, *Political Liberalism* (New York: Columbia University Press, 1993).

12. Martha Nussbaum, 'Conversing with the Tradition: John Rawls and the History of Ethics', *Ethics* 109, no. 2 (January 1999): 424–30.

13. Eva Kittay, *Love's Labor: Essays on Women, Equality, and Dependency* (New York: Routledge, 1999).

14. Berger, *The Disarticulate*, 177.

15. Ibid., 178.

16. Ian Finseth, 'The Civil War Dead: Realism and the Problem of Anonymity', *American Literary History* 25, no. 3 (September 2013): 536.

17. Colin D. Halloran, 'I Remember the Parades', *Drunken Boat* 24. Available at: <http://d7.drunkenboat.com/db24/home/colin-d-halloran> (last accessed 24 February 2022).

18. Amir Eshel, *Futurity: Contemporary Literature and the Quest for the Past* (Chicago: University of Chicago Press, 2007), 4–6.

19. David Grossman, 'Writing in the Dark', *New York Times Magazine*, 13 May 2007; cited in Eshel, *Futurity*, 3.

20. Valerie Hope, 'Trophies and Tombstones: Commemorating the Roman Soldier', *World Archaeology* 35, no. 1 (2003): 87.

21. Ibid., 86.

22. Ibid., 90.

23. Philip Meters, *Behind the Lines: War Resistance Poetry on the American Home Front since 1941* (Iowa City: University of Iowa Press, 2007), 3.

24. Jim Murphy, *The Boys' War: Confederate and Union Soldiers Talk about the Civil War* (New York: Clarion Books, 1990), 37.

25. Nina Silber and Mary Beth Sievens (eds), *Yankee Correspondence: Civil War Letters Between New England Soldiers and the Home Front* (Charlottesville: University Press of Virginia, 1996), 28.

26. Currall, 'Burying the Dead'.

27. Wilfred Owen, *The War Poems*, edited by Jon Stallworthy (London: Chatto and Windus, 2006), 29.

28. Jay Winter, *War Beyond Words: Languages of Remembrance from the Great War to the Present* (Cambridge: Cambridge University Press, 2017), 144–5.

29. Reynolds, *The Long Shadow*, 181.

30. Adrian Caesar, *Taking it Like a Man: Suffering, Sexuality, and the War Poets* (Manchester: Manchester University Press, 1993), 71; Winn, *The Poetry of War*, 15, 19; Silkin, *Out of Battle*, 70; Leed, *No Man's Land*, 80–2.

31. For a more thorough discussion of the ethnic and racial makeup of the British military see David Omissi, *Indian Voices of the Great War: Letters 1914–18* (New York: Palgrave, 1999); and Santanu Das, *Race, Empire, and First World War Writing* (Cambridge: Cambridge University Press, 2011).

32. David R. Segal and Mady Wechsler Segal, 'America's Military Population', *Population Bulletin* 59, no. 4 (December 2004): 20–3; Amy Lutz, 'Who Joins the Military?: A Look at Race, Class, and Immigration Status', *Journal of Political and Military Sociology* 36, no. 2 (2008): 169–74.

33. For a discussion of ghosts and apparitions as a post-traumatic symptom see Adrienne Harris, Michael S. Roth, Daniel G. Butler, Douglas Kirsner and Don Troise, 'Ghosts in Psychoanalysis', in *Ghosts in the Consulting Room: Echoes of Trauma in Psychoanalysis*, edited by Adrienne Harris, Margery Kalb and Susan Klebanoff (Oxford: Routledge, 2016), 115–39. Cathy Caruth cites the manner in which Freud addressed the continuous desire to write the history of Moses that was eventually published as *Moses and Monotheism* as 'an unlaid ghost'. See Cathy Caruth, *Unclaimed Experience: Trauma, Narrative, and History* (Baltimore: Johns Hopkins University Press, 1996), 21).

34. Of ghosts as the unburied dead in Homer, see Sarah Iles Johnston, *Restless Dead: Encounters Between the Living and the Dead in Ancient Greece* (Berkeley: University of California Press, 2013), 9–10; and in a more contemporary context, Ann Fabian, 'Introduction: Ghosts of the Unburied Dead', in *The Skull Collectors: Race, Science, and America's Unburied Dead* (Chicago: University of Chicago Press, 2010), 1–9.

35. Walid Khalid Abdul-Hamid and Jamie Hacker Hughes, 'Nothing New under the Sun: Post-Traumatic Stress Disorders in the Ancient World', *Early Science and Medicine* 19 (2014): 555.

36. Ibid., 556.

37. See, for example, Robert J. Ursano, Ronald C. Kessler, Murray B. Stein, James A. Naifeh, Pablo A. Aliaga, Carol S. Fullerton, Nancy A. Sampson, Tzu-Cheg Kao, Lisa J. Colpe, Michael Schoenbaum, Kenneth L. Cox, Steven G. Heeringa, Army Study to Assess Risk and Resilience in Servicemembers Collaborators, 'Suicide Attempts in the U.S. Army During the Wars in Afghanistan and Iraq, 2004 to 2009', *JAMA Psychiatry* 72, no. 9 (2015): 917–26; and James A. Naifeh, Holly B. Herberman Mash, Murray B. Stein, Mary C. Vance, Pablo A. Aliaga, Carol S. Fullerton, Hieu Dinh, Gary H. Wynn, Tzu-Cheg Kao, Nancy A. Sampson, Ronald C. Kessler and Robert J. Ursano, 'Sex Differences in US Army Suicide Attempts During the Wars in Iraq and Afghanistan', *Medical Care* 59, no. 2 (February 2021): S42–S50.

38. Brian Turner, *Here, Bullet* (Farmington, ME: Alice James Books, 2005), 20.

39. Turner, *Phantom Noise*, 7.

40. Samina Najmi, 'The Whiteness of the Soldier-Speaker in Brian Turner's "Here, Bullet"', *Rocky Mountain Review* 65, no. 1 (2011): 57.

41. Roy Scranton, 'The Trauma Hero: From Wilfred Owen to *Redeployment* and *American Sniper*', *Los Angeles Review of Books*, 25 January 2015. Available at: <https://lareviewofbooks.org/article/trauma-hero-wilfred-owen-redeployment-american-sniper> (last accessed 24 February 2022).

42. Jane Marcus, 'Review of *Virginia Woolf and War*', *The Journal of English and Germanic Philology* 92, no. 4 (October 1993): 579.

43. Najmi, 'The Whiteness of the Soldier-Speaker', 71.

44. Frederick Foote, *Medic Against Bomb: A Doctor's Poetry of War* (West Hartford, CT: Grayson Books), 55.

45. Ibid., 41, emphasis in original.

46. Ibid., 17.

47. Ibid., 45–6.

48. Ibid.

49. 'Fix Me Dummy', *You're the Worst*, directed by Wendy Stanzier (Los Angeles: FX, 2016).

50. Leed, *No Man's Land*, 124.

51. Ibid., with additional material from source text: Fritz Kreisler, *Four Weeks in the Trenches: The War Story of a Violinist* (Boston and New York: Houghton Mifflin, 1915), 2.

52. '5G', *Mad Men*, directed by Lesli Linka Glatter (New York: AMC, 2007).

53. Mena, *The Shape of Our Faces No Longer Matters*, 55.

54. Ibid.

55. Maximilian Uriarte, *The White Donkey: Terminal Lance* (New York: Little, Brown, and Company, 2016).

56. Derrida, *Monolingualism of the Other; or, The Prosthesis of Origin*, 48.

57. Robert Pogue Harrison, *The Dominion of the Dead* (Chicago: University of Chicago Press, 2003), 158.

58. Berger, *The Disarticulate*, 2.

59. Ibid., 11.

CHAPTER 6

Body and Metaphor

According to the *Oxford English Dictionary*, prosthesis is the 'replacement of defective or absent parts of the body by artificial substitutes'.[1] That definition provides an apt description of the function of post-war poems I discuss in this book: objects meant to replace an essential component of human life that has been 'impaired' to varying degrees during war. And just as the prosthesis, in the physical sense, is meant to allow a person to regain some, but not all, of the functions lost by injury, so the poetic prosthesis represents an attempt at an artificial, or wrought, linguistic prop. This literary, linguistic tool, as I have discussed in previous chapters, allows soldiers to write or speak after war, despite the fact that their vocabulary has been booby-trapped by wartime experience. War veterans, through the use of the prosthesis, create a mangled, artificial, uncomfortable mode of describing the violence they have experienced, the death they have seen, and at the same time demonstrate what violence has done to their ability to communicate, a duality that serves as a significant feature of what we call 'poetic language'. Poetic speech, in terms of these veterans' poems and in general, then, is a kind of stylised failure, an object that both achieves its purpose and fails, akin to that wonderful line from Wallace Stevens: 'The poem must resist the intelligence / Almost successfully.'[2] As such, the poem or prosthesis bears the marks of success – in relating something about one's painful past, in gaining a sense of artistic agency – as well as the failure of a persistent phantom pain, flashbacks, hyper-vigilance and the continued and frustrating inability to describe that past 'correctly' or to remember 'well'. At one at the same time, then, the prosthesis enables the stepping out of death into renewed movement and communication while serving as a constant reminder, an index, of the loss that triggered its creation. This is the source of that oscillation or 'irony' that was the subject of Chapter 4, one also evident in the 'results' provided by the prosthesis: improved functioning alongside the constant presence of pain.

In their attempt to describe indescribable wartime scenes, soldiers will be moved to use benign words such as Randall Jarrell's 'hose'. However, the manner in which they use such words will reflect the duality in which they are trapped and from which they will attempt to escape. Standing in a back yard, either unable to use the hose in the necessary manner or finding it very difficult to do so, veterans are faced with a form of disability: not, to be sure, a disability that always manifests physically or externally, as the soldier I have chosen here as a more general example is able to lift the tool and make use of it physically, whether it is a hose or a word. But it is a disability nonetheless since, again, when it extends to the countless words, idioms and slang touched by violence, veterans are eventually forced outside of their own mode of communication, stranded on an island of personal experience and fear, where every word, innocent as it may seem, could set off an explosion. The bridge out of this solitude is the construction of a poetic prosthesis. However, this oscillating bridge between the past and the future results in one other significant bridge or connective tissue that this book hopes to aid in constructing, and that is the theoretical and perhaps clinical bridge between trauma and disability: between these veterans' commitment to their own experience of failed communication and seclusion, and the desire to return to some semblance of life after war.

For veterans, the impetus to write is an event or experience in the past, during their military service. It is that historical incident that serves as the accident, as Merleau-Ponty states, that extinguishes the human flame – an act of Force, per Simone Weil, that objectifies the human, which turns that which is alive into a passive, motionless object. And yet, as in Weil's reference to those who become objects in life, or the stirring image of the dead-while-alive military veteran, the object-soldier lives and moves, torn between the part that is alive and the part that has been killed. The poetic prosthesis, then, by combining the accident of history and the anguish of the individual, is an attempt to consolidate these two poles through the creation of poetic art, using everyday, communal language and bending it to point toward individual emotion. This is, in other words, the role and use of literature, if that use was not hitherto already made clear, and serves as a working definition of literature as well, at least for me: the effort to gauge the tension between communal and personal, and thus the ability to speak of both at the same time. In this context, and before I address the manner in which literature bridges the gap between traumatic experience and the experience of disability, I would like for a moment to elicit yet another field, that of memory studies, more specifically that of memoir and life writing, which seem to me to be especially pertinent here. And as Jennifer Jensen Wallach writes in the introduction to her study of African American life writing, it is the poetic or literary element of life writing that initiates the desired movement:

> A full-fledged understanding of a particular historical moment must capture the complexities of the cognitive and the affective, the factual and the imaginary, perceptions and misperceptions. These elements are constitutive of a complex historical reality, which exists *from* the perspectives of the people who inhabited a past social world. The facts and feelings of historical agents are not responses to a preexisting social reality. Rather, they *are* reality.[3]

Aside from my slight aversion to Jensen Wallach's use of 'historical agents', the essence of this statement speaks volumes to me of the value of writing by individuals who experience history and who are crushed by it, specifically veterans and their family members And this is the reason for my dedicating this chapter to trying to understand why it was that two fields so closely associated by individual pain and the experience of disability – namely, trauma studies and disability studies – were so suspicious of the literary.

Indexical poetics, by its very investment in the index, shares trauma studies' interest in the traumatic event and the representational challenges that event presents. That problematic was first established in Freud's later conception of trauma in *Beyond the Pleasure Principle*, and worked out further through later theoretical accounts such as Cathy Caruth's *Unclaimed Experience*, Kelly Oliver's *Witnessing*, Elaine Scarry's *The Body in Pain* and Shoshana Felman and Dori Laub's *Testimony*, as well as Ruth Leys' polemic with the Freudian tradition in *Trauma*. An event violently disrupts one's ability to lead the same life; unprocessed and perhaps unprocessable pain lingers, isolates and paralyses. These, I think, should all be familiar phenomena at this point and it is quite clear that the concept of trauma, as well as trauma studies as a whole, has had an important role in contributing to my own understanding of the injury to language and the need for a poetic prosthetic. However, at the same time, indexical poetics is also invested in the reanimation of that stalled movement, of mimicking and recreating movement through the poetic prosthetic object, and thus also in the possibility of an afterlife. This kind of moving on is, in fact, hinted at in Freud's discussion in *Beyond the Pleasure Principle* of 'children's games'[4] as one way of dealing with trauma, an idea very much in tune with my own focus on concepts such as 'movement' and 'play'. However, as I shall discuss later, that has not been the focus of the trauma theory tradition.

In that regard, then, indexical poetics, as it is invested in a reading embedded in the past and the effect of that past, is simultaneously preoccupied with the tool aspect of the aesthetic object, its function as a kind of prop that enables a return to communication, albeit of a very different kind, and a way back into the community. That same community, moreover, either writes off war veterans as 'lost' or is completely blind to the disability they carry since it often bears no physical or external markers – such as the lack of scars or signs addressed in Ex-Officer's poem 'Coward'. Indexical poetics is, then, also embedded in the theoretical, social and aesthetical debate forwarded by disability studies, especially such ideas as Tobin Siebers's notion of 'disability aesthetics', Rosemarie Garland-Thomson's concept of the 'normate', Mitchell and Snyder's writings on the 'narrative prosthesis', James Berger's work on the 'disarticulate' and 'care' – as evident in the previous chapter – Donna Haraway's 'cyborg' and, naturally, David Wills's work on the prosthetic. Disability studies seemingly mends the gap left by trauma studies in that it does not centre on personal disability; rather, it is that field, most invested in the afterlife of disability, of life with disability. This is the kind of limping life, moreover, that is afforded by the prosthesis.

However, as this chapter will show, despite the parallels between indexical poetics and these theoretical contexts as a mode of reading and understanding these prostheses, indexical poetics lies in a middle ground between both fields and is somewhat set apart, serving what I hope to be an important role in oscillating between those two poles. While both trauma studies and disability studies share a commitment to the manner in which the personal affects the poetic, the focus for trauma studies has inherently been on the personal experience of trauma and its destructive consequences, whereas disability studies has concentrated, for the most part, on the social and often political ramifications of the link between disability, representation and society – so, the veterans' experience of being isolated and outside of language, along with an apt depiction of their struggles to fit into the fabric of society. Secondly, while trauma studies, by and large, views the event of trauma as a representational crisis or obliteration of the ability either to represent or to communicate trauma, thus is invested in the event as ending a way of life – the soldier returning different, his personality changed in the wake of war – disability studies is occupied more with the post-event, often to the exclusion of the event of disability itself from its discussion. If wartime trauma is an epistemological apocalypse, in other words, disability studies and its focus on, say, the lives of soldiers at home after war, are inherently post-apocalyptic. To use Kelly Oliver's concepts, while trauma studies is focused on subjectivity – the experience of being disabled – disability studies is invested in the subject position – the reality of disability in society. While one mourns what had been lost, the other picks up from the moment and/or experience of loss, pushing back against the social and political stigma of loss and disability in a society seemingly bent on idolising the complete and 'healthy'.

Given the nature of injury I describe in this book, conceived as an assault on language, communication and one's sense of life or humanity, it is intrinsically tied to questions of trauma and the discussion of war as one kind of post-traumatic event. Whether through strict psychoanalytical terms or theories influenced by Freud, the traumatic event is that which infiltrates the psyche's defences, wreaking havoc in the subject's psychic economy, creating a compulsion to repeat, revisit and experience trauma. From the point of view of the crisis of war, veterans are struck by an inability to incorporate death and memories or experiences with death back into post-war home life, leading to nightmares, flashbacks, erratic and violent behaviour, suicidal ideation and hypervigilance, with returning veterans avoiding small spaces or crowded restaurants and flinching at exhaust pipe backfire. Describing the disastrous effects of such hyper-vigilance, Jonathan Shay writes of his war veteran patients that they 'scan the rooftops of the low-rise buildings near the clinic for snipers and look in the spaces between parked automobiles for people crouching for attack'.[5] However, a discussion of the traumatic effects of wartime experience would be incomplete, at best, if not also supplemented by a look into the way of life formed following war, a life marked by the attempt to come back. That form of life is a significant part of my discussion of poetic prosthetics, both in the analysis of the wartime social setting and its effect on individual experience, and in the thrust of this entire book as a whole – that the poetic prosthesis aims to re-establish a link to one's identity and surrounding social setting. And yet, despite drawing its influence from both fields, indexical poetics is also set apart from both traditions, mainly in the stress I place on the value of poetics, of the artistic representation of wartime experiences, especially given the anti-representational tendencies in both trauma and disability studies: more specifically in the resistance expressed by both trauma and disability studies, for different reasons, to the figurative and metaphorical.

Against Poetry

Deeply rooted in the psychoanalytical tradition, trauma studies, as it later came to be called, saw its rise in the wake of the First World War via the Freudian analysis of wartime neuroses, and further developments in Freudian and Lacanian theory following the Second World War and the Holocaust. Throughout its development, however, trauma studies' focus has, to a point, remained the unknowability of the traumatic event, accessed only via the circumventive paths of dreams, obsessive repetition, and symptoms one would associate with the modern contemporary category of PTSD. As Freud writes in *Beyond the Pleasure Principle*, the foundational text of later trauma theory written in the aftermath of the Great War, trauma is that force pressing into the system, overriding its defences and throwing it into disarray. As such, it can never be known *per se*, or represented – only found in its effects, in the wound it leaves in its path. As Caruth writes in *Unclaimed Experience* (1996), one of the more influential works in this tradition:

> [Trauma] is always the story of a wound that cries out, that addresses us in the attempt to tell us of a reality or truth that is not otherwise available. This truth, in its delayed appearance and its belated address, cannot be linked only to what is known, but also to what remains unknown in our very actions and our language.[6]

The double bind of the unknowability of the traumatic event and the importance of symptoms in the attempt to 'point toward' that event has given rise to a focus on figurative language, specifically metaphors, in any depiction or analysis of trauma. If any attempt to depict traumatic experience, whether to oneself or others, is tantamount to a sign pointing to an unknown referent, then figurative language, and specifically metaphors, become useful tools, if not emblems of the dynamic of trauma itself. The shift into metaphor, the very use of metaphor, is an indication of the inability to discuss trauma and traumatic events or their lingering effects in any 'direct' way.

The 'wound that cries out', then, is not a representation of the moment of injury, since we do not and cannot have access to that moment, but a signifier, a signpost, that points at a missing, unknown and horrific signified or meaning. The problem becomes more complex, moreover, when considering the causality, or lack thereof, set up by Freud in *Beyond the Pleasure Principle*, in which evidence of the traumatic event is always discovered belatedly, through the weeping of the wound. One compelling example of this elusive structure, one that further distances our ability to know or represent trauma, whether as event or as effect, is provided by Freud himself. Interestingly, it is a moment, not uncommon in Freud's work and in the psychoanalytical tradition writ large, of literary analysis in service not only of exposing the workings of the psyche but of dealing with the subject of war. In the excerpt discussed, Tancred, the hero of Tasso's epic poem set during the Christian Crusades in the Holy Land, *Gerusalemme Liberata* ('Jerusalem Delivered'), finds himself, time and again and inadvertently, wounding and killing his beloved Clorinda, a Christian warrior maiden who had joined the Muslim ranks:

> Its hero, Tancred, unwittingly killing his beloved Clorinda in a duel while she is disguised in the armour of an enemy knight. After her burial he makes his way into a strange magic forest which strikes the Crusaders army with terror. He slashes with his sword at a tall tree; but blood streams from the cut and the voice of Clorinda, whose soul is imprisoned in the tree, is heard complaining that he has wounded his beloved once again.[7]

Freud's analysis of Tancred's tragic repetition of the horrible act of killing Clorinda identifies the unconscious tendency to repeat horrific experiences from the past that seems to override Freud's earlier conception of the 'pleasure principle', or the psyche's motivation to reject what does harm to it and accept only those elements that causes it pleasure. The compulsion to repeat a past catastrophe, a very real part of the form of life after war – flashbacks, nightmares – is, then, that which points toward an earlier event or experience which itself, as Freud writes, points at the undercurrents of the unconscious. It is not in the Freudian tradition, even the event itself that we encounter in our analysis of our own acts of repetition, but the pull and influence of an element to which we have very little access, if any. As Caruth writes in *Unclaimed Experience*, trauma, paradigmatically speaking, as an 'accident', as it emerges in Freud's discussion of trauma in *Beyond the Pleasure Principle*,[8] does not simply represent the violence of a collision but also conveys the impact of its very incomprehensibility. 'What returns to haunt the victim', Caruth writes, 'is not only the reality of the violent event but also the reality of the ways that its violence has not yet been fully known.'[9] Writing along the same lines, Avital Ronell adds:

> The 'technical' difficulty consists in the fact that trauma can be experienced in at least two ways, both of which block normal channels of transmission: as a memory that one cannot integrate into one's own experience, and as a catastrophic knowledge that one cannot communicate to others.[10]

From this point of incomprehensibility, I suggest, the path seems quite direct to what could be the enshrinement of the unknowability of the traumatic event as an index of its 'reality' for, quite simply, one cannot represent, communicate or articulate what one does not, and patently cannot, know. My own delineation of these ideas, with its obvious faults and simplifications, nonetheless lays bare what could be called the mystical or moral aspects of this type of discourse regarding trauma, and perhaps a mysticism inherent to the aftermath of violence: mystical since the event in question cannot be named, and moral since the naming of it, as proven by the continued failures to do so 'accurately', represents an ethical transgression. In perhaps the most famous reference to the possibility of a post-traumatic crisis of representation, Theodor Adorno asserted that 'To write poetry after Auschwitz is barbaric,'[11] linking the inability to represent with an ethical imperative: it is not only that one cannot write poetry after the horrors of the Holocaust, but it is that in the post-Holocaust world, one *should not*. The circularity of this notion, advanced by trauma studies, that the traumatic is somehow real is criticised by Ruth Leys in her 2000 book *Trauma: A Genealogy*.

Leys, positioned perhaps at the other pole of contemporary discourse concerning trauma in the humanities, criticises Caruth's analysis of trauma as a crisis of representation, mainly what she perceives as the 'realness' of post-traumatic experiences and memories. In *Trauma: A Genealogy*, Leys argues against the concept of traumatic repetition as 'literal, nonsymbolic, and nonrepresentational'.[12] Her argument rests on two major thrusts: firstly, she argues against the claim that post-traumatic repetitions such as the nightmare or the flashback are *real* or *literal* iterations of an unrepresentable event; and secondly, while advancing the Freudian notion of belatedness – the event, itself too violent and fast to be understood or known at the moment of its taking place, is experienced only after the fact – Caruth and other interpreters of Freud's work create a direct causal chain between a source event and its repetition. In other words, the repetition is belated; it is a kind of literal return of an event, and once returned, paradoxically, it is directly and, again, literally related to that event.

There are ways in which Leys's criticism of Caruth's notion, or at least her own interpretation of Caruth's notion, is relevant to the discussion of post-war soldier poetry. This is generally so, since the irony which I claim to be so central to the workings of the poetic prostheses is the result of a tension, a distance, between what is perceived to be 'real' – that is, indices existentially tied to their referent – and the imagined or social – symbols, the meaning of which, for the most part if not exclusively,[13] is socially dependent. A literal understanding of this attempt, a literality standing at the heart of Leys's criticism of Caruth, would be, to use Peirce's terms, to claim that the traumatic and the indexical are coterminous – as identical, to use another literary moment, as the fatal link between Ahab's harpoon and the plunging white whale. On a larger or more theoretical scale, treating these poems as pure indices of the traumatic experiences divests them, as I have already argued, of their aesthetic status as poems at all and of their function as post-war prostheses for, if they are nothing but reactions in a vaguely constructed chain reaction, they no longer represent a distinct kind of post-war work – the creation of art after war – and thus are relegated to the category of symptom or reflex.

However, the indexical, or literal to use Leys's term, is nonetheless an indispensable component of this new machine, making it impossible to banish completely the notion of 'literality' or a play with that term, as it seems Leys's analysis aims to do. In fact, the indexical, or ontological – what *really* happened in war, plays a major part in the experience of the prosthetic, mainly since the need for prosthesis is both ontological and epistemological, both real (a leg is missing, for instance) and unreal (a phantom leg continues to haunt its former 'owner'). In fact, if there is a way in which both Caruth's and Leys's work could be said to be participating in the discussion of the prosthesis, it could be in the complication that the traumatic event presents in understanding the difference, both in language and in action, between real and unreal, safe and dangerous. A problematic is created around the blurring of what is perceived to be a 'natural' or at least pre-war state of affairs, one of clear divisions between safety and danger, and based on positivist notions of knowledge and learning – the more you live and experience, the more adept you become at living. The moment, event or prolonged exposure perceived by the individual to be responsible for such an undermining of a sense of security with one's own language is the 'accident' or 'surprise' that cannot be subsumed, as yet another instance of learning. Information, via content, is not received, as the experience disrupts, via Ronell's insight, the very ability to process information, or evaluate the relation between the experiencing body and either its temporal or its spatial context. In Freudian terms, this event could be described as the sense data bypassing systems of representation and meaning, and directly invading and subverting consciousness. However, whether adhering to the Freudian narrative of trauma or not, the effect of this disruption could be said to manifest in a difficulty to consolidate body and context, experience and language, or to perceive them as being possible at the same time and in the same place.

As the Freudian tradition then develops further through the work of Jacques Lacan and others, this element of unknowability remains and, as Berger argues in his essay, becomes a theoretical focal point. It is the trace of an encounter, if we were to refer to the Lacanian development of this idea, with the *real*. As Berger writes, while psychoanalysis, whether Freudian or Lacanian, naturally has had a vested interest in the clinic and the working through of trauma, these tendencies may have, in their later interpretations and manifestations, been replaced by a fascination with an inability to work through, and an almost ethical prohibition against representation:

> In contemporary trauma studies, the problematics or impossibility of working through is often given greater emphasis than any consideration of what working through might actually consist of. Žižek, for instance, following Lacan, has tended to regard any symbolic articulation as yet another symptomatic–ideological suturing of the traumatic wound of the real that is the unspeakable, abyssal center of every symbolic order. Similarly, Eric Santner has written of the 'narrative fetish' that simulates a condition of wholeness and denies the continuing effects of trauma.[14]

Thus, trauma studies' double bind of unknowability and representational crisis has led to a tendency to focus on what could be the inaccessibility of the event and the shift triggered by that discussion into a focus on the end of a personal history, on the obliteration of experience, the cleaving of the subject. As Berger again writes:

> In spite of its extensive use of metaphor of damage and recuperation, and of its function as a theory of metaphor, trauma studies does not employ figures suggesting disability. In this regard, trauma studies is actually more apocalyptic in attitude than it might like to admit. Its concern is with absolute catastrophe, obliteration, absolute transformation, total alterity.[15]

Trauma theory's emphasis on trauma as an end to personal history and its preoccupation with the metaphor could be read as a focus, at least a theoretical one, on what had been obliterated by trauma, as opposed to the form of life that persists following the traumatic event. That traumatic event, in other words, in its very inaccessibility marks it as somehow a 'realer' and more authentic event or experience than the symbolic life, to use Lacanian terms, that protects the ego from being exposed to that real. However, as Berger argues, this apocalyptic aspect of the Freudian understanding of trauma, at least in the manner in which that aspect has taken on a greater and greater role in later iterations of trauma studies, renders the traumatic event so destructive, and so 'real', that it signifies nothing short of a sublime end. Beyond that end, beyond this naggingly persistent obstacle of fragmentation and unknowability, nothing can be certain – nothing, at least, but aporia and the mystic pull aporia has had on psychoanalysis and, in turn, the critical tradition since the Second World War.

Within the context of discussing the lives of soldiers after war, however, and given this notion of end or, at the very least, a deeply seated scepticism regarding the possibility of moving on in both a personal and a communal fashion, there is a long way in which trauma is essential in understanding about the sense of 'end' in veterans' writing. A view into that life is available, as I have argued, through the use of the poetic prosthesis, not through an emblem that points at a wound but one that opens up a space in which past pain is introduced. In the poetic text written by Iraq veteran Brock Michael Jones titled 'Explaining the Unexplainable', there is a very clear sense of something ending, without any idea of how life would go on. Describing the aftermath of a soldier who had 'disappeared' after being killed in an explosion, Jones describes the charred aftermath of death where it is not very clear if there is room for even the slightest, most feeble life to grow:

> There's this scout in Bandit Troop lost one of his buddies that way: one minute he was there and the next . . . gone. They searched for three days, never found so much as a finger. Apparently a few weeks later the scout started hearing his old pal's voice coming from down in one of the piss tubes where the whole camp would go three, four times a day to take a leak. And so when he recognized his buddy's voice coming out of that three-inch pipe, he wouldn't let anyone else near the place, said there was no way he was going to let anyone piss on his friend. MPs finally had to get physical with him and he held so tightly to that one piss tube that he pulled it out of the ground as they dragged him off. It took four of those police to pull it out of his arms. They pulled the other pipes out of the ground and spread fresh dirt over the holes and made some poor private dig three more PVC pipes into the ground over closer to the chow hall.[16]

It is quite easy to see how a moment like this, a happening like this, a keeping of faith with the dead, a caring for the dead, would draw one into a world of nothing but death. Do the new pipes help the scout live with the memory of his friend? Do the voices persist? Does he live? All of those questions remain unanswered. And yet, despite the seeming finality present in today's war poems it still seems that the way trauma studies has and does address the so-called end of experience in the wake of trauma leaves much to be desired. What does life after war or trauma look like? Is it liveable? Is it life? Are all questions asked about the after-effects of trauma, but seldom raised in the context of the theoretical discussions of the rift itself. They were relegated, to an extent, to the social sciences, the medical sciences, and the post- and counter-Freudian branches of psychiatry and psychology. However, while the possibility of a horizon of human action and knowledge remains murky in con-temporary trauma studies, precisely that horizon, or at least part of it, represents the epicentre of ongoing work in disability studies.

Ultimately, later trauma theory's apparent neglect of post-traumatic life – the aspect, paradoxically, that preoccupied Freud in *Beyond the Pleasure Principle* and later – was augmented with the rise of disabil-ity studies. The focus in disability studies had been not so much on the existential event of becoming disabled but on what happens next, whether through the experience of disability or the manner in which disability is treated and stigmatised by society: not the unknowable traumatic moment at war, in other words, but the difficulties of living with its scars, both visible and invisible. Drawing its influence more from the discourse of the social sciences and theoretical interventions in the social sciences, such as by Michel Foucault, Edward Said and Alain Badiou, than from psychoanalysis, disability studies seems poised to fill the gap left by trauma studies precisely because of its emphasis not on the obliteration of life but its stubborn persistence, as well as its social realities. Thus the resistance found in disability studies to the traumatic treatment metaphor, similarly to other identity-based theoretical inter-ventions, is grounded in psychoanalysis's perceived focus on individual emotional and psychic experience, one both detrimental to an under-standing of a wider political reality and, in some cases, directly partici-pating in political oppression.[17]

One standout example of such an intervention, and the manner in which it resists psychoanalytical models of the psyche, is Garland-Thomson's conceptualisation of the 'normate'. Writing in *Extraordinary Bodies*, Garland-Thomson argues for the existence of a social understand-ing of disability that serves to sustain and demarcate a zone of socially constructed normality she dubs as the 'normate'. The normate, as Garland-Thomson argues, points precisely to the inorganic, artificial reality of the oppressive category of normality, or, said otherwise, exposes that claim for organity or completeness as part of the oppressive mechanism meant both to prop up those considered normal and to oppress those labelled disabled. And much along the lines of Said's attack on orientalism, as both socially and culturally constructed and politically motivated,[18] Garland-Thomson's analysis targets those cultural, social and scientific institutions whose work culminates in stigmatisation and political oppression of those excluded from the normate, such as people with disabilities. And just as, for Said, anthropologists and authors who had written about the Orient in the service, seemingly, of culture, only to bolster a larger mechanism of political oppression still further, Garland-Thomson aims at dismantling those same social agents of the oppression of the disabled. I will approach Garland-Thomson's attack on literature and metaphor as part of this analysis later on in this chapter, but for now it suffices to say that Freud and the Freudian tradition are marked, and quite sharply so, in *Extraordinary Bodies*, as part of that self-same hegemonic oppressive mechanism, much in keeping with a tradition of feminist critique of Freudian psychoanalysis.[19] As Garland-Thomson writes:

> The modern secular world's method of labeling disability dangerous is to term it pathological rather than evil or immoral. Freud's essay on 'The Exceptions,' for example, labels disabled people psychologically pathological. Conflating the inner and outer selves, Freud concludes that 'deformities of character' are the results of physical disability.[20]

Thus, not only does Freud, in this line of thought, participate in the erection of the normate and oppression of the disabled, but he does so according to what Garland-Thomson identifies as a general Western tradition that associates what it considers as exterior deformities with moral corruption. Later, Garland-Thomson writes:

> Western tradition posits the visible world as the index of a coherent and just invisible world, encouraging us to read the material body as a sign invested with transcendent meaning. In interpreting the material world, literature tends to imbue any physical difference with significance that obscures the complexity of their bearers.[21]

Thus, Freudian psychoanalysis and its later iteration in theory vis-à-vis trauma studies both negate the agency of social change and make up a significant part of the same medical–oppressive apparatus that services the normate while stigmatising and marginalising the disabled. The stage, for Garland-Thomson, and for other leading voices in the history of disability studies, is not the stage of the psyche, which is another expression of the intrusiveness of the heuristic/diagnostic political impulse of the normate, but that of the politicised, gendered, racialised and disabled subject.

However, while the social, personal, emotional and intellectual aspects of disability take centre stage, they do so with a healthy dose of distrust, if not disdain, for that most central of trauma-theory features, the metaphor, a position seen already in Garland-Thomson's analysis of the normate's propensity to mark the physically different as morally corrupt through its medical and literary representations. Given the social reality of disability, and in the context of post-war writing, metaphors not only become suspicious but also, to an extent, signify the societal oppression of the disabled. As Garland-Thomson argues, in the real-world semiotic game, as well as in the literary one, the disabled person is nothing but pure metaphor: blindness indicates corruption; a missing limb points to a moral undoing or, in the case of war veterans, the ravages of war. The social body uses the disabled as symbols, thus consistently erasing individual experiences of disability and dehumanising the disabled. Far from being a tool by which to gain access into an inaccessible experience, then, the literary treatment of disability, in a move that seems to take more than a page from Foucault's post-Gramsci discussion of hegemony and Said's attack on the Western artistic representations of the Orient in *Orientalism*, necessarily partakes in a larger social project of erasing the lived experience of individuals with disabilities through symbolic artistic representations used to prop up the 'normate'. It is not a porthole into the shock and unknowing of pain and trauma but a social stigma placed on the disabled, and through which, as Garland-Thomson argues, what she calls 'the normate, the space of normative bodies and behaviors', defines itself.

To sum up, and to return to Berger's article 'Trauma Without Disability, Disability Without Trauma', the two fields have drifted far apart, in essence serving similar yet complementary and at times oppositional roles in viewing the place and state of the disabled, traumatised person in society. And yet, despite these differences, both have adopted an anti-representational stance, whether for ontological/psychological or social/ethical reasons. The reality, which is defined on either psychological or social bases, of experience evades representation, making every instance of representation either a pre-ordained failure, as in the case of trauma theory, or an act of political oppression, as in Garland-Thomson as well as other disability theorists. As Berger writes:

> Trauma theory is, in many ways, ultimately a theory of metaphor; it is a way of thinking about how some extreme event or experience that is radically

non-linguistic, that seems even to negate language, is somehow carried across into language. Disability studies, conversely, devotes much of its practical and theoretical energy toward disputing the uses of metaphor with reference to the disabled, regarding metaphor as irremediably tied to oppressive ideological systems.[22]

Since metaphor, its uses, and its representations of disability, or the inability to depict disability, serve as a central bone of contention between trauma and disability, it would, then, be a productive site for an attempted reconciliation. This would be a reconciliation not in the hopes of successfully integrating psychoanalysis with disability studies – an aim, I must admit, which is far beyond the scope of this book – but as a result of the intuition that there is a benefit in addressing the destruction of trauma, of discussing it in terms of something lost, as well as addressing life after that loss: of allowing, again, one to oscillate with the other.

One manner of addressing that reconciliation from a disability studies standpoint is spelled out in David T. Mitchell and Sharon L. Snyder's influential *Narrative Prosthesis*. First and foremost, Mitchell and Snyder, similarly to Garland-Thomson, warn against the toxic social effect of literature's ongoing fascination with disability. Through their concept of 'narrative prosthesis', their study identifies a long-running usage of the deformed body or the disabled body as a tool of generating narrative drama. Using the example of the one-legged soldier in the children's story 'The Steadfast Tin Soldier', Mitchell and Snyder highlight the aesthetic pitfalls of such a rudimentary and dismissive use of physical difference for the sake of narrative suspense, as well as their possible social ramifications: the dismissal of the disabled body as a symbol of the narrative mechanism, all the while glossing over the intricacies, ambiguities and pain of the experience of disability.[23] While Mitchell and Snyder stop short of damning all representation of the disabled as collaborating with a larger mechanism of oppression, they do warn against an artificial and irresponsible use of disabled figures in the attempt to 'ratchet' narrative, one that in itself serves to diminish the humanity of disabled characters, both real and imagined.[24]

However, elsewhere Mitchell and Snyder point at the kind of artistic representation that could, in fact, achieve the representation of disability by providing a kind of oscillating and unstable map of meaning: the kind of unstable space, moreover, that at first glance seems to resemble that of the poetic prosthetics and of the soldier poems discussed here. As they write:

> This textual performance of ever-shifting and unstable meanings is critical in our interpretive approach to the representation of disability. The close

readings that follow hinge upon the identification of disability as an ambiva-
lent and mutable category of cultural and literary investment. Within literary narratives, disability serves as an interruptive force that confronts cultural
truisms. The inherent vulnerability and variability of bodies serves literary
narratives as a metonym for that which refuses to conform to the mind's
desire for order and rationality. Within this schema, disability acts as a metaphor and fleshy example of the body's unruly resistance to the cultural desire
to 'enforce normalcy'.[25]

The ever-shifting, ever-oscillating space of meaning, in which signs fade
in and out of their function, is quite similar to the mechanical breakdown
and description I propose as indexical poetics. And in creating this new
field or space of meaning, I would argue, the kind of oscillation Mitchell
and Snyder propose would also fit with yet another important aspect of
the poetic prosthesis, and really with poetry more generally, which is the
generation of new meanings out of the 'waste' of language. This is metaphor, then, not as a way of anchoring a known tradition of meaning-
making or of gesturing toward that tradition – disabled equals morally
corrupt, for instance – but as a way to give new meaning to a novel, and
in this case quite violent, experience; metaphor, then, as a new meaning
breaking through or, as Eric J. Leed writes in the context of World War I,
words 'used, verified, integrated into an historical experience to acquire
meanings and associations that they did not previously have'.[26] However, while this dream-like lack of semantic stability is inherent both to
Mitchell and Snyder's notion of a successful metaphor of the manner in
which disability challenges norms and concepts of the body, and to the
prosthesis that stands at the heart of this book, there remains one significant difference: the past, the manner in which individual experience is
shaped by that past, and the past's wound-like persistence.

While Mitchell and Snyder indeed highlight the kind of stand-in function of texts about and out of disability, the function of the metaphorical
machine for them is, ultimately, a social one. The disabled body, most
often is misrepresented and glossed over in the service of providing 'narrative prosthesis', even when adequately represented, serves, yet again, as
first and foremost a disruptor of social norms, concepts and systems of
meaning. By insisting on marking the disruption of disability as somehow epistemologically and politically cogent, Mitchell and Snyder, similarly to Garland-Thomson, create a landscape in which, as Berger writes
in his 2016 *The Disarticulate*, even a successful depiction of disability
via an ever-oscillating hermeneutics glosses over the *particular, individual
experience of pain, negativity, inadequacy, and unease* that too are part of the

story of disability in general, and in the case of war veterans, particularly. Moreover, there is a glossing over not only of that individual experience of the past; there is also no room for a discussion of the ways in which that pain is intertwined with the moral obligation to speak for those who cannot speak for themselves, who did not gain access to a voice of disability. In the case of war veterans, this role could be said to be filled by the war dead, or those traumatised beyond the ability even to attempt a written depiction of their experiences.

Thus, as similar as Mitchell and Snyder's formulation is to my own notion of an ever-oscillating, tension-sustaining indexical poetics, this last point bears further iteration. If the ethics posited by the writing and reading of prosthetic texts are defined by oscillation and by a persistent experience of unease and disruption, then the inability, firstly, to articulate the manner in which that pain is itself part of the unpredictable hermeneutics of the text, and secondly, is a persistent feature of that symbolic mechanism amounts to what I would claim is only a partial reading. It is partial not because Mitchell and Snyder somehow miss the ambiguity and complexity of representing disability experiences; they do, in fact, point to precisely that ambiguity in their work. However, ultimately, it is partial since that complexity is, again, used as a kind of social corrector, as opposed to a mode of reading that exposes both the social aspects of what I refer to as post-disability solipsism and dehumanisation, and the personal experience of limit, tension and pain that is as personal as the social cry for communication with others.

As with Garland-Thomson, then, as well as other noted disability thinkers such as Donna Haraway, the sense of personal agony and incoherence that disability brings about, especially in the context of traumatic experiences, is morphed into a kind of socially conceived 'superpower': the disabled body as that which, via disruption, clarifies the inconsistencies and oppressive nature of the normal–disabled social categories. I say this not to insist, as Berger writes, on concepts such as 'pathology' or 'deficit',[27] but on 'pain': that the disruptive nature of the prosthetic transfer or dream in question is not only the constant oscillation and disruption of the symbolic order of meaning, and thus of social norms, but is itself disrupted by the index of a concrete past, pain and loss. This is the figure of, if you will, the constant spanner in the poetic works, that which Wills so poignantly describes as his father's experience of the spasm of phantom pain. Thus, an over-reliance on metaphor renders the traumatic event, the index of past pain, as entirely illegible, solipsistic and thus antisocial and inaccessible, while an over-reliance on the social function of the disabled body, as disruptor of norms, renders the pain of that invisible, if not politically ineffective in some cases. The way out of this double bind of anti-figuration, I argue, is double too: an understanding of the transformative function post-war figuration can have as a way to re-enter the social sphere while retaining the wounds of the past and, at the same time, an emphasis on mutual dependency and care.

Bridging the Gap

While disability studies and trauma studies stand at opposite ends of the social and personal experience of war, and while both fields seem to shun the moral and political ramifications of attempts to represent pain and disability, they do provide an olive branch of sorts that gets us closer to the notion of representation as actively participating in disability that this book puts forth. One such moment from the standpoint of trauma studies is the work of Dominick LaCapra, particularly in his 2001 book *Writing History, Writing Trauma*. LaCapra's concept of trauma includes a direct attack on what I have called above, following Berger, trauma theory's focus on the obliteration of experience:

> Some of the most powerful forms of modern art and writing, as well as some of the most compelling forms of criticism (including forms of deconstruction), often seem to be traumatic writing or post-traumatic writing in closest proximity to trauma. They may also involve the feeling of keeping faith with trauma in a manner that leads to a compulsive preoccupation with aporia, an endlessly melancholic, impossible mourning, and a resistance to working through.[28]

What LaCapra calls a 'preoccupation with aporia' marks the limits drawn here to trauma studies' ability, by and large, to detach itself from the moment of disaster and move on to life after disaster. And while LaCapra describes the tendency to attach to the traumatic epicentre through the idea of 'fidelity', one that emphasises the moral obligation to remain in pain, I would add, as I have discussed earlier, that this obligation is coupled with a sense of trauma and the traumatic event being 'realer' than everyday life: that to stay near the 'melancholic' is, in some way, to remain within the orbit of an index of reality, despite the pain that comes with that proximity. As a counter to that tendency, LaCapra discusses an emphasis on writing as a way of 'working through': to shift, in other words, from the apocalyptic to the slow drudge of post-apocalyptic life through works of history, poetry and even criticism, a category of post-traumatic text that would, I believe, include this very book. For

LaCapra, as he later writes, this preoccupation is rooted in the under-standing of trauma as a mystical experience that locates meaning in the site of paradox:

> I think one is involved here in more or less secularized displacements of the sacred and its paradoxes. The hiddenness, death, or absence of a radically transcendent divinity or of absolute foundations makes of existence a fun-damentally traumatic scene in which anxiety threatens to color, and perhaps confuse, all relations. One's relation to every other – instead of involving a tense, at time paradoxical, interaction of proximity and distance, solidar-ity and criticism, trust and wariness may be figured on the model of one's anxiety-ridden 'relation without relation' to a radically transcendent (now perhaps recognized as absent) divinity who is totally other.[29]

These last comments, I would argue, link to the former discussion of the role of the metaphor in trauma studies, specifically as a symptom of unknowability and destruction: the use of figurative language in soldier poetry – 'I was a coffin' – as an indication that the 'true' experience was not able to filter through. By doing so, by privileging the obtuseness of metaphor, a general corruption takes place, in which the very act of speaking and writing, to use LaCapra's words, turns into 'relation without relation'. And while LaCapra does indeed address the limits of an 'aporia-based' study of traumatic experience, a criticism shared, albeit from a different angle, in Leys's *Trauma*, his case is a somewhat isolated one. While it would seem that this correspondence would lead to a kind of joining of the two fields, the different theoretical footings (psychoanalysis and post-Freudian thought being one glaring difference), as well as the different focal points (psychic trauma versus physical disability), have left them quite apart.

Moreover, in terms of my discussion of post-war writing as a prosthetic that places significant stress on the index or the 'actual event', LaCapra's embedding of the work of post-traumatic writing in a historiographical mode is another important aspect of his work: in other words, the role of real events in one's personal past that lead to a variety of modes of writing created in the wake of that event, be those works historical, critical or artistic. And herein also lies what LaCapra calls 'fidelity to the past': the struggle to speak after war, after trauma or from the standpoint of disability, is not just the metaphysical undoing of language and experience but also bears the weight of moral obligation, of speaking for others who cannot document their own experiences, those whom Berger identifies as the 'disarticulate'. Thus the pull of the historical is not just the ever-elusive, representation-resistant disaster, but also the obligation to a community of likewise silenced individuals, whether they have been silenced by social norms, the impact of trauma or political marginalisation. Ultimately, this is that part of the work of history and personal history that I identify as the indexical aspect of post-war poetic prosthetics: the index both locating a concrete place and time of happening and, at the same time, indicating the impossible moral weight on words to say anything more meaningful than, for instance, Brian Turner's 'it happened there'. However, while LaCapra's theory of trauma writing brings us closer to the middle ground fashioned by indexical poetics, Wills's 'prosthesis' and Berger's 'care', it is Tobin Siebers's concept of 'disability aesthetics' that provides the other pole, the symbolic, through its emphasis on the aesthetic, as opposed to ethical, role of disability.

Siebers's *Disability Aesthetics*, published in 2010, argues for the centrality of the disability experience not only serving as a theme in literature and the arts but also participating in the fundamental act of experiencing any aesthetic object, as such. In one noted example, Siebers attributes the artistic importance and merit of the Venus de Milo precisely to the manner in which the work oscillates between the beauty of the torso and the shock of the missing limbs. Thus, perhaps standing as a kind of polar opposite to Garland-Thomson's warning against the social cost of representing disability, Siebers inserts disability into the heart of any artistic representation, identifying the very ability to experience and evaluate works of art as involved in recognising that those works 'summon images of disability. Most frequently, they register as wounded or disabled bodies, representations of irrationality or cognitive disability, or effects of warfare, disease, or accidents.'[30] Siebers's theory, then, could be said to echo somewhat the relationship the 'wound' has to meaning in trauma theory only from an aesthetic point of view – that which is beautiful in modern art revolves around, or is experienced in contrast to that which is disabled: 'It is often the presence of disability that allows the beauty of an artwork to endure over time.'[31]

Siebers's 'disability aesthetics', then, dovetail with LaCapra's theory of post-traumatic writing to produce something along the middle ground offered by Wills's notion of the prosthetic text. If, as LaCapra states, the work of writing after trauma is a part of working through trauma and, moreover, can result in a variety of textual production, one possible outcome of that effort is the kind of art Siebers identifies as summoning 'disability' and, importantly for this book, as representing the personal aftermath of war. In at least one significant way, then, my discussion of post-war soldier writing is also an attempt to break down what it is about the machine that makes it 'work' – as a prop that imitates the action of a lost original in order to regain some of its function but also, and perhaps inherently, makes it beautiful. It is here that the discussion of the poetic prosthesis is an attempt both to analyse its parts – index, symbol, and the icon that results from the tension between the two poles – as well as to try to understand the effect – dream, icon, prosthesis.

The personal pull soldiers feel toward their past, the pain of the index and the moral duty to speak of others' experiences of that past, is an intrinsic part of any prosthetic work, one that is either marginalised or dismissed, by and large, in disability studies. On the other hand, the transformation of that past into a new present, one infused with pain as well as rejection by one's community, is an important aspect since it is that community to which war veterans strive to return, albeit on new terms. The result is a discussion of both the immutability of the past and its surprising mutability – from an anchor of specific experience, weighed down all the more by the moral duty to represent that reality to others who had not experienced it, to an act of performance, play and transformation. As Berger writes in 'Disability without Trauma, Trauma without Disability':

> We can understand a present situation only in relation to some past event; yet, because this past event has, through its overwhelming violence and horror, obliterated itself, it can only be encountered by means of its effects in the present. And these effects are not direct: transmission is achieved through transformation and metamorphosis.[32]

The past and its violence and horror are precisely the focus of trauma theory and represent that field's visible contribution to the indexical poetics this book puts forth. At the same time, as Berger writes, the marks of that obliterated and obliterating past are very much alive in the present, whether in the form of visible, physical disability or the oppression of past trauma on the mind of those who return from war.

In terms of what I have been claiming thus far, it is precisely the signs that represent the attachment and influence of the past, the index, that are primed and, as Berger writes, set to undergo metamorphosis through the act of burying the index, as I discussed in the previous chapter. However, it is, as I have argued in the Introduction and Chapter 1, a very elusive brand of metamorphosis, since the physical shape, at times, does not shift at all. In other words, the challenge the prosthesis presents is not the wholesale demolition of communication in the wake of war, nor the successful creation of a private mode of communication that somehow supersedes communal language; it is, rather, the presentation of the dream or diagram of language, perhaps one akin to the 'dream of life' of Jarrell's gunner, in a manner which exposes the mechanical nature of that dream, all without changing language or words in any radical way. It is, at the very same time, both literal and figurative, indexical and symbolic, with the spectre of its ever-shifting locus of meaning the effect of precisely this coupling: a coupling that Schlegel, in his discussion of irony, termed the constant tension between the inability to communicate – a kind of communication, if we are to take Peirce's cue, that is inherently communal – and the absolute necessity to communicate. This duality seems to me to be at least partially linked to the motion between moored and unmoored that Merleau-Ponty identifies as the essence of cave art and perhaps also to his definition of life as a relation or movement. To return, for a moment, to Schlegel:

> Irony sustains and provokes a feeling of the irresolvable conflict between the conditioned and the unconditioned, between the necessity and the impossibility of a complete communication. Irony is the freest of all forms of license since it allows one to go quite beyond oneself, but is equally the most binding since it is unconditionally necessary.[33]

The importance of Schlegel's definition, in the recognition of the simultaneous plasticity and immutability of communication, is, of course, as a way to assuage at least some of Garland-Thomson's concerns regarding the role of representation or metaphor. Under this understanding of the form and function of the poetic prosthesis what takes place is neither representation – a relation of a copy to an original – nor the 'real' or traumatic signified – in the psychoanalytical tradition – but both at one and the same time. Both, in addition, are positioned in such a manner as to produce some new meaning, some new picture of reality, and in this case the reality of disability, that is the result not of pinning down the image of the disabled but the constant stop-start oscillation Mitchell and Snyder describe when added to the tremors and convulsions of pain described by Derrida and Wills. Perhaps one useful example of the way in which something can change without changing, as the structure of the prosthetic diagram creates tension resisting radical transformation, echoes Wittgenstein's discussion of 'secondary sense' and 'aspect dawning' in his *Philosophical Investigations*.

With his discussion of aspect dawning – seeing a picture or image as something else without losing the original image – Wittgenstein reiterates, albeit differently, the notion of viewing language as a diagram or picture. Looking at the diagram of a cube, to use Wittgenstein's example, we can see it as a cube, as a cube with a visible missing side or with the side not in our line of sight, as a cube made of glass and so on. What enables this constant shift in what we see, I argue, is the result of an image of reality quite similar to that insisted upon by Wittgenstein in his earlier work, the *Tractatus Logico-Philosophicus*. If we were to view a picture of an iron cube, for instance, these shifting aspects would be harder, although far from impossible, to trigger for, as in his earlier work, the *Tractatus*, the prerequisite of such shifting is viewing the scheme of a cube. Once naked form is achieved, what Peirce calls a 'diagram',[34] the image suddenly lends itself to be viewed differently. As Meredith Williams writes, the example of a cube 'serves to highlight the fact that any picture, chart, schema (i.e., any *isolable* representational object) is susceptible to more than one interpretation, to more than one use'.[35] Thus the effect of a poetic text of the kind this language of war creates, like the cube, is far from being realistic in a detail-specific manner but instead serves as a launching pad for innumerable aspects of one experience of war. This shift to a new kind of seeing – as proposed in Weigl's proclaimed shift from 'life' to 'poetry' – is one which, as Stephen Mulhall states, manifests 'the nature of our normal relationship with language – we directly perceive the written and spoken elements of language as meaningful words and sentences, not as sounds-or-marks-to-be-interpreted.'[36] Literature, for Wittgenstein, is that special kind of linguistic activity where the meaning of a proposition is not derived solely from the context of a specific picture, as in ordinary language games: 'When I read a poem or a narrative with feeling, surely something goes on in me which does not go on when I merely skim the lines for information.'[37] Wittgenstein likens this manner of experiencing language to seeing a painting, in which the work allows, unlike ordinary language games, the experience of its totality as well of its composite elements in isolation: 'If a sentence can strike me as a painting in words, and the very individual word in the sentence as like a picture, then it is no such marvel that a word uttered in isolation and without purpose can seem to carry a particular meaning in itself.'[38]

Nothing changes, then, and everything changes. In Mena's poem Kyle dies, and remains dead, and the hose used to wash out the remains of a soldier is the same hose. The facts remain the same, the words remain the same, and yet something seems to happen, as I have been arguing, when facts and words are placed in a certain fashion, made to work off each other, subvert and pull at each other. As I have already stated, this is related to the work of burial. But for now I would like to end this chapter with Berger's discussion of what seems like the similar phenomena of what he calls 'metaphor' and ' catachresis', which pushes forward the work I believe figurative language to do in the life of soldiers after war:

> Metaphor, as I argue in this book, does not work by means of simple sub-stitution. Its mechanism is closer to that of catachresis, in which a word is reconfigured to denote some entity that has not yet been adequately con-ceptualized and that has, at present, no word that signifies it. Metaphor as catachresis is a creative and maieutic, not simply a manipulative, act; it brings something into the world . . . Poetics as catachresis as I have tried to describe it makes possible new perspectives and thus new knowledge. This knowledge, of course, can be evaluated and critiqued. It may be determined that it is ethically untenable, or so incompatible with other, prior knowledge that it ought to be rejected – deemed to be not knowledge at all, but a fantasy deriv-ing from ideological or other unconscious forces that ought to be exposed and condemned. That process is certainly within the purview of disability studies, but does not involve a critique of the practice of metaphor per se – which, as the work of thinkers as disparate as Derrida, Lakoff and Johnson, Ricoeur, and Black demonstrates, is an essential, if not the essential, element in human thought.[39]

What Berger calls 'metaphor' here seems to align closely with my own concept of indexical poetics, if not my own, quite intentional, emphasis on what Wills would call 'kinetics': the work of putting things back together, of recreating a process that some 'accident' had ended and that, as Berger states, has been argued as being essential to human thought. However, if I were to dovetail that intuition, along with my own discussion of the seeming necessity to articulate wartime experiences as a way out of a 'bestial' or 'death-like' solipsism, it would seem that I am willing to go one step further, that the process initiated by the prosthesis is one without which the human is not experienced as such any more – not an essential element, then, of human thought, but that which marks the human and re-establishes a lost humanity.

Notes

1. 'Prosthesis, n.' *OED Online*. June 2018. Oxford University Press. Available at: <http://www.oed.com/view/Entry/153069?redirectedFrom=prosthesis> (last accessed 25 February 2022).
2. Wallace Stevens, 'Man Carrying Thing', in *The Collected Poems of Wallace Stevens* (New York: Vintage Books, 1982), 350.

3. Jennifer Jensen Wallach, *Closer to the Truth than any Fact: Memoir, Memory, and Jim Crow* (Athens: University of Georgia Press, 2008), 3–4.

4. Freud, *Beyond the Pleasure Principle*, 8–11, 29.

5. Jonathan Shay, *Odysseus in America: Combat Trauma and the Trials of Homecoming* (New York: Scribner, 2002), 63.

6. Caruth, *Unclaimed Experience*, 4.

7. Freud, *Beyond the Pleasure Principle*, 16.

8. Ibid.

9. Caruth, *Unclaimed Experience*, 6.

10. Avital Ronell, *Finitude's Score: Essays for the End of the Millennium* (Lincoln: University of Nebraska Press, 1998), 314.

11. Theodor W. Adorno, 'Cultural Criticism and Society', in *Prisms*, translated by Shierry Weber Nicholson and Samuel Weber (Cambridge, MA: MIT Press, 1983), 34.

12. Ruth Leys, *Trauma: A Genealogy* (Chicago: University of Chicago Press, 2000), 272.

13. Julia Kristeva, *Revolution in Poetic Language*, translated by Margaret Waller (New York: Columbia University Press, 1984), 72.

14. James Berger, 'Trauma Without Disability, Disability Without Trauma: A Disciplinary Divide', *JAC* 24, no. 3, Special Issue, Part 2: Trauma and Rhetoric (2004), 568.

15. Ibid., 569.

16. Brock Michael Jones, 'Explaining the Unexplainable', *Mobius: The Journal for Social Change* 22, no. 2 (Summer 2011). Available at: <https://mobiusmagazine.com/poetry/explaini.html> (last accessed 25 February 2022).

17. Liz Bondi, 'Locating Identity Politics', in *Place and the Politics of Identity*, edited by Steve Pile and Michael Keith (London: Routledge, 1994), 86–9; Judith Butler, 'Agencies of Style for a Liminal Subject', in *Without Guarantees: In Memory of Stuart Hall*, edited by Paul Gilroy, Lawrence Grossberg and Angela McRobbie (New York: Verso, 2000), 30–8; Lois McNay, 'Subject, Psyche, and Agency: The Work of Judith Butler', *Theory Culture and Society* 16, no. 2 (1999): 183–90;

18. Edward Said, *Orientalism* (London: Penguin, 1977), 9–15.

19. See, for example, Simone de Beauvoir, *The Second Sex*, translated by Constance Borde (New York: Vintage Books 2009), 73–86; Kate Millett, *Sexual Politics* (New York: Columbia University Press, 2016), 176–203; and Luce Irigaray, *Speculum of the Other Woman*, translated by Gillian Gill (Ithaca, NY: Cornell University Press, 1985).

20. Rosemarie Garland-Thomson, *Extraordinary Bodies: Figuring Physical Disability in American Culture and Literature* (New York: Columbia University Press, 1996), 37.

21. Ibid., 11.

22. Berger, 'Trauma Without Disability, Disability Without Trauma', 563–4.

23. David T. Mitchell and Sharon L. Snyder, *Narrative Prosthesis: Disability and the Dependencies of Discourse* (Ann Arbor: University of Michigan Press, 2000), 54–57.

24. Ibid., xxiii–xiv.

25. Ibid., 48.

26. Leed, *No Man's Land*, 77.
27. Berger, *The Disarticulate*, 160.
28. Dominick LaCapra, *Writing History, Writing Trauma* (Baltimore: Johns Hopkins University Press, 2001), 23.
29. Ibid., 23.
30. Tobin Siebers, *Disability Aesthetics* (Ann Arbor: University of Michigan Press, 2010), 2.
31. Ibid., 5.
32. Berger, 'Trauma Without Disability, Disability Without Trauma', 565.
33. Schlegel, *Philosophical Fragments*, 13.
34. Peirce, *The Writings of Charles S. Peirce: A Chronological Edition*, vol. 5, 163.
35. Meredith Williams, *Wittgenstein, Mind, and Meaning: Toward a Social Conception of Mind* (London: Routledge, 1999), 158.
36. Stephen Mulhall, *On Being in the World: Wittgenstein and Heidegger on Seeing Aspects* (New York: Routledge, 1990), pp. 40–1.
37. Ludwig Wittgenstein, *Philosophical Investigations*, translated by G. E. M. Anscombe (Upper Saddle River, NJ: Prentice Hall, 1958), 214e.
38. Ibid., 215e.
39. Berger, *The Disarticulate*, 149.

Conclusion: Leaving the Island

People aren't supposed to look back. I'm certainly
not going to do it anymore.
I've finished my war book now. The next one
I write is going to be fun.
This one is a failure, and it had to be, since it was
written by a pillar of salt. It begins like this:
Listen:
Billy Pilgrim has come unstuck in time.
It ends like this:
Poo-tee-weet?

— Kurt Vonnegut, *Slaughterhouse Five*[1]

I will begin this somewhat odd concluding chapter to my book by
stating what may have been obvious to some of my readers until this
point: the work of prosthesis-making and the mechanical vocabulary it
seems to invite, including, as I have mentioned, my own use of the term
'prosthesis', is not without its limits. I do not write this to be contrary to
my own argument and in that way perhaps controversial, but because I
find, as I have hinted, a few unresolved issues and limits not only to the
work of prosthesis-making but also to the very discourse of the prosthesis.
And while I stand behind my description of the prosthesis and its inner
workings and the manner in which I describe the actions taken by soldiers
to return to society and language through the mechanism of poetry, I
would like to articulate the possible costs that description, reliable as
it may be, may incur. These concerns include, but are not limited to:
firstly, the mechanical breakdown that is part and parcel of Peirce's
analysis of language and Wills's discussion of the prosthesis exposes a

predominantly masculine propensity for discussing injury, disability, trauma and their relation to language in explicitly mechanical terms in a manner that may result in aversion to 'non-mechanical' or 'organic' aspects, including, but not exclusive to, sexuality; secondly, the work of constructing prostheses necessarily involves the begrudging endurance of the familial or social security network that is, for the most part, left out of the work of prosthesis itself, with family members often portrayed as malicious agents who, in some cases, brought about the soldier's decision to enlist; thirdly, emphasis is placed on the most extreme of encounters with the dead and thus the most extreme linguistic shifts and, as a result, I too am propping up the myth of the (male) soldier and his bewildering encounter with death; and fourthly and finally, the notion of care I advance in this book, as it relates to a care for the dead, both includes men only and bears noxious resonances of ancestor worship. If I were to sum all these concerns in one, it is the sense that the work male soldiers do after war is not a reaction to or departure from whatever chauvinistic and individualistic position they may have had before the war and that shifted after it, but a different thing of the same type: male solitary work that results in violence against all those identified as unmale, all while further bolstering a male inner circle that may or may not be coterminous with Garland-Thomson's 'normate'. However, this is all very easily said but, as I mentioned at the end of the last chapter, not as easily done or demonstrated. That demonstration will be performed by a discussion of the literary text that served as my own post-war lifebuoy: Daniel Defoe's *Robinson Crusoe*.

I will be the first to admit that a discussion of contemporary post-war writing and its function as prosthesis does not seem to necessitate an intervention from an early eighteenth-century travel narrative. However, despite the wide historical and generic gap between *Crusoe* and the contemporary works of soldier writing that stand at the heart of this book, Defoe's text provided for me personally, if I may insert my own index at this point of my own theoretical prosthesis, a compelling example of the manner in which the poetic not only allows for the expression of disability but also is perhaps one important way in which disability has been read and received by the non-disabled. It should be noted: not only important for it to be received by others because I wanted my own story to be told – indeed, that was important enough – but because I felt I had to tell stories for others as well: for my less literarily inclined comrades and, in what seems like something of a theme following Wills's writings, for my father as well. I cannot speak for others, soldiers or otherwise, but it was only after war that I found myself thinking about my father's war – the 1973 Yom Kippur War – and my own attempt to speak of my war turned in effect to the attempt to tell my father's story or, said otherwise, tell myself the story my father never told, or perhaps one I had not understood. There is an importance to this type of father–son hereditary track, of course, one also tied to what I have mentioned as the possible noxious effect of an adoration of the past and of past ancestors[2] and the centrality of masculinity and the male line.[3] But I will get to that later on in the chapter. For now I will only say: reception is key not only because others will receive your post-war prosthesis, but because one's own prosthesis is, in its own way, already a form of reception. Personally, I was able to come to terms with that act of writing as reception only through my own non-academic writing, a semi-autobiographical novella published three years after the completion of my PhD. But that book had not yet been written when I returned from war in the middle of my BA studies. The book that was there, however, was *Robinson Crusoe*. While I was not at first able to come to terms with the effect of my reading of *Crusoe*, under the guidance of the intellectually unstoppable forces that are Milette Shamir and Shirley Sharon-Zisser, and later through the supervision of Karen Alkalay-Gut, it has become clear that Crusoe's unhappy adventures on his (almost) lonely island served as my first foray into trying to make sense of post-war life.

On a basic level, the plot of Defoe's novel provides a perfect diagram of post-war writings' philosophical, emotional and linguistic underpinnings: a protagonist goes out to seek adventure, suffers an unexpected blow and is then left to deal with the solitude of its aftermath. That person attempts, firstly, to make a life out of that solitary predicament, only to fail ultimately, and as a result of that failure reconnects with other humans and, lastly, with community. The former failure and latter success are, of course, intrinsically tied, representing the failure of what could be called the non-communicational or personal model, in which one deals with a seemingly incommunicable experience by never talking about it. In the novel this tendency can be seen in the failed attempt to keep a 'personal history' through the writing of a journal, and the attempt to 'talk' to Crusoe's parrot, Poll, a conversation composed of Crusoe and Poll echoing each other's words.[4] The failure of this attempt is marked by Crusoe's encounter with the footprint in the sand, a shocking event that leads him almost immediately to seek out human companionship and to his encounter with Friday. The success, then, of that mode of communication which does enable a discussion of the experience, along with the damage it introduced into communication, is what we could call most generally literature, and specifically the text of *The Adventures of Robinson Crusoe.* I felt there was merit in understanding Defoe's novel – paradigmatic example as it is of a very contemporary cultural thrust, discussed most vividly in the context of the rise of the English novel – as a discussion of a transhistorical predicament of being set off from society and language and the kind of work necessary to return to both language and, irrevocably, community. And, moreover, I felt that there is value in setting an image of the kind of event that ends life's movement and the kind of work that reinitiates that movement through a literary text. In the spirit of Wills's dictum, that the transfer of the ghost of meaning is invisible or ambiguous in the text, the only way to exemplify that movement is through a text created, albeit fictionally, about separation from society and the return to that society through art.

Similarly to those soldiers whom I discuss in this book, Defoe's fictional world delineates a loss of security that is not strictly theoretical but bears real-life ramifications. Thus, after the violent storm, Crusoe finds that he alone survived, bringing about what I what argue is the immediate manifestation of a disruption in the once secure link between signs and the objects they pertain to name or describe:

> I walked about the shore, lifting up my hands, and my whole being, *as I may say*, wrapt up in the contemplation of my deliverance, making a thousand gestures and motions *which I cannot describe*, reflecting upon all my comrades that were drowned, and that there should not be one soul saved but myself; for, as for them, I never saw them afterwards, *nor any sign of them*, except three of their hats, one cap, and two shoes *that were not fellows*.[5]

Upon first realising that he has survived a near-death experience, Crusoe, not unlike myself at that period of coming to terms with my military experience in the summer of 2006, immediately appears confused in relation to words and signs. Defoe's protagonist exhibits two major features of what I considered to be a soldier's insecurity with language: firstly, an explicit qualification of the ability to delineate experience ('as I may say'; 'I cannot describe'), and secondly, an implicit instability in the link between sign and referent to the point of preventing a definitive interpretation ('I never saw them afterwards, nor any sign of them'; 'two shoes that were not fellows'). Coming to terms with his loss, Crusoe both uses 'gestures' he cannot describe, and exhibits an ability to separate signs from objects – 'shoes' and 'fellows'. However, the description of Crusoe's landfall and 'salvation' also includes an ironic investigation of language, with the phrase 'two shoes that were not fellows' possibly being read as either 'shoes that turned out not to be people' or 'shoes that did not make up an identical pair', meaning two shoes coming from two different people. In both cases, the word being highlighted, 'fellows', is used in an idiomatic way and is subsequently taken apart to discover its possible literal meanings while, somehow, being left untouched. A similar kind of linguistic investigation via disintegration can be seen in Currall's 'Burying the Dead', which takes a 'secure' use of language to task by literally exposing the multiplicity of meanings it glosses over:

> Burying the dead is a metaphor.
> They don't literally mean bury the dead
> Try not to think too much about it
> They mean put things to rest
> Pull your socks up
> Stop harping on
> Get on with it
> Let things lie
> Get a grip
> Forget.
>
> They've never buried the dead.
>
> Literally.[6]

While this is not a physical island on which soldier poets such as Currall are stranded after war – surrounded, as they are, by people in both the war and home environments – Crusoe's predicament throughout the novel serves as a powerful symbol for a real-life experience of linguistic exclusion. Defoe's imaginary island is thus quite real to soldiers writing poetry after war, stranded because they cannot use words to communicate certain facts and events in a way that would seem meaningful or correct, a failure embedded in words' apparent inability to stick 'securely' to their respective referents ('shoes' and 'fellows'). This experience of being set apart from the human sphere, as I have argued above, along with a strangeness or unsettling of reality, is a recurring one in these poems, as exemplified in 'A Soldier's Winter', which I briefly discussed earlier, posted online by its author Chris from Kandahar:

> What is this cold?
> Where is this white
> Is this real, or just a fleeting moment of life, of my life

I see no longer the greens and reds,
Where have the autumn leaves gone?
This must be the first signs of a new winter?

I see trees, I see sky, I see clouds,
All winter white,
Can I reach upward to touch the falling flake?
I try but never seem to connect,

And as I lay there staring at the sky
Is my body cold?
As I lay I hope I am not forgotten
But here I am alone.
I close my eyes and try to think of home
Is this really happening to me?

This isn't real this is only a dream
I never have felt this way before, cold, weak and exposed,
but strangely at ease
With a tear I draw my parting breath
I'm looking down on my body below

I understand now this is winter . . . this is my winter.[7]

Chris's poem is a poetic reimagining of Crusoe's inability to connect to disjointed, solitary and progressively homogenous surroundings, what Weil describes as 'the contradiction lodged within the soul [which] tears it to shreds'.[8] Pointing at a gap between the speaker and his world, the poem destabilises the words meant to signify, and that all addressees can understand, while injecting personal meaning and experience into those elements that 'pin down' the description, also seen in earlier discussions of poems such as Lynn Hill's 'Capacity' and Graham Barhart's 'Everything in Sunlight I Can't Stop Seeing'. As early as the first stanza of Chris's poem, words are used to disorient as opposed to creating any fixed, concrete meaning. Thus, instead of providing a place or naming a sensation or experience, the poem's first lines, along with their manipulation of what I have referred to as indexical poetics, replace 'reality', or 'realness', two concepts intrinsically tied to indices and their existential, almost physical, connection to their referents, with a sense of unreality and detachment.

This literary bewilderment, the framework of which is provided by the interplay between words, continues with a stark separation between all he sees and what he feels. Regarding the outside world, the soldier demonstrates that he retains the ability to label the outside world: 'I see trees, I see sky, I see clouds' or 'staring at the sky'. However, the ability to classify and name is deemed worthless in his attempt to understand the link between his environment and the manner in which he experiences it ('I try but never seem to connect'; 'Is my body cold?'), leading to an escalating sense of isolation and estrangement. The perceived gap between internal and external leads the speaker to question the reality of his surroundings, calling it a 'dream'. In addition, the wintry external world, that which words are meant to describe and differentiate, is covered with a layer of white snow, signalling, as Mary Favret claims in her essay concerning a tradition of war writing linking the annihilation of war to that of winter, the growing inability to differentiate, along with the fear that inability brings of disappearing under a chaotic, unordered reality.[9] Ultimately, however, the dream-like sensation spreads to his own body, his physical presence, as an object under observation, on a par with the trees, sky and clouds he sees but cannot touch: 'With a tear I draw my parting breath / I'm looking down on my body below.' An inability to consolidate external and internal coherently leads the speaker to feel estranged even from that object that he has hitherto considered to be an index of himself, creating a terrifyingly small deserted island on which to dwell. Furthermore, Defoe's depiction shows that the deserted island is dangerous not only because it cuts one off from society and from a sense of belonging to one's surroundings, but also because it tempts one to believe that one could build a new home on that island, away from one's community.

Crusoe's response to his calamitous separation is to try to build a new life on his island, positioning himself as the maker of a new, private world. Interestingly, this was also what I myself had done through the earlier philosophy of Ludwig Wittgenstein. As luck would have it, the period following my return from war was filled with equal parts Crusoe and Wittgenstein, a fact that ultimately culminated in my 2008 essay on how *Crusoe* can be read as narrating the theoretical upheaval Wittgenstein took upon himself in his shift from the logical and solipsistic *Tractatus*, the foundations of which were laid as a result of Wittgenstein's experiences in World War I, to the later social, language-game and community-centred work.[10] As that essay claimed, expressing in theoretical terms what I had felt at the time, the attempt to live alone with unspeakability does not result in a liveable way of language or, for that matter, life, but something resembling a spiritual solitary confinement. In *Crusoe* this failed attempt to live outside language ends as violently and traumatically as the first ejection from language, a parallel with a soldier's choice to sidestep the tension created by a gap with one's surroundings by avoiding that gap – building a home on the deserted island. That failure is marked, more than any attempt to speak with parrots, by Crusoe's encounter with a paradoxical index – an impossible footprint.

While walking on the shore of his island, Crusoe stumbles upon a revelation: 'the print of a man's naked foot on the shore'.[11] The indexical, and paradoxical, evidence of human life on an island – indexical because the footprint is a paradigmatic example of indexical signs, paradoxical since it is only one footprint – sends Crusoe crashing, to paraphrase Wittgenstein, into the limits of his language. The phantom of the past, in other words, that had been repressed in the attempt to 'live alone', has made, to use Wills's term, a 'wretched pass', creating an after-effect as fearful, if not more so, than his initial desertion:

> After innumerable fluttering thoughts, like a man perfectly confused and *out of myself*, I came home to my fortification, not feeling, *as we say*, the ground I went on but terrified to the last degree, looking behind me every two or three steps, mistaking every bush and tree, and fancying every stump at a distance to be a man; *nor is it possible to describe* how many various shapes affrighted imagination presented to me, how many wild unaccountable whimsies came into my thoughts by the way.[12]

This second breakdown is not the result of Crusoe's detachment from reality and estrangement from language, as in Chris's poem and Crusoe's lament upon his arrival on the island, but the undoing of that tool which was meant to safeguard the survivor from being shipwrecked ever again. The space of new symbols, all 'self made', meant to safeguard him from ever making 'the same mistake again', comes crashing down, resulting in a heightened and even more confusing linguistic separation:

> When I came to my castle, for *so I think I called it* ever after this, I fled into it like one pursued. Whether I went over by the ladder . . . or *went in at the hole in the rock, which I called a door*, I cannot remember; no, nor could I remember the next morning, for never frightened hare fled to cover . . . with more terror of mind than I to this retreat.[13]

As Defoe's narrative shows, Crusoe's encounter disorients him ('a man perfectly confused and out of myself') and he feels a perplexity which induces paranoia ('fancying every stump at a distance to be a man'), amnesia ('I cannot remember') and, finally, linguistic insecurity and scepticism, or at least the creation of a certain critical distance from what used to be one's common-sense language use ('my castle, for so I think I called it', 'the hole in the rock, which I called a door'). This encounter, complete with its description of sudden terror, ghosts and the apparent inability to speak, echoes Merleau-Ponty's notion of an accident that extinguishes the human flame. The deserted man, thus, finds himself imperilled on both sides: he can neither reconnect with society in the manner to which he was accustomed (the ship cannot be rebuilt and sailed back home, the 'fellows' cannot be made to live again), nor build a language or a life by himself that is only of himself, evidenced by the failure of that attempt, one that has found its philosophical echo in Wittgenstein's argument against private language in his later work, *Philosophical Investigation*.

Bereft on both sides, haunted by past ghosts and by his detachment from his home, Crusoe is forced to find a new way. The only way back from the island, in the face of such a failure, is by forging a text that uses the placeholders provided by indices and physical experience with the social conventions of the symbol to renew movement through the poetic text – a prosthesis. This is not a prosthesis referring to any specific, denotable meaning, but which stands for an experience – namely, the experience of losing language and humanity – a new means of communication that is forever haunted by the trauma of communication breakdown. What is noteworthy, moreover, in the manner in which Crusoe returns to society is both the tool through which that return is accomplished – a linguistic breaking down and resewing of his time on the island – and his means of returning – care and dependency.

Male Care, Master Care

There are many possible issues regarding the limits of care that *Robinson Crusoe* can illustrate, especially in its relation to the examples of soldier writing I have discussed thus far in this book, but I would like to focus on two such concerns that I feel are of the utmost importance to the questions I have raised thus far. The first is that care often, though not always, entails a relationship of power over others, and the second is that the individuals involved in providing care for each other, whom I shall call 'care group', and who exhibit care in terms of highlighting codependency and vulnerability, are all individuals who identify as men, to the exclusion and sometimes detriment of any who are identified by the care group as anything other than male. As I discussed in the previous chapter, care giving and the related concept of compassion have both come under attack within the realm of disability studies, and, more often than not, from a feminist or at least an anti-patriarchal position. The argument, as articulated, again, by such thinkers as Berlant, Garber, Vogler, Garland-Thomson and, perhaps obviously, Judith Butler, runs along the lines that the sense of care put forth in disability studies and, cast more widely, within the context of identity-based theory serves as a tool for divesting those to whom care must be given of their rights and political power, all under the umbrella of general and seemingly positive such terms as 'care' and 'compassion'. To care for the disabled, in political and social terms, is to make sure they are out of the normate's sight, or, said differently, used strategically in order to further establish the lines between normate and the perceived abnormal, a theoretical continuation of a line that passes, it seems, through Foucault's work on insanity and modern scientific discourse. And while I proposed, and still in fact do propose, considering care as a valuable term in our discussion of war veterans and the writings they produce after war, and thus perhaps not accepting the full brunt of the criticism I have just articulated, there is just reason to be, for a lack of a better word, careful of care.

In *Robinson Crusoe* at least some of these problems become evident and gain a noticeably racial and gender-based character. Crusoe leaves his home in direct defiance of his father, and yet by doing so, also leaves his mother, who is described as begging the young man to stay, having lost an older son to the Thirty Years' War.[14] It is also clear, however, from this initial interaction that Crusoe's debate on the intellectual and spiritual level of accepting the advice to maintain the 'middle path in life' is with his father, his mother playing a marginal sentimental role. And while Crusoe's mother is the first and most important female figure in his adventures, she is the last as well, as Crusoe's efforts to reinsert himself into society include a care group composed exclusively of men. His first attempt at a relationship of care is with the slave boy Xury,[15] whom Crusoe quickly sells back into slavery. Later, already on the island, the rest of the creatures with whom Crusoe attempts to connect include what seems to be a male parrot, as well as a touching scene involving the care and, appropriately, burial of an old 'he-goat' Crusoe finds on the island.[16] Eventually, Crusoe forms the closest relationship to a true care-based codependency, the community of men assembled on the island, revolving around the nuclear coupling of the new Adam and Eve of the island, Crusoe and Friday.

However, immediately upon its formation, the bond between Crusoe and Friday is tinted in yet another shade: colonial and racial mastery. Friday represents the closest example to a relationship of codependency and care in the novel, with Crusoe often describing his slave as his friend, stating that the island native was, in fact, superior in both physical and intellectual terms.[17] Friday is, in no uncertain terms, Crusoe's equal, and equal in his need for care as well, as both men had been separated from their homes by force of storm/war, and depend on each other to survive and escape the island successfully. And yet, despite the extent to which Crusoe depends on Friday upon his re-entrance into the social world, he remains Friday's master, a fact that will not change for the duration of the novel. Crusoe's mastery over a racialised colonial other, first through Xury and later Friday, is of course a well-known feature of the twentieth-century critical and theoretical reception of the novel.[18] What my analysis hopes to add to that understanding, however, is the notion of Crusoe and Friday's politically uneven relationship as perhaps also a feature of post-war care and, more precisely, that mode of care I have called care for the dead.

This sense of authority over others in the newly formed care group is, in its own way, a replication of the kind of authority exerted by more traditional familial groups, such as the one Crusoe was escaping upon embarking on his high-seas adventure. The interdependent relationship of care Crusoe establishes with Friday mirrors, then, the action of the prosthetic text in that it enacts a replacement of a lost original, with two significant differences: the new unit does not include non-male members – a fact that is true both in its original state and then with the inclusion of later arrivals – nor, as Christopher Flint claims, 'complications' of biological attachment:

> In dealing with Friday, Crusoe arrogates the paternal role without testing the basis and nature of fatherhood. He assumes the privileges that family confers upon the patriarch without facing the biologic complications. To locate himself in and demonstrate his power over a world that seems always to subordinate him, Crusoe fabricates a family that reflects his authority but does not then challenge his claim to that authority.[19]

Thus the care group established in order to rise out of the deathly hollows of post-disaster solipsism mimics the structure and function of family, only without the family unit's gender variety. It thus represents the freedom of the group from a former, ostensibly flawed or lost model, all while seemingly basing that notion of freedom on a departure from the biological and, most notably, from the female.

And this point is related to the one I have made regarding the lessons of war and the potential of seeing war as a teaching or disillusioning mechanism. If, as some works of post-war writing seem to indicate, war exposes the toxicity of male aggression and propensity for violence, the lesson learned seems to be that the only group that can advance an end to that aggression is like-minded, war-experienced men or, in the case of *Robinson Crusoe*, other untethered, isolated and disaster-stricken men. Women and all that is perceived as non-masculine are altogether excluded from the horizon of the new post-war family. And this new family is of special concern, mostly for how quickly Crusoe seems to dispatch with it in order to seek new adventure, which, in the wider context of this book, amounts to returning headlong into war. This is how Crusoe describes his family toward the end of the novel:

> In the meantime, I in part settled myself here; for, first of all, I married, and that not either to my disadvantage or dissatisfaction, and had three children, two sons and one daughter; but my wife dying, and my nephew coming home with good success from a voyage to Spain, my inclination to go abroad, and his importunity, prevailed, and engaged me to go in his ship as a private trader to the East Indies; this was in the year 1694.[20]

Just as the younger Crusoe had completely ignored the pleadings of his mother, bent, as it were, on proving his father wrong, so the older Crusoe remains tone deaf regarding the female members of his immediate group. His wife's death is summarily described mid-sentence, and his abandonment of three young children barely an afterthought. Female and non-male figures, thus, not only do not feature prominently as possible care givers or as possible members of care groups, but they are often completely excluded from the prosthetic narrative created in the wake of personal disaster.

In the post-war poetry written by men all relationships are masculine, and those relationships that are other than masculine are described as either a force of necessity, a burden or an afterthought and, worse still, as a threat and a target. And this male-centric, master-and-servant aspect of post-disaster care is also a prominent feature for many of the post-war writings I read and discuss in this book. Male relationships of care and support are highlighted; non-male figures are almost entirely absent or, ultimately described as burdens. In some cases, moreover, post-war trauma could be said to contribute to increased violence in veterans' households, or, at the very least, act as a mediating factor to said violence,[21] a phenomenon Jonathan Shay dubs 'coldness and cruelty to nearest and dearest'.[22] One example of this toxic reaction to family upon the return from war is the manner in which Abe, Uriarte's protagonist

Figure 5.4 Uriarte, *The White Donkey*.

in *The White Donkey*, physically and emotionally shuts out his girlfriend as he is frozen in a grief-stricken stupor, until he finally exits the room only to discuss his experiences at the grave of his dead comrade, Garcia. In fact, the two female characters in *The White Donkey*, Abe's girlfriend and mother, are not only excluded but also berated in the most explicitly misogynistic terms. Non-male individuals, then, are either seen as the object of impossible desire or are completely outcast from the post-war care groups, at least as those are represented in post-war writings.

It should be noted that these remarks do not amount to a glowing endorsement of the exclusivity of the heteronormative family structure; nor does they advance the idea that family or care groups must include gender and sexual variety. They do, however, point to at least one recurring blind spot in post-war writing, of which Crusoe here stands as a somewhat paradigmatic exemplar: the long and difficult journey that is taken, and perhaps must be taken, from a point of language-less, dead or animalistic solipsism to a reintroduction into society is not one that necessarily obliterates or even challenges some of the core values its reception history seems to think. Men coming out of war, in other words, and even those creating the kind of literary or poetic prosthesis necessary to perform that task, remain reclusive and exclusive in terms of the intimate relationships they foster after war. Crusoe returns from the island completely engrossed by his experiences to the point of never attaching to the family he forms in its wake. Abe, in the name of what I have called 'caring for the dead', shuts off his family in order to find Garcia's grave. Turner's speaker in 'At Lowe's Home Improvement Center' deals with nothing but male characters in his bid for post-war redemption. Mena's speaker grapples with Kyle's death and Kyle's death alone. This is in addition to several of the other works I have discussed in this book that make no reference to female family members at home, female civilians under attack, or the experience of re-encountering non-male individuals, in many cases, upon their return home. Perhaps a paradigmatic moment of such abandon, if I am to return to the spectre of post-World War I writing, is the ending of Hemingway's *A Farewell to Arms*, in which the war-stricken, thoughtful male protagonist deserts the body of his wife and child, who had both died in childbirth: 'But after I had got them out and shut the door and turned off the light it wasn't any good. It was like saying goodbye to a statue. After a while I went out and left the hospital and walked back to the hotel in the rain.'[23] The female body, in all its postpartum abjection, to use Julia Kristeva's concept, is rejected in many post-war prostheses, as sexual relations are replaced with those of male care, what Kristeva calls 'fear of procreation'.[24]

It should be said these observations do not conclude the redundancy of the prosthesis-making process. As I have claimed throughout, it is a process that successfully extracts veterans from death back into a limping life. However, that second part of the work of the prosthesis, the reading of it, is not to be taken for granted and is essential in a successful return to family and social circles. To address the wider effects of soldiers' return home, as seen in my discussion of the work of Kate Gaskin and Elyse Fenton, for instance, is also to take heed of the strain even the act of trying to stay alive puts on family members, friends and spouses. Writing in a post on *The New York Times* blog *At War*, Jackie McMichael writes of the struggle to find care for her veteran husband, dealing with the bureaucratic process of diagnosing her partner's trauma as well as with the reality of being his care taker, a mass of tension and anxiety that ultimately led to their divorce:

> Veterans need to learn how to reintegrate into their families and how to take care of those families again; how to trust their spouses again. As a caregiver, you are put in a position of authority over your spouse, doling out daily 'what to do's,' managing the finances. What toll does that take on a marriage that is supposed to be built on equal partnership? At the same time, the caregiver feels forgotten, berated and belittled because his or her complaints pale in

comparison to the pain, emotional or otherwise, of the veteran. What happens when we get sick? Surely we do not want to be told, as some spouses are, 'It's not like you're dying! I know guys whose legs have been blown off.'[25]

The distance described here between the drama of war trauma and the everyday struggle of illness or care taking forms a line in the sand between the veteran and his partner. And yet what McMichael describes in her writing is a continuation of war by other means. It is worthwhile, I think, taking note of the effects these separate experiences and events have not only on those soldiers who experience them, but also on those who await their return and eventually are committed to facing the consequences of that return, the very act of prosthesis-making being one of those many consequences. Those outcomes, as I have discussed in Chapter 4, have their own poetic shape, and it is at this point that I would like to return to one of the poets discussed previously, Elyse Fenton.

Fenton, whose partner was deployed to Iraq in 2005, addresses the struggle to return to a sense of normalcy and connection after war in her two published poetry volumes, *Clamour* (2010) and *Sweet Insurgent* (2017). More than just sharing the anxieties of family members as they await the fate of loved ones in peril, Fenton's poems often address the toll war takes not only on the returning soldier but on his family as well. In 'Refusing Beatrice', Fenton's speaker anxiously awaits as her partner is deployed in Iraq, assuming the role of Dante's Beatrice – passively waiting for her lover to go through hell. However, as opposed to Beatrice, she has no plan of hell and cannot be there if and when the voyage out fails:

You've got no itinerary. Just an armored car
To ferry you down the graveled airport road, a Chinook

Gut-deep in the green swill waiting to dislodge.[26]

In this contemporary equivalent of the 'waiting partner', all Fenton's Beatrice can do is, perhaps not unlike her namesake, hope for small miracles:

And if the updrift's whirlwind
    Doesn't make the sniper miss, if your helicopter lifts
        From Baghdad as doomed as the Chaldean sun

I won't be there to see the wreckage
    Or papery flames, the falling arsenal of stars –[27]

'Refusing Beatrice', then, gives a sense of the tense anticipation, the expectation that at any moment the world may end, that is the lot of military families, one given voice in Alexandra Hyde's wonderful essay on the parallel lives led by military families. Writing of family members hearing of a fatal incident in Afghanistan that may involve their loved ones, Hyde depicts the impossible reality of dual awareness, of the home and of war, bringing the war, effectively, to the home. The event, she writes,

> becomes manifest in the temporal form of waiting and is spatially reinscribed in unexpected places, such as the driveway of a suburban house in Germany where Hannah waits for the appearance of the families liaison officer whom she imagines will tell her the news of her husband's death.[28]

As MacLeish writes of the constant strain of uncertainty exerted on military families: 'The possibility of loss – of a loved one's life, of the reliable connection that lets you know you can expect to hear from them, of, indeed, everything – hovers constantly, compounding the more immediate loss of separation and absence.'[29] And yet, as seen in my earlier discussion of Fenton's 'Conversations', a helicopter burning to the ground is not the only type of wreckage those families may yet witness, with those returning from war in 'one piece'. The shock, or at least part of it, may actually be, as is the case with the veterans themselves, that they had survived war, a tremor that, for veterans, may spell survivor's guilt and, for their families, as Fenton writes beautifully in 'Infidelity', a different sort of guilt, that of expecting death, of a premature farewell from the presumed to be almost dead partner:

> When you were in Iraq I dreamed you
> dead, dormant, shanked stone
>
> in a winter well, verb-less object
> sunk haft-deep through the navel
>
> of each waking sentence. I dreamed
> myself shipwreck, rent timbers
>
> on a tidal bed, woke to morning's cold
> mast of breath canted wide as a search light
>
> for the drowned. Dreamed my crumbling
> teeth bloomed shrapnel's bone light

bricks mortared into a broken
kingdom of sleep where I found you

dream-sift, rubbled, nowhere.
Forgive me, love, this last

infidelity: I never dreamed you whole.[30]

More than just anxiety and the toll that anxiety takes, Fenton's voice here discloses the inability to stay in that ruthless in-between of hope and despair. To give up, in this case, on her partner is to imagine him dead, perhaps as a kind of release from unbearable uncertainty. And yet what these dreams of death and annihilation create is a reality in which life is not the expected outcome of war, one that possibly makes it difficult to readjust to a reality in which the object of all that anxiety returns home alive. This uneasy in-between state, in other words, bleeds into life after war, following homecoming, to create the site of estrangement and distance I have already addressed in Fenton's poem 'Conversations':

Each eggplant that I pick
is ripe and sun-dark in its own inviolable
skin. Except there is no inviolable anything
and you've been home now for a year.[31]

That lack of intimacy or distance is highlighted through the use of a language of separation, from the 'disparate' and 'across an ocean' of the first stanza, to the solitary picking of the eggplant – perhaps a symbol of ripe sexuality or desire – that closes the poem. Moreover, it is the desire for intimacy, responsibility for the loss of which, it seems, falls on both partners, which marks Fenton's poem as being so radically different from the soldiers' writings I have discussed throughout the book. While Crusoe is numb to his wife's death following his return from the island, and as Abe shuts the proverbial door to exclude his partner and mother, Fenton's speaker, who feels as split and undone by war's effects on her world, turns to intimacy as a way to resolve the seeming unbridgeable gap between her returning partner and herself. 'There is no inviolable anything', Fenton's speaker says as she holds the 'sun-dark' eggplant, a seemingly benign and matter-of-fact statement that, however, rings as a desperate challenge against the walls of silence and the rejection of sexual intimacy that seem to shroud many works of male soldier writing.

The Ghost and I

To take heed of the limits, dangers and possible blind spots of the idea of the prosthetic and that of care for the dead does not mean to abandon the prosthesis altogether. I would like to end this book, then, with one other form of oscillation, of which I have written much in this book, that speaks both to the inherent structure of the prosthesis and to the standstill of post-war social and familial life I have described in the above section. And I would like to do that by putting forth an oscillation that is not only internal to the work of writing after war but also, to risk another instance of mechanisation and separation, between reading and writing, between addressing the community through an act of writing and by being addressed by that same work. The soldiers who write these prostheses are also readers, either of their own texts or of the tradition with which they find themselves engaged. Soldiers return from war, if I may now cautiously use this trope, in pieces, and create texts that mend those pieces, momentarily, as in a dream, together. However, their actions, whether in war or after, do not take place in a social or political vacuum; they can, and do, have an influence, sometimes a negative one, on those they perceive to be unworthy of participating in a relationship of care. Thus, again, to write the prosthesis truly is also to read the prosthesis, and the oscillation that takes place between reality and fantasy, index and symbol, life and death, self and others, and must continue also between the writers and readers, whether those readers are fellow soldiers, civilians who have never experienced war, civilians under attack in war, members of the community that identify as male or otherwise, sexual and life partners, and the writers themselves. When enacted, moreover, this oscillation between reader, text and writer enables – and this as opposed to the warnings of thinkers such as Garland-Thompson – a view into the ever-oscillating reality and unease of post-war disability. Thus there is room to comment, I believe, on the reception pole of that work of art or, in other words, art's ability to take in readers who are not disabled themselves and introduce them to the ghost hovering between the different poles of disability that I have addressed throughout the book: indexical, symbolic, personal, social, language and silence.

Wills's conceptualisation of the prosthesis as that text informed by the dead and the alive, and characterised by the constant motion of kinetics and ghostly transfer, was the main theoretical vehicle connecting the work of art to the disabled body it pertains to represent and, in a way, to the reader. That reader, in Wills's case, is Wills himself, and his difficulties in reading his father's disjointed and painful prose. However, while Wills's work was instrumental, along with that of Siebers and Berger, linking individual pain to aesthetics and disability, it could be said to have a precursor of sorts in Wolfgang Iser's theory of reception and his foundational essay 'The Play of the Text'. In that work Iser describes the importance of the reader in understanding the work of art – that it is art, so to speak, is triggered through the encounter with the reader in a manner that resembles Wills's theory, at the very least through Iser's shared fascination with what could be termed a preoccupation with kinetics and the ambiguity of ghostly transfer he terms 'play'. At the centre of Iser's notion of play is a release from the pressures and expectations of what he calls a closed heuristic system, one which he identifies with Greek and medieval modes of interpretation, and which we could link to the figure of Graham Barnhart's father looking for the 'right word'. No longer is the text comparable with a reality it pertains to represent, but with a world created through the endless interaction or oscillation between the reader and the text, one he terms play:

> When the closed system, however, is punctured and replaced by open-endedness, the mimetic component of representation declines and the performative one comes to the fore. The process then no longer entails reaching behind appearances in order to grasp an intelligible world in the Platonic sense, but turns into a 'way of world-making.' If what the text brings about were to be equated with world-making, the question would arise whether one could continue to speak of 'representations' at all. The concept could be retained only if the 'ways of world-making' themselves became the referential object for representation.[32]

Where my own formulation and, I believe, that of Wills as well would stop short is, I would argue, the discarding of the notion of representation, a complete rejection of a relationship between reality and text. Iser's rejection is all the more clear in a short passage from later on in the essay, regarding the advantages of play over closed interpretation: 'Play does not have to picture anything outside itself. It allows the author–text–reader to be conceived as a dynamic interrelationship that moves toward a final result.'[33] With this statement I return to a point I made in the Introduction, regarding the appeal of Peirce's semiotics as opposed to Saussurian and post-structuralist semiology. The reason for that is embedded in the notion that the indexically poetical text is anchored in experience, is triggered by experience and can never, even in the midst of its iconic dream, conceive of a reality in which the past or reality has no influence or does not exist. So, contrary to Iser's formulation, indexical poetics is committed to a sense of past and personal pain, even if that commitment is ethical more than anything else.

However, having said that, I would like to point out that Iser's highlighting of 'world-making' as the central axis around which the work of play revolves, as opposed to an exclusively representational impulse, is very much in line with what this book has been arguing. The post-war poetic prosthesis, while born out of the desire to represent war, is equally founded on the failure of that attempt, at least in an exclusively referential way. It is an oscillation between said and unsaid, symbolic and indexical, that undermines what has been said and foregrounds moments of indexical lack of meaning. The result is not a representation of war but a diagram, a dream, that is both, like the cave paintings in the quotation from Merleau-Ponty's in the Introduction, moored to the past and to reality and somehow hovering above it, a space all of its own. And this disabled beginning of the work of post-war writing, and the stuttering, limping dream it puts forth, also go some way towards articulating the manner in which Siebers saw art as invested inherently in disability, in projected disability and in conjuring images of disabled bodies, for art– and post-war writing exemplifies this well enough – is born out of disability and allows a way into disability that would have been otherwise impossible.

Thus, to return to *Robinson Crusoe*, the way off the lonely island is the poetic, the work of art that is created out of an impulse to document as well as liberate, to bury others and oneself. But, as I have suggested here in this Conclusion, literature, through reading, is also the way *into* disability, perhaps the main or only path into an experience of life with disability and of the limits of our own ideas of ability and the interplay of our body with the bodies of others. Art, specifically verbal art, is thus that artificial space of 'diagram' or 'dream', a tension between personal experience and communal communication that allows the discussion of the middle stance in regard to language: one, as in the case of the poems discussed here, brought on by the onset of personal trauma, that the literary text allows for a simultaneous move away from either 'reality' or 'fantasy' in the attempt to create a new space in which signs and meaning are something with which one can play. A similar sentiment is expressed by Richard Kuhns:

The symbols in the text do not refer to other orders of reality, nor to a private fantasy system of the writer, but rather to the structure and the ultimate meaning to be found in the text itself . . . The language of the text – that is, that language which *is* the text – is a language about itself because it explores how and in what way what it offers may be meaningful. And it considers seriously the possibility that it itself may be without meaning. One purpose of the text then is to provide evidence for its own meaningfulness, and that implies offering to the reader a method for reading.[34]

In the new diagram of relations between words and things, between real and unreal or between probable and impossible, a prosthetic space of distance is created, producing a manner of communication that simultaneously serves as a comment on communication. It is for that reason that I felt it necessary to present a literary symbol, an icon for this state of being thrust out of language or community through a literary text concerning that experience– namely, Defoe's *Robinson Crusoe*. Being a poetic text, *Crusoe* allows a material discussion of an essentially philosophical or existential problem: that of being torn from language and community, with its attempt to live 'privately', the failure of that attempt, and an ultimate return to society via the testimony of the fictional, iconic, text. The literary text, in other words, is the only kind of language – prosthetic, ironic and poetic – where boundaries can be undone and language discussed. As psychoanalyst John P. Muller writes of his own use of Conrad's *Heart of Darkness* to discuss Lacanian psychoanalysis, 'It may be hard to experience the progressive loss of boundaries as the Real is approached; it has, however, been powerfully conveyed in certain literary works.'[35]

As claimed throughout, this book reads poems written after war as attempts at sites of sustained, ironic tension between indices and symbols, one which requires a certain form of reading as well, a reading in which the tension between these poles stands at the centre of the work, as opposed to an attempt to envelop individual poems within the boundaries of any one overarching theory. This requirement is, of course, linked to the understanding of these poems as questioning the ability of language itself, let alone theoretical linguistic constructs, from categorising or even describing their experience with language in a manner which could be considered accurate, final or secure. The sense of an obliteration of the ability to feel secure in one's frameworks of life is expressed perhaps most vehemently by Czech thinker Jan Patočka, discussing the writing of World War I veteran and mystic Pierre Teilhard de Chardin,[36] and the effect the frontlines have on the ability to latch on to a positivistic ideology or system of belief: 'The motives of the day which had evolved the will to war are consumed in the furnace of the front line, if that experience is intense enough that it will not yield again to the forces of the day.'[37] Patočka's reading of Teilhard's wartime experiences, as well as those of German writer Ernst Junger, seem, perhaps too often, to idolise an encounter with absolute violence as 'freeing' soldiers from these ideologies, as a spiritual experience of release. And yet while I would shy away from the determinism implied in Patočka's reading, understanding that not all war veterans write poetry or find themselves at odds with their ideology following war, it is still valuable in discussing in terms of the wider form disillusionment may take in the wake of war – not one's disillusionment from any one specific theory, a trait shared by many war poems – but from theory as such, from the ability to adhere securely to a set system, including language. This, I would argue, is the 'irony' which war teaches. This is not to say that war cannot produce theory, or that those who experience the frontlines do not formulate new, perhaps even more 'secure' theories in the wake of war (one can only think of a soldier whose patriotism is enhanced by war and who chooses to proceed in a military career, for example). What I would argue, nonetheless, is that the writing of poetry after war, whatever the message of the poetry may be, while also engaged in an attempt to 'make sense' of war or 'describe' it, is, to varying degrees, first and foremost an attempt to speak, to make words. Thus, instead of choosing any one theory to decipher or expose a general theme concerning the poetry written by soldiers after war, I have relied on both the semiotic interplay of signs and the concept of 'irony' in order to state only one overarching statement concerning online soldier poetry: that the poems represent, in vastly differing and unique ways, attempts to use signs and language to fashion a prosthesis of their own. And that they, and in fact all of us, would do best to read the poems along those lines as well as directing the veterans themselves toward the responsibility for reading their own prosthesis.

So, while any one of the soldier poems I have discussed could be said to conform to any of several theoretical frameworks, the kind of analysis I have attempted and the brand of reading it promotes attempt to circumvent a theoretical interpretation of these poems, choosing to read them as prostheses enabling the use of language. It is a reading that is ironic as well, in that it allows the gap between personal experience and communication to remain, and only presents the various ways in which that gap is dealt with in the poetry written by soldiers after war. I mean ironic, it should be added, in two ways: an understanding that irony could be, for some, a sustained mode of being and thought; but also in the sense of rejecting the impulse to find a 'theory of war poetry' and insist on seeing how the tools presented in this book enable us to see each poem as fashioning different kinds of prostheses, only using similar tools – the tools at hand. As Shay writes, this kind of reading amounts to listening to a unique experience of a gap between experience and communication, before rushing to categorise or judge either that person's experience, or the vessel with which he is dealing with that experience:

> [H]ealing from trauma depends upon communalization of the trauma – being able safely to tell the story to someone who is listening and who can be trusted to retell it truthfully to others in the community. So before analyzing, before classifying, before thinking, before trying to *do* anything – we should *listen* . . . At its worst our educational system produces counselors, psychiatrists, psychologists, and therapists who resemble museum-goers whose whole experience consists of mentally saying, 'That's cubist! . . . That's El Greco!' and who never *see* anything they've looked at.[38]

Ultimately, this book, born out of my own experiences with violence, the fear of violence and the idea of war, is meant to provide yet another tool to disrupt the 'connoisseur' in the quotation from Shay, who manages only to peg veterans further into set, abstract, 'real' categories, while ignoring, if not annihilating, personal suffering and transformation. It sets out to read the irony that sets one poem, one prosthesis, one soldier apart from another, and the ability to see the personal, singular effort that is the attempt to write oneself back into language, community and life. And, lastly, as this final chapter has attempted to do, it attempts to begin to trace the collateral damage the act of prosthesis-making itself can bring about, and to encourage a continued communal oscillation during the constant work of the prosthesis. And all in an effort to initiate the post-war play or oscillation that enables the return to life, as limping as that return may be.

Notes

1. Kurt Vonnegut, *Slaughterhouse Five* (New York: Dial Press, 2009), 28.
2. Emilio Gentile, 'Fascism as Political Religion', in *Fascism*, edited by Michael S. Neiberg (London: Routledge, 2017), 229–51; and David McCrone, *The Sociology of Nationalism* (London: Routledge, 1998), 44–63.
3. Sandro Bellasai, 'The Masculine Mystique: Antimodernism and Virility in Fascist Italy', *Journal of Modern Italian Studies* 10, no. 3 (2007): 314–35.
4. Daniel Defoe, *Robinson Crusoe* (Hertfordshire: Wordsworth Classics, 2000), 109.
5. Ibid., 34, emphasis added.
6. Currall, 'Burying the Dead'.
7. Chris from Kandahar, 'A Soldier's Winter'.
8. Weil, 'The *Iliad*, or the Poem of Force', 9.
9. Mary Favert, 'Still Winter Falls', *PMLA* 124, no. 5 *Special Topic: War* (2009): 1549.

10. Ron Ben-Tovim, '*Robinson Crusoe*, Wittgenstein, and the Return to Society', *Philosophy and Literature* 32, no. 2 (2008): 278–92.
11. Defoe, *Robinson Crusoe*, 117.
12. Ibid., emphasis added.
13. Ibid., 188, emphasis added.
14. Ibid., 13–14.
15. Ibid., 24–6.
16. Ibid., 136.
17. Ibid., 170.
18. Alastair Pennycook, *English and the Discourse of Colonialism* (London: Routledge, 2001), 10–16; and Brett C. McInelly, 'Expanding Empires, Expanding Selves: Colonialism, the Novel, and *Robinson Crusoe*', *Studies in the Novel* 35, no. 1 (2003): 1–21.
19. Christopher Flint, 'Orphaning the Family: The Role of Kinship in Robinson Crusoe', *ELH* 55, no. 2 (1988): 393.
20. Defoe, *Robinson Crusoe*, 234.
21. See, for example, Michelle D. Sherman et al., 'Domestic Violence in Veterans with Posttraumatic Stress Disorder'; and Mark W. Miller, Erika J. Wolf, Annemarie F. Reardon, Kelly M. Harrington, Karen Ryabchenko, Diane Castillo, Rachel Freund and Richard E. Heyman, 'PTSD and Conflict Behavior Between Veterans and their Intimate Partners', *Journal of Anxiety Disorders* 27, no. 2 (2013): 240–51.
22. Shay, *Odysseus in America*, 137–40.
23. Hemingway, *A Farewell to Arms*, 320.
24. Julia Kristeva, *The Powers of Horror*, translated by Leon S. Roudiez (New York: Columbia University Press, 1982), 77–9.
25. Jackie McMichaels, 'After Divorce, Losing Veterans' Support Along with a Spouse', *The New York Times*, 29 May 2015. Available at: <https://atwar.blogs.nytimes.com/2015/05/29/after-divorce-losing-veterans-support-along-with-a-spouse/> (last accessed 11 March 2022).
26. Elyse Fenton, *Clamour* (Cleveland, OH: Cleveland State University Press, 2007), 28.
27. Ibid., 28-9.
28. Hyde, 'The Present Tense of Afghanistan', 862.
29. MacLeish, *Making War at Fort Hood*, 96.
30. Ibid., 73.
31. Ibid., 64.
32. Iser, 'Play of the Text', 206–7.
33. Ibid., 207.
34. Richard Kuhns, *Structures of Experience: Essays on the Affinity Between Philosophy and Literature* (New York: Basic Books), 220.
35. Muller, *Beyond the Psychoanalytic Dyad*, 76–8.
36. Pierre Teilhard de Chardin, 'La Nostalgie du front', in *Ecrits du temps de la guerre* (Paris: Grasset, 1965).
37. Jan Patočka, 'Wars of the Twentieth Century and the Twentieth Century as War', in *Heretical Essays in the Philosophy of History*, edited by James Dodd, translated by Erazim Kohak (Chicago: Open Court, 1996), 130.
38. Shay, *Achilles in Vietnam*, 4–5, emphasis in the original.

INDEX